The Endurance of Family Businesses
A Global Overview

The Endurance of Family Businesses is a collection of essays offering an overview of the importance and resilience of family-controlled large businesses. Much of economic and business history research neglects family businesses, considering them an inefficient form of business organization. These essays discuss the strengths of family businesses: the ways family firms have managed, financed, and governed their corporations, as well as the way in which they structure their relationship with the external environment, from the government to the company's stakeholders. Family businesses have learned new ways of organizing their resources and using their accumulated know-how for new markets and institutional environments. This volume combines the expertise of well-known scholars who specialize in business history, economic history, management, and consulting to provide an interdisciplinary perspective on family businesses. Contributors provide a global view by taking into account Asian, American, and European experiences.

Paloma Fernández Pérez is Professor in the Department of Economic and Business History at the Universitat de Barcelona. She received one of the first ICREA Academia awards from the Catalan government in 2008 and is on the editorial council of the journals *Business History* and *Investigaciones de Historia Económica*. She founded and coordinates the Network of Interdisciplinary Research in Family Firms. Her last book is *La última globalización y el renacer de los grandes negocios familiares en el mundo* (2012).

Andrea Colli is Professor of Economic and Social History in the Department of Policy Analysis and Public Management at Bocconi University in Milan, Italy. He is a member of the Editorial Review Board of *Family Business Review*. He is the author of *Business History: Complexities and Comparisons* (with Franco Amatori, 2011).

The Endurance of Family Businesses

A Global Overview

Edited by

PALOMA FERNÁNDEZ PÉREZ
Universitat de Barcelona

ANDREA COLLI
Bocconi University, Milan

CAMBRIDGE
UNIVERSITY PRESS

CAMBRIDGE
UNIVERSITY PRESS

32 Avenue of the Americas, New York NY 10013-2473, USA

Cambridge University Press is part of the University of Cambridge.

It furthers the University's mission by disseminating knowledge in the pursuit of
education, learning and research at the highest international levels of excellence.

www.cambridge.org
Information on this title: www.cambridge.org/9781107480513

© Cambridge University Press 2013

First published 2013
First paperback edition 2014

A catalogue record for this publication is available from the British Library

Library of Congress Cataloguing in Publication data
Fernández Pérez, Paloma, 1964–
The endurance of family businesses : a global overview / Paloma Fernández Pérez,
Universitat de Barcelona, Andrea Colli, Bocconi University.
pages cm
Includes index.
ISBN 978-1-107-03775-5 (hardback)
1. Family-owned business enterprises – Case studies.   I. Colli, Andrea, 1966–   II. Title.
HD62.25.F47   2014
338.6–dc23   2013007438

ISBN 978-1-107-03775-5 Hardback
ISBN 978-1-107-48051-3 Paperback

Contents

Figures and Tables

FIGURES

TABLES

vii

Contributors

Remei Agulles is a research assistant in the Department of Entrepreneurship at IESE Business School and a Ph.D. candidate at the Universitat Internacional de Catalunya. She holds a degree in Philosophy from the University of Navarra. Her current research interests involve knowledge-sharing in service multinationals, learning in practice, new professions, and professionalization processes.

Christine Blondel is Adjunct Professor of Family Business at INSEAD Business School (France, Singapore, Abu Dhabi), where she codirects the "Family Enterprise Challenge" executive program. She coordinated INSEAD activities in the field of family firms from their creation in 1997 until 2007. She advises several family firms. Her research interests are large, long-lasting family firms, family business governance, women in the family business, Fair Process (*Family Business Review*), and the sale of the family business. She is the lead author of *L'Entreprise Familiale sauvera-t-elle le Capitalisme? Portraits* (Editions Autrement). She was one of the founders of IFERA (the International Family Enterprise Research Academy) and is actively involved in the Family Business Network.

Pramuan Bunkanwanicha is an Associate Professor of Finance at ESCP Europe–Paris Campus, where he teaches Corporate Finance, Emerging Markets Finance, and International Finance. He received his Ph.D. in Economics from Université Paris 1 Panthéon-Sorbonne. Prior to joining ESCP Europe, he was a visiting scholar at Columbia Business School and Yale University. He was also a visiting professor at Hitotsubashi University and Boston College. His research lies at the intersection of family business, political connections, and finance. His research has been published in peer-reviewed finance journals such as the *Review of Financial Studies* and the *Journal of Financial and Quantitative Analysis*.

Lucia Ceja is a researcher for the Family-Owned Business Chair at IESE Business School. She obtained her Ph.D. in Work and Organizational Psychology from the University of Barcelona. Her current research interests within the family business field involve the genesis and development of psychological ownership in the next generation, management of values, family governance, and the application of coaching psychology to family business success. Within the field of organizational behavior, she is interested in the temporal evolution of employee well-being and the development of intervention programs aimed at fostering employee flourishing. Her work has been published in journals including *Journal of Organizational Behavior*, *Human Relations*, *Journal of Happiness Studies*, *Nonlinear Dynamics*, *Psychology*, and *Life Sciences*.

Andrea Colli teaches business and economic history at Bocconi University, Milan. He has published extensively about family firms and small- and medium-sized enterprises. Recently, he has published, with Franco Amatori, *Business History: Complexities and Comparisons* (London: Routledge, 2011).

Susanna Fellman (Dr. of Social Sciences) is Professor of Business History in the School of Business Economics and Law at Gothenburg University. Fellman has published extensively on the professionalization and modernization of management. She has also worked on labor market and industrial relations issues and on the Nordic model of capitalism. Her current research interests are especially related to cartels and competition policy in a historical perspective.

Paloma Fernández Pérez is Professor on the Faculty of Economics and Business at Universitat de Barcelona in Spain. Her current research interests include family businesses in emerging economies of the past and present, entrepreneurial networks, and intangible assets. Her most recent book is *La última globalización y el renacer de los negocios familiares en el mundo* (Bogotá: Universidad de los Andes/Cátedra Corona, 2012). She coordinates the *Network of Interdisciplinary Research in Family Firms* (available at http://www.ub.edu/histeco/p4/eng/researchers .php). She co-organizes (with A. Lluch) a research project of twenty researchers from eleven countries that studies large family businesses in

Latin America, Portugal, and Spain in the twentieth century and serves on the editorial boards of *Business History*, *Investigaciones de Historia Económica*, and *Entrepreneurial History Discussion Papers On-line*.

Esteban García-Canal is a professor of Management and International Business at the University of Oviedo (Spain). He is also President of the International Management Division of ACEDE and a member of the Institute of Business and Humanism at the University of Navarra. His research interests include strategic alliances, organizational design, international strategy, and emerging market multinationals. He has published in the *Strategic Management Journal*, *Academy of Management Perspectives*, *Research Policy*, *Journal of Management Studies*, *Journal of International Management*, and *Harvard Business Review*, among others.

Mauro F. Guillén is the director of the Joseph H. Lauder Institute at the University of Pennsylvania, a research and teaching program on management and international relations. He holds the Dr. Felix Zandman Endowed Professorship in International Management at the Wharton School and a secondary appointment as professor of sociology at the University of Pennsylvania. He also serves on the World Economic Forum's Global Agenda Council on Emerging Multinationals. He received a Ph.D. in sociology from Yale University and a doctorate in political economy from the University of Oviedo in his native Spain.

Vipin Gupta, Ph.D., Wharton School, is Professor and Co-director of the Global Management Center at the California State University San Bernardino. He has made significant contributions to the science of culture, sustainable strategic management in emerging markets, managing organizational and technological transformations, and entrepreneurial and women's leadership, and is a pioneer in the field of culturally sensitive models of family business around the world. In addition to about 150 publications, he has authored or edited sixteen books, including the seminal GLOBE book on culture and leadership in sixty-two societies, eleven on family business models in different cultural regions, two on organizational performance, one on the MNCs in China, and an innovative strategy textbook. Dr. Gupta has been a Japan Foundation Fellow and a recipient of the Society for Industrial Organizational Psychologists' coveted Scott M. Myers Award for Applied Research in 2005.

Harold James is Professor of History and International Affairs and the Claude and Lore Kelly Professor of European Studies at Princeton University. He was educated at Cambridge University and was a Fellow of Peterhouse for eight years before coming to Princeton University in 1986. His books include a study of the interwar depression in Germany, *The German Slump* (1986); an analysis of the changing character of national identity in Germany, *A German Identity 1770–1990* (1989); and *International Monetary Co-operation since Bretton Woods* (1996). He was also co-author of a history of Deutsche Bank (1995), which won the *Financial Times* Global Business Book Award in 1996. More recently, he has written *The End of Globalization: Lessons from the Great Depression* (2001); *Europe Reborn: A History 1914–2000* (2003); *Family Capitalism* (2006); *The Roman Predicament: How the Rules of International Order Create the Politics of Empire* (2006); and *The Creation and Destruction of Value: The Globalization Cycle* (2009). His study of the European Monetary Union was published by Harvard University Press in the fall of 2012. In 2004, he was awarded the Helmut Schmidt Prize for Economic History and in 2005 the Ludwig Erhard Prize for writing about economics. His current work is concerned with the history of European monetary union. He is director of the Center for European Politics and Society at Princeton. He is also Marie Curie Visiting Professor at the European University Institute and writes a monthly column for Project Syndicate.

Christopher Kobrak is a professor of finance at ESCP Europe, Paris and of business and financial history at Rotman School of Management, University of Toronto. An International Fellow at the Centre for Corporate Reputation, Oxford University, he serves on the editorial boards of several business history journals. His publications include *Banking on Global Markets: Deutsche Bank and the United States, 1870 to the Present* and *European Business, Dictatorship and Political Risk, 1920–1945* (edited with Per Hansen), as well as journal articles on a wide range of business and financial topics.

Marina Niforos is the Managing Director of the American Chamber of Commerce (AmCham) in France and the former Executive Director of the INSEAD Center on Diversity and Leadership. While at INSEAD, she participated in and managed global research projects such as the INSEAD/WEF collaboration on the Corporate Gender Gap. Her last publication on women in the family business was her chapter contribution for *Father-Daughter Succession in Family Business: A Cross-Cultural Perspective*, in which she examined the generational evolution in concepts of leadership and the changing role of women in assuming corporate management responsibilities in the context of the family business in Latin America through a specific case study on Peru. In 2012, she co-authored the joint report by AmCham and the Business Industry Advisory Committee to the OECD "Putting ALL Our Minds to Work: Harnessing the Gender Dividend, A Business Case."

Nuria Puig is Professor of Economic History and Institutions at the Universidad Complutense de Madrid, Spain. Her research focuses on the long-term effects of foreign investment and the role of business groups and family firms in twentieth-century Spain. Her last publication, "Globalization and the Organization of Family Philanthropy: A Case of Isomorphism?" (*Business History* 55(1), 2013), examines the development of family foundations in the United States, Germany, and Spain. She is the principal investigator of two publicly funded research projects, BOLDE (Business Organization in Late Developing Economies, www.bolde-project.net) and FILT (Foreign Investment and Local Talent, www.filt-project.com) and serves on the editorial boards of *Business History Review* and *Revista de Historia Industrial, Economía y Empresa*.

Carlo Salvato is an Associate Professor of Strategic Management and Entrepreneurship at Bocconi University in Milan, Italy. His research focus is on entrepreneurial capabilities in closely held firms. He is an associate editor of the *Family Business Review* and a board member of the Family Firm Institute (FFI), and he was elected PDW Chair and future Chair of the Entrepreneurship Division of the International Academy of Management.

Pramodita Sharma is the Sanders Professor for Family Business at the School of Business Administration, University of Vermont. She serves as the Academic Director of the Global Successful Transgenerational Entrepreneurship Practices (STEP) project. Sharma is the co-founder of the Family Enterprise Research Conference. She is the editor of the *Family Business Review* (FBR) – a Top 20 Business journal.

Hans Sjögren is Professor of Economic History and Institutional Economics at Linköping University and Adjunct Professor at Stockholm School of Economics. He has published extensively in the fields of business history and economic history, for example, on corporate governance, family business, financial crises, economic crime, entrepreneurship, and innovation.

Josep Tàpies is a professor in the Department of Strategic Management and holds the Family-Owned Business Chair at IESE Business School. He gained a Ph.D. in Industrial Engineering at the Polytechnic University of Catalonia (UPC) and an MBA at the ESADE Business School. As an expert in family-owned businesses, he teaches several courses and is a frequent speaker at family-business programs organized by business schools worldwide, such as AESE in Portugal, CEIBS in China, IDE in Ecuador, PAD-University of Piura in Peru, ISE in Brazil, IAE in Argentina, ESE in Chile, and INALDE in Colombia. He has also been a member of the academic board of IPADE in Mexico and ESE in Santiago, Chile.

Abbreviations

AESE	Associação de Estudos Superiores de Empresa
AGD	Aceitera General Deheza
AIdAF	Associazione Italiana delle Aziende Familiari
ALSA	Automóviles Luarca SA
AmCham	American Chamber of Commerce
BCG	Boston Consulting Group
BOLDE	Business Organization in Late Developing Economies
CASE	Culturally sensitive Assessment Systems and Education
CEIBS	China Europe International Business School
CEO	Chief Executive Officer
CPA	Certified Public Accountant
CSP	Corporate Social Performance
CSR	Corporate Social Responsibility
DNA	Deoxyribonucleic acid
EFB-GEEF	European Family Businesses
ESADE	Escuela Superior de Administración y Dirección de Empresas
ESE	Escuela Superior de Empresas
FB	Family Business
FBN	Family Business Network
FBR	*Family Business Review*
FBS	Family Business Studies
FFI	Family Firm Institute
FILT	Foreign Investment and Local Talent
FIM	Family Involvement in Management
FIO	Family Involvement in Ownership

F-PEC	Family: Power, Experience and Culture
GAS	G.A. Serlachius Ab
GEEF	Groupement Européen des Enterprises Familiales
GLOBE	Global Leadership and Organizational Behavior Effectiveness Program
GM	General Motors
HBS	Harvard Business School
HP	Hewlett-Packard
IAE	Instituto de Administración de Empresa
ICADE	Instituto Católico de Administración y Dirección de Empresas
IDE	Instituto de Dirección de Empresas
IEF	Instituto de la Empresa Familiar
IESE	Instituto de Estudios Superiores de la Empresa
IFERA	International Family Enterprise Research Academy
IMD	International Institute for Management Development
IMEDE	Institut pour l'Enseignement des Méthodes de Direction de l'Entreprise
IMF	International Monetary Fund
IMI	International Management Institute
INALDE	Instituto de Alta Dirección de Empresas
INI	Instituto Nacional de Industria
INSEAD	Institut Européen d'Administration des Affaires/European Institute of Business Administration
IPADE	Instituto Panamericano de Alta Direccion de Empresas
IPFB	International Program for Family Business
IPO	Initial Public Offering
MBA	Master of Business Administration
MIT	The Massachusetts Institute of Technology
MNC	Multi National Corporation
NX	National Express
NYSE	New York Stock Exchange
OECD	Organisation for Economic Co-operation and Development
PAD	Programa de Alta Dirección
PDW	Professional Development Workshop
PEC	Power, Experience and Culture
R&D	Research and Development
S&P	Standard and Poor's
SME	Small- and Medium-sized Enterprise

SOM	School of Management
STEP	Successful Transgenerational Entrepreneurship Practices
UFSAL	Universitaire Faculteiten Sint-Aloysius
U.S.	The United States of America
WEF	World Economic Forum

Introduction

A Global Revolution: The Endurance of Large Family Businesses around the World

Paloma Fernández Pérez and Andrea Colli

This book is about the dynamic evolution of one of the most popular, debated, and controversial forms of business ownership and management: family firms, in particular, those of large dimensions.

Family businesses are as old as humankind, and their relevance worldwide has been acknowledged and studied by a diverse group of social scientists, particularly historians, management scholars, and economists. The advent of the large corporation, as a result of the spread of mass production and distribution techniques, together with the creation of a new class of professional managers during the second half of the twentieth century, seemed to pose serious challenges to the survival of large family firms. In addition to this, the first oil crisis of the 1970s – which heavily hit OECD (The Organisation for Economic Co-operation and Development) economies – and, above all, the strong financial deregulation of the 1980s and 1990s meant new challenges for family firms, which were more exposed than others to the profound changes in the economic framework. Many economic and business history books indicate that, among the many consequences of the Second Industrial Revolution that spread through the diffusion of the technologies of mass production and distribution, calling for new organizational structures based on the skill of professional managers, was the decline of the role of the family as the provider of both financial and human capital in complex businesses (Chandler, Amatori, and Hikino 1997). Research written and published in the 1960s and 1970s addressed the rise of the modern professional corporation, pointing out the difficulties that traditional family businesses experienced in adapting to these changes (Chandler 1962, 1977). The basic idea was that, in industries characterized by economies of scale and economies of scope, a process of convergence in organizational and ownership structures was unavoidable – the future was the large, vertically integrated managerial multidivisional corporation, a reality requiring financial and managerial resources that could hardly be provided by a single family, even if it were wealthy, or by a skilled and talented individual. In terms of ownership, the solution was the fragmentation of capital among a multitude of shareholders, who were barely interested or totally disinterested in being involved in the management of the corporation: it was the rise of the public company.

However, despite a diffused feeling of convergence in corporate forms, research published since the late 1990s has stressed the enduring presence of family-controlled large businesses in many industries all over the world, in both developed and emerging economies (see, e.g., Jones and Rose 1993; Rose 1995; Colli 2003; Fernández Pérez 2012). Studies in management (Whittington and Mayer 2000), finance (La Porta et al. 1999), and corporate governance (Barca and Becht 1998) all simultaneously realized that large firms around the world were only partially converging toward the model of the public corporation. Both cross-sectional and longitudinal research demonstrated that concentrated ownership and management were the rule, in both advanced and emerging countries, and among the main owners family firms were still present. Family-controlled large business groups are considered to be a relevant feature and one of the distinctive advantages in emerging economies (Guillén 2001; Colpan, Hikino and Lincoln 2010). Even very recently, the public company has received some bad press; even though it is considered as an engine of modern economies, it shows serious weaknesses when compared with other ownership structures, including those based on families and dynasties, not only in developing economies, but also in mature ones (*The Economist*, May 19, 2012).

Was this not a contradiction of previous research that seemed to bury family businesses as an unsuitable and inefficient form of business organization? How was it possible that the old and traditional family firm that seemed to be in decline before the 1970s was showing such strength in the complex world of the third wave of globalization, a world dominated by transnational corporations and global networking after the 1980s? All of these questions are undoubtedly relevant to scholars, especially to business historians. However, besides these questions, one more general question surrounds the whole issue, one that is certainly crucial for public opinion: Why, if family businesses have dominated, and, indeed, still dominate the world, should one dedicate time to them at all?

A first consideration, common to almost all the publications and research in the field, is that family ownership is not only resilient among large firms, but also often connected to good levels of performance – not only economic performance, as some econometric evidence shows (Barontini and Caprio 2005), but also other types of performance.

To stress the vitality of family ownership as a management model that is particularly efficient under some conditions is not, however, the primary purpose of this book, which is instead to demonstrate that one must study family businesses because, notwithstanding their predominance and relevance, there is an enormous lack of reliable, comparable information about them. The diffusion of limited liability since the mid-nineteenth century allowed family businesses, particularly large businesses, to increase their anonymity, hiding themselves in official statistics at all administrative levels, where issues concerning ownership were far less important than those of a fiscal nature or those related to employment levels or other measures of productivity. Hence, official statistics regarded the nature of ownership as a factor that could have an influence on performance as irrelevant until very recent times, when legislation started to increase disclosure requirements. As a consequence, historical research on family firms (including the largest ones) still lacks an acceptable and comparable quantitative basis, on which it would be possible to build a shared definition of family ownership. Several chapters in this book clearly reveal the difficulties in properly defining what a family business is – something that is even more problematical when the historical perspective is introduced.

And the differences in the perception and the definition of what family ownership is, and of what a family firm or a family group is, are relevant for many reasons, not least because the different typologies of family ownership may influence our understanding of the process of internationalization and the growth of firms. In addition, the debate about the nature of family ownership is connected to a broader discussion of the diversity and ongoing changes of family models in the world. Demographers, anthropologists, and sociologists have all thoroughly studied how the introduction of birth control, new models of families, the massive incorporation of women into the salaried labor market, new sexual habits, the increase in life expectancy, the reduction in female fertility, and the increase in the age at first motherhood had an impact on the way in which families organize succession, inheritance, and business among generations and between genders. New families in changing societies have yielded new rules of internal government, new types of networking activities, and new ways of planning the continuity of the essence of the family across generations.

As the chapters in this book suggest in a more or less explicit way, this transformation is clearly evolutionary and dynamic, and something that calls for a multidisciplinary investigation. First of all, it has taken place on a world scale and in the long run (during the last century), which means that a dynamic approach, carried out on the basis of the existing case studies, is needed for its analysis. Second, this process has changed the family firm in a profound way from a microeconomic point of view. This "revolution" has concerned all the fundamental aspects of corporate life and culture, as well as the relationships between the family and the firm itself.

An interdisciplinary approach to this topic is even more necessary, given the past attitudes of scholars interested in family firms from different fields. Management scholars and business historians, albeit with different concepts, sources, and methods, and usually with very different goals, mainly resorted to case-study research. Broadly speaking, approaches from strategy and management research rarely take into account path dependency and historical rigidities. Case studies and essays written by consultants, advisors, and management scholars between the 1970s and 1990s immediately caught the impact of the changes in the external environment that took place after World War II in the structure, strategies, and organization of large family firms throughout the world (Gersick et al. 1997). Very little was done, however, to place these observations in a medium- to long-term perspective, or to analyze the changes in a global context: changes that have, in fact, constituted a process of global revolution that has taken place in large family businesses on different continents.

Business historians, on the other hand, usually provide a wealth of empirical data with little connection with theoretical debates and suffer from a sort of analytical weakness in formulating their research questions. Furthermore, their research perspective has never been truly international, rarely dealing with the key issues relating to leadership, training, or succession.

To move a step beyond in the analysis of this process of evolution, the chapters of this book, written by a variegated group of business historians and management scholars, explicitly combine concepts from management literature with the long-term view of business history, in a perspective that is global, longitudinal, and interdisciplinary. In the editors' opinion, this is the only way in which to understand fully the various aspects of the transformation of large family firms from "traditional" to "modern" organizations in which the relationship between the family dimension and that of the business shows a complex architecture. This transformation has been shaped differently in different sectors of activity, and in different environments; subsequently, the chapters of the book are explicitly comparative and take into account Asian, American, and European experiences.

The sections of this book broadly address different aspects of this evolution, while the individual chapters address the more specific issues. The first section (Chapters 1–4) is dedicated to key theoretical issues and debates concerning the evolution and structural transformation of large family firms. In Chapter 1, Fernández Pérez and Puig show how, despite the growing interest toward the topic from the early 1990s onward, family business research was not at all a new field of study. During the last century, historians and management scholars devoted time and energy to assess the various aspects of large, family-run corporations, in an effort to understand their evolutionary patterns in greater depth. One interesting example of this process is the debate concerning the individuation of a shared definition of what a family business is. As suggested by Sharma and Salvato in Chapter 2, the "tormented" individuation of a common definition says much of the evolutionary process of family firms and of family capitalism, which lies at the core of Harold James's analysis in Chapter 3, which is built around three cases of long-lived family firms in Europe. In James's perspective, longevity and sound performance are closely related to the ability of families to evolve in their relationship with the business, which, in the end, leads to a reduction of risk and uncertainty. In the last chapter of the section, however, Colli suggests a more balanced approach. The performance of family firms depends, in fact, on a delicate equilibrium between the positive and negative influences of the family presence, which, in its turn, evolves continuously during the natural process of expansion of the business activity.

Chapters 5 to 8 address exogenous, environmental conditions that have affected the process of transformation of many large family firms from traditional structures to modern institutions, given the institutional constraints provided by the environment. The chapters by Gupta, by Guillén and García-Canal, and by Sjögren, though focusing on particular countries, develop comparisons with other parts of the world and show that many large family firms have successfully made considerable efforts to transform traditional locally oriented strategies into global ones. In the course of this process, many firms disappeared, but some survived thanks to a complex learning process in which they modified their relationship both with the state and with other firms (Chapter 5 by Sjögren). In other cases, this evolutionary process has resulted in the birth of multinational family corporations characterized by a considerable competitive strength in global markets, through a great diversity of organizational skills and network capabilities (Chapter 6 by Gupta and Chapter 7 by Guillén and García-Canal). Besides some specific topics, these chapters highlight how successful large family firms were able to modernize their structures and strategies under the pressure of changing external economic and political conditions. The same dynamics can be individuated in industries, such as banking, and, in particular, in private banking, as analyzed in Chapter 8 by Kobrak and Bunkanwanicha, in which kinship qualities in business represent a much-needed counterweight to the social costs of uncritical reliance on market corrections.

The "global (r)evolution" under review is clearly not the exclusive outcome of exogenous pressures. The last section of the book focuses on some relevant, endogenous determinants of the transition process. The evolving cultural foundations and values of enduring large family firms, of which the changing contribution of women is a significant component, are examined in Chapter 9 by Blondel and Niforos and in Chapter 10 by Agulles, Ceja, and Tàpies. One relevant consequence of this cultural transformation concerns the prevailing management models among family firms. Professionalization (addressed by Susanna Fellman in Chapter 11) – that is, the increasingly diffuse employment of professional managers in key positions alongside family members and owners – is probably the most significant and celebrated outcome of the cultural transition in the variegated world of family firms.

The first relevant message delivered by the chapters in this book is that family firms confirm their dynamic nature and their ability to adapt to changing conditions in their external environments. Many examples mentioned in this book refer to longeve family firms of considerable dimensions. In some cases, they dominate their respective fields or are included among the global leaders in their sectors of activity. Their history bears witness to an outstanding ability to evolve and change in their intimate structure following the transformations occurring within the family, within the family business, and in the relationship between the family business and the changing environment, maintaining, however, at the same time, their identity in relation to a dynastic motive, or, as pointed out in the chapter by Sharma and Salvato, their "essence." The company histories mentioned in the chapters by Sjögren, by James, and by Guillén and García-Canal concerning large and longeval European family firms show successful cases of companies that were not only able to change some structural features (enhancing the professionalization of family members, successfully hiring outsiders, diversifying their activities from their original core business), but also able to preserve the family mission and essence – as examined in greater detail by authors dealing with the intimate aspects of the interaction between the family dimension and the entrepreneurial one, as the chapters by Gupta, by Blondel and Niforos, and by Agulles, Ceja, and Tàpies all show.

The second relevant contribution of this book – which clearly emerges from the chapters by Colli, by Kobrak and Bunkanwanicha, and by Guillén and García-Canal – is the emphasis on a critical approach to the universality of standard rules for success among family firms active in similar sectors and activities. These three chapters present significant examples that show how family resources can make a significant difference in the case of specific activities, adding a strategic asset and explaining how the familiar/family nature of business contributes to the reduction of uncertainty and risk in environments with imperfect market information and weak institutional protection of investors.

The third contribution of this book is to demonstrate the key role played by the professionalization of management in the course of this "global revolution," as suggested in the chapters by Fernández Pérez and Puig, and by Fellman. According to the latter, professionalization – that is, the hiring of professional managers and their insertion in key positions in the business alongside selected family members – is a function of a country's education policy, which impacts on the potential amount of professional managers available to firms, included those that are family owned. However, education alone is not the only factor that explains professionalization in family firms. Country-specific factors (as the Finnish case demonstrates) play a similar role to education in explaining the differences in the rate of professionalization of family firms among different countries and cultures.

The fourth contribution of this book is to frame the process of the transformation of large family firms in a long-term perspective. Theories and perspectives about family firms develop, in fact, together with the topic itself, as the various chapters point out. A more detailed knowledge of the evolutionary patterns in family business studies is thus a key element in our understanding of the process of the transformation of family capitalism. In their chapter, Fernández Pérez and Puig examine the strong connections between the changes in the economic and political framework in developed Western countries in the late 1970s and during the 1980s, the evolving nature of large family firms, and the creation of incentives to the institutionalization of family business research in the world. New challenges for family firms resulted in new directions for academic research. Deregulation and privatization all over the world, growing fiscal pressure in developed countries, the opening of new global markets, and the creation of big regional blocks in the world economy offered new challenges to family business leaders, who were, however, able to count on a bigger and better pool of professional consultants and advisors. The incentives to institutionalize family business research in universities, associations, and business schools, and also to standardize knowledge that could be efficiently used by family business consultants around the globe was thus strengthened. In the end, families, businesses, society, and the academic world established a new era of fruitful dialogue.

In synthesis, this book addresses some topics that are currently at the core of the research into family firms, framing this in a comparative and historical perspective, with a particular emphasis on the transformation in crucial and critical variables to interpret the changing nature of family capitalism. These include professionalization, the changes in the nature and structure of the family, the transformation in gender roles, the transformation in financial markets, the increasing relevance of cultural capital and reputation, the strategic role played by social capital, for instance, in the process of international expansion, the changes in leadership education and transmission, and, last, but not least, the political implications of personal/family control over large companies in both the developed and developing economies.

The main assumption underlying this book is that something occurred to the intimate nature of large family firms in the course of the last decades, that is, in the way in which families have managed, financed, and governed corporations. Family companies also changed their relationships with the external environment, from the government to the vast array of stakeholders. New ways of organizing resources and of using accumulated know-how have been put in place. Family firms have been able to count on better formal business education, political support from local and global institutions, as well as on improved legal and financial tools. Consultants have increasingly provided their services to family leaders. These changes have taken place in different parts of the world, at different moments, and in different circumstances. It has been a slow but pervasive "global revolution" for many large family businesses, a process of change in their ownership, governance, and organizational structures, which resulted into the emergence of a new typology of family firm, characterized by the professionalization of family members and by the hiring of skilled professionals, without implying the vanishing of family control or influence over the firm and its policies. For those firms that successfully underwent this process of change, the outcome has been growth and increased market power.

Far from being passive organizations, the case studies presented in this book suggest that family firms have been well aware of the need to change their traditional organizational forms by adapting to the changing environment. Many were active actors seeking to influence the evolution of the environment when searching for a new internal organization able to adjust to the external new conditions.[1]

This book poses many questions and aims to encourage new research agendas. The evidence reported in the chapters contests the idea that family firms are a transient stage of development of business in the world, and suggests that, on the contrary, they are an example of successful adaptation to changes in the environment. From a normative point of view, this book confirms the extent to which, among large companies, family ownership and management are today sustainable during the process of growth much more than in the past. In other words, institutional and "environmental" factors allow family firms to endure, provided that the families consciously adapt their culture and values to the external constraints and opportunities.

References

Barca, Fabrizio, and Marco Becht, eds. (1998). *The Control of Corporate Europe.* Oxford: Oxford University Press.

Barontini, Roberto, and Lorenzo Caprio. "The Effect of Family Control on Firm Value and Performance. Evidence from Continental Europe." June 2005, EFA 2005 Moscow Meetings Paper. Available at: http://ssrn.com/abstract=675983 or http://dx.doi.org/10.2139/ssrn.675983 (Accessed 9 September, 2012).

Chandler, Alfred D. (1962). *Strategy and Structure: Chapters in the History of the American Industrial Enterprise.* Cambridge, MA: The MIT Press.

Chandler, Alfred D. (1977). *The Visible Hand: Managerial Revolution in American Business.* Cambridge, MA: Belknap Press.

---

[1] This active role of large family businesses facing the new waves of globalization of the economy and the new institutional changes affecting different parts of the world during the last century has been assumed and developed by a line of scholars whose theoretical contributions have influenced the different chapters of the book (Jones and Rose 1993; Rose 1995; Chua et al., 1999).

Chandler, Alfred D., Franco Amatori, and Takashi Hikino, eds. (1997). *Big Business and the Wealth of Nations*. Cambridge, MA: Cambridge University Press.

Chua, Jess H., James J. Chrisman, and Pramodita Sharma (1999). "Defining the Family Business by Behavior." *Entrepreneurship Theory and Practice*, 23(4): 19–39.

Colli, Andrea (2003). *The History of Family Business*. Cambridge: Cambridge University Press.

Colpan, Asli M., Takashi Hikino, and James R. Lincoln (2010). *The Oxford Handbook of Business Groups*. Oxford: Oxford University Press.

Fernández Pérez, Paloma, ed. (2012). *La última globalización y el renacer de los grandes negocios familiares en el mundo*. Bogotá: Publicaciones de la Cátedra Corona de la Facultad de Administración de la Universidad de los Andes.

Gersick, Kelin E., John Davis, Marion Hampton, and Ivan Lansberg (1997). *Generation to Generation: Life Cycles of the Family Business*. Cambridge, MA: Harvard Business School Press.

Guillén, Mauro F. (2001). *The Limits of Convergence, Globalization and Organizational Change in Argentina, South Korea, and Spain*. Princeton, NJ: Princeton University Press.

Jones, Geoffrey, and Mary B. Rose, eds. (1994). *Family Capitalism*. London: Routledge.

La Porta, Rafael, Florencio Lopez-de-Silanes, and Andrei Shleifer (1999). "Corporate Ownership around the World." *Journal of Finance*, 54(2): 471–517.

Rose, Mary B., ed. (1995). *Family Business*. Cheltenham: Edward Elgar Publishing.

"The Big Engine That Couldn't: public companies Have Had a Difficult Decade, Battered by Scandals, tied Up by Regulations and Challenged by Alternative Corporate Forms." *The Economist*, May 19, 2012. Available at: http://www.economist.com/node/21555552 (Accessed 9 September, 2012).

Whittington, Richard, and Michael Mayer (2000). *The European Corporation*. Oxford: Oxford University Press.

PART ONE

THEORETICAL ISSUES AND DEBATES

I

The Emergence of Family Business Studies

A Historical Approach to Pioneering Centers, Scholars, and Ideas

Paloma Fernández Pérez and Nuria Puig[*]

THE INTEREST OF MANY DISCIPLINES IN FAMILY BUSINESS

Family business has been on the research agenda of academic anthropologists and historians since at least the nineteenth century. Families and their different systems of self-definition and alliance, and the functionality of for both social and economic life, have been the focus of a number of dissertations of European and North American scholars since the 1940s. Most of them based their new theories about kinship on extensive field research developed in South America, Africa, Oceania, and Asia (Evans-Pritchard 1940; Lévi-Strauss 1947; Radcliffe-Brown and Forde 1950; Goody 1983). Kinship systems, descent groups, lineages, phratries, and other forms of family organization were studied, and debates among proponents of structuralist, functionalist, and other theoretical approaches flourished in the second half of the twentieth century. The changes experienced in marriage, family, and kinship in the second half of the twentieth century also attracted the attention of sociological studies, particularly in the United States (Smith 1999).

History has paid attention to the evolution of family systems of organization and the structures of social life, particularly after the 1940s.

* The authors are grateful for comments on an original version of this chapter received at the Workshop "Global Revolution. Endurance and Transformation of Large Family Firms in the World," held at the University of Barcelona on October 30, 2009. We also thank Miguel Ángel Gallo, Alfredo Pastor, John Davis, Alden G. Lank, Ivan Lansberg, and Judy Green for their kind cooperation. All errors are, of course, ours. Financial assistance has been received at different stages of the research and writing process from Spanish public research projects ECO2008-00398, ECO2009-10977, and ICREA (Institució Catalana de Recerca i Estudis Avançats) Academia 2008 award.

Most of the great works written from the end of the Second World War until the end of the 1970s focused their attention not on the people of distant Asia, Oceania, or Africa, but on America and Europe. French, British, North American, and German social historians all published volumes on marriage, sex, childhood, divorce, and culture for periods since the Middle Ages (Ariès 1960; Flandrin 1976; Stone 1977; Goody 1983; Ariès and Duby 1986; Gies and Gies 1987). They paid close attention to concepts and methods from more theoretically grounded disciplines that were used to deal with families in the past in a more quantitative way, such as the influential Cambridge Group of Demography led by Peter Laslett (which was interested in the study of household formation and the evolution of fertility rates). Classical, social, historical, and demographical studies focusing on families and their businesses developed during the golden age of capitalism of the 1950s and 1960s, in a context of a rapid increase of household consumption (led by decisions made by women as consumers) and the emergence of women in the labor market (with its concomitant implications in changes in traditional marriage and fertility patterns and in family structures). Changes in family systems and family patterns, which affect social and economic life, are still an outstanding subject of study among social historians interested in the interaction between family life and social evolution, and between family networks and economic growth in a path-dependent evolutionary perspective (Ozment 1983; Lewin 1987; Casey 1989; Fernández Pérez 1997; Chacón et al. 2003; Rodríguez 2004; Chacón and Hernández 2007; García González Cuenca 2008).

Economic and business historians began, between the late 1940s and the late 1970s, to study the success of the large U.S.-style corporations in the world, with debates about the contribution of family-owned and family-managed businesses to the economic growth, or decline, of Western capitalist economies (Fernández Pérez 2003). The crisis of the 1970s, the beginning of the privatization process, and deregulatory legislation, as well as the effects of new technologies of information and communication, in both traditional and new businesses throughout the world, led to the success of flexible forms of business organization after the 1980s. From the 1980s onward, an increasing number of economic and business historians started to research the theoretical foundations and/or the history of family firms and family business groups in their countries (Casson 1999).

Owing to the nature of anthropological and historical research, which requires – above all in the field of history – some distance between the researchers and the subjects of their study, in relation to the process of analysis and the interpretation of the empirical data, the interests of researchers very often have been very different from the objectives and needs of the family business stakeholders under study. Furthermore, anthropologists and historians have not been interested in institutionalizing their particular field of research through the creation of special chairs, centers, associations, and publications focusing on family business research, with only a few remarkable exceptions.[1] In comparison with the family business studies developed by scholars of management, many of whom have consulting experience, which we analyze in the following section, family business studies are only a marginal topic of study in these disciplines, with isolated and dispersed practitioners.

THE INSTITUTIONALIZATION OF FAMILY BUSINESS STUDIES

Another type of family business researchers, who were much more interested in the personal and professional needs of the people involved in a family business, or in the contribution of family businesses to economic growth and development in the world, flourished in the late 1940s and early 1950s, particularly from the late 1970s, in schools and faculties of economics, business, sociology, law, and psychology. Though different in academic training, work methodology, and objectives, a common denominator of this second type of family business scholars is that they had – and continue to have – an interest in understanding family business needs and professionalize their educational and professional methods to meet these needs. In this process, scholars from different disciplines and countries have organized the institutionalization of a new subject of study. This process has encouraged the professionalization of family business studies since the late 1970s – first, through academic efforts to standardize definitions, concepts, and theories, and second, through the institutionalization of family business programs, associations, centers of study and research, and publications – in order to organize the creation and dissemination of ideas. There is an effort toward the standardization of knowledge, which may guarantee the quality of the services provided to family business stakeholders in different regions of the world (Sharma et al. 2007).

[1] Two outstanding exceptions have been *The Journal of Family History*, which began publication in 1976, and the University of Murcia group of study and publications about the history of the family from a social and political historical perspective, created in the late 1980s by Francisco Chacón. Among demographers, the Cambridge Group studied household composition and evolution in international comparison, led by Peter Laslett.

The chronology of the key developments in the emergence of family business research as an institutionalized field of study, under this second type of approach, is already well known (Jones and Rose 1993; Rose 1995; Sharma, Chrisman, and Chua 1996, 1997; Colli 2003; Colli, Fernández Pérez, and Rose 2003; Fernández Pérez 2003; Sharma et al. 2007). As a result of this existing knowledge, we already know about the origins of family business research as a new scientific field of study in the world, from the first doctoral dissertation that specialized in the subject, completed in the United States in 1953; to the first European dissertation on the legal situation of family firms, written by an Asian author in 1963; to the first consulting firm in Brazil in the early 1970s; to the first European programs and chairs in the late 1980s; and to the 128 family business centers and 50 premiere business schools with family business programs in 2008.[2]

This section provides a short description of the most outstanding North American and European drivers of knowledge about family business research, whose contributions led to the institutionalization of a type of professional family business research closely linked to the interests and needs of family business stakeholders and to the professional study of the contribution of family businesses to economic growth and development. The following section presents the key ideas that composed the first body of knowledge about family businesses taught at the first European chair of family firm studies, in Barcelona, in the 1980s and 1990s. This chapter thus adds an analysis of the historical context, and a new ideologically based perspective, to the existing literature about the origins of family business studies, which has concentrated on the description of the "infrastructure" of centers, associations, and publications (Sharma, Chrisman, and Chua 1996, 1997; Sharma 2004; Sharma et al. 2007).

The Historical Context

The fact that the institutionalization of Family Business Studies (FBS) took place in the United States requires a few observations about the U.S. economic and social context. After the Second World War, a combination of factors created the conditions that led to a need for a specialized body of knowledge, with formal training methods and practitioners. The demand grew between the 1950s and 1970s because many family firms

---

[2] Panikkos Poutziouris, "The Family Business Academy: Trends and Practices," unpublished speech delivered at the Family Business Conference, Budapest, September 11, 2008; and Sharma et al. 2007.

created at the end of the nineteenth century and in the first decades of the twentieth century, as well as firms created after the 1929 crisis, were experiencing conflicts in their transition to second, third, and even fourth generations of family control. According to a 1971 survey of the approximately 1 million registered corporations in the United States, around 980,000 were family owned or controlled (*Industry Week*, 1971, cited in Beckhard and Gibb Dyer 1981: 1). After the 1970s, these family businesses – some of them new fortunes (the Buffets, the Gateses), some the continuation of late-nineteenth century family businesses (the Fords, the Rockefellers), and some heirs of postwar businesses (such as the Waltons of Wal-Mart) – were confronting the need to justify their wealth in terms of democratic values, to protect their fortunes from the folly and extravagance of their descendants, and to protect their descendants from the corruption of wealth (Marcus and Hall 1992; Hall and Marcus 1998). Moreover, the macroeconomic environment was changing, with President Richard Nixon abandoning the existing Bretton Woods system of international financial exchange by unilaterally canceling the direct convertibility of the U.S. dollar to gold, which had served to guarantee monetary stability in the world, and the impact of the oil crisis in many oversized multinational corporations. Debts, bankruptcies, and monetary problems added new financial problems to the traditional three challenges that had confronted U.S. family firms from the time of the late-eighteenth century Bostonian dynasties. The traditional use of spendthrift trusts, charities, and acts of philanthropy to reduce taxation and organize the professionalization of management and its separation from ownership, which had previously been so common in the United States, shifted to the use of professional experts from different fields – lawyers and psychologists – after the 1970s and 1980s. In addition, U.S. family firms were becoming older,[3] and, with them, the number of family managers also grew, in transition from the founder's stage to the brothers' and cousins' consortium's stages, thus presenting a much more complicated scenario that was plagued by conflict.

Conflict in the succession of family firms, as family business specialists have frequently indicated (Jones and Rose 1993; Colli, Fernández, and Rose 2003), involve financial, psychological, managerial, labor relations, and strategic problems. Traditional family firms previously washed their dirty laundry in private without external consultants, but North American family firms, particularly those of medium and large size, had

---

[3] An overview of the year of foundation of the 150 oldest U.S. family firms, available at: www.familybusinessmagazine.com/top150html, is revealing in this regard.

experienced a process of professionalization, with many of their junior family members holding degrees from the prestigious business schools and many external consultants managing trusts and charitable foundations, as well as family offices (in existence since the nineteenth century at least), according to Marcus and Hall (1992) and Hall and Marcus (1998). It was relatively easy for U.S. family business stakeholders (easier than for European, Asian, or Latin American family business stakeholders in the 1970s) to understand and, above all, to accept that the continuity of the family firm also needed professional assistance.

From the early 1970s, the economic crisis hit big corporations hard, and unemployment grew; in this context, popular opinion was increasingly against tax deduction policies that favored the charitable donations of wealthy individuals and corporations. Tax policies had progressively benefited the old dynasties in the 1970s. Top marginal tax rates for the wealthiest of the country had consistently declined in the last third of the twentieth century under a series of new liberal republican governments. It had descended from the 91 percent top marginal tax rate established in Eisenhower's time in the 1950s (it had ranged from 63 to 79 percent during the New Deal policies of the 1930s), to an average of 70 percent during Nixon's presidency in the 1970s, and to around 50 percent in Ronald Reagan's presidency during the 1980s.[4]

On the other hand, the crisis hit both public and private firms and corporations hard as well, owing to rising prices and the devaluation of the U.S. dollar with the collapse of the Bretton Woods system. Productive activities suffered from increasing prices and a reduction in profits. At a political revel, and to confront the popular discontent with a set of policies that could simultaneously satisfy both the wealthy and the lower and middle classes, a coalition of members of powerful entrepreneurial dynasties of the country and members of the government and key public and private institutions joined forces in the 1970s (e.g., in the File Commission of 1973–75 and in the Independent Sector Association of the early 1980s), creating a positive environment in which family business consultants, and family business studies, could emerge in the United States.[5]

---

[4] Available at: http://politics.gather.com/viewArticle.action?articleId=281474977623449 (Accessed July 23, 2010).

[5] Commission on Private Philanthropy and Public Needs. Giving in America. Toward a Stronger Voluntary Sector. Report of the Commission on Private Philanthropy and Public Needs, 1975. Available at: https://archives.iupui.edu/handle/2450/889 (Accessed July 26, 2010). Details in Fernández Pérez (2012).

The Institutionalization of Family Business Studies

In the early 1980s, the family firm started to be seen as a unique business form. According to John Davis (interviewed May 13, 2009), one of the main drivers of FBS in the United States, a few people were showing professional and academic interest in Family Business (FB), a quite discredited topic at the time, when the big managerial firms were seen as superior. In Davis's words, FB people saw (and see) themselves as "business doctors" who solved problems, performed research, theorized, and published articles on family firms. From the beginning, the legitimization of family business studies was a professional *and* academic process that took place, first and foremost, in the United States. A summary of the chronology of all the key events and dates of this process has recently been published (see Table 1 in Sharma et al. 2007), and so we concentrate on the dominant ideas of the key drivers of the institutionalization of family business studies, many of whom were interviewed especially for this chapter.

A founding meeting took place in 1982, organized by Richard Beckhard and Ivan Lansberg (Kaslow 2006: 4). Barbara S. Hollander, the founder and first president of the Family Firm Institute (FFI), explained in 1993 that "What was needed was a mechanism that would bring together the people who were looking at the major questions and issues related to family business" (Lansberg 1993). Hollander was just finishing her dissertation on Levinson Steel, a large manufacturer of steel products founded in Pittsburgh by Jewish immigrants and a complex organization with more than forty-five shareholder cousins. To discuss her research, she contacted Dick Beckhard, Elaine Kepner, Gibb Dyer, and Ivan Lansberg, all of whom were involved in a project at the Massachusetts Institute of Technology. In addition, she interviewed John Ward at Loyola, John Messervey in Chicago, Leon Danco in Cleveland, Fredda Herz in New York, John Davis at the University of Southern California, and Peter Davis at Wharton.

In 1983, Hollander, Aaron Levinson, and some of the aforementioned scholars created a group that donated the money needed to incorporate the FFI. One faculty member from the MIT Sloan School of Management (Richard Beckhard), Hollander, Elaine Kepner, and the two businessmen, Aaron Levinson and George Raymond, each contributed U.S.$2000 to help defray what would become the FFI's start-up expenses. Additional friends of Lansberg, including John Davis, Kelin Gersick, Ernesto Poza, John Ward, and Joe Astrachan – the latter then an organization behavior doctoral student at the Yale School of Management – set out to design an institute that would "bring together consultants, bankers, academics, lawyers, family therapists, and accountants to talk about family business" (Kaslow 2006: 4). Two meetings helped the creation of the FFI, one in Safety Harbor, Florida, in 1985, and another at University of Southern California in November 1985. A charter was drawn, and Barbara Hollander was chosen as the first president. The Founding Board consisted of the seven founders and fifteen additional members. From 1987 to 1991, Rod Correll was executive director and the FFI was housed in his consulting offices in Johnstown, New York. Membership grew to more than 400 people by 1990, and went beyond 770 active members by 1992, including consultants, educators, and family business owners (Kaslow 2006). The FFI held its first meeting in Los Angeles in 1984. Four years later, the *Family Business Review* was launched under the editorship of the Yale consultant Ivan Lansberg (Hollander and Elman 1988; Lansberg 1988).

In 1991, Rod Correll, who had been the executive director of FFI from 1987, resigned. He was replaced by Judy Green, and the FFI headquarters moved to Boston. Soon after, the newly elected president of the FFI, Craif Aronoff, stressed the educational goals of the institute (Kaslow 2006: 10). Green (interviewed July 30, 2009) shed light on the early transformation of the FFI, as she confirmed that business owners were being "kicked out" when she arrived. Commenting on this important move, Ivan Lansberg (interviewed July 20, 2009), explained that, although the FFI was built on three pillars (consultants, academics, and business owners), these foundations had soon started to crack. Their interests diverged, and business owners, despite the drive and initiative of Levinson and Raymond, felt increasingly uncomfortable. Hence, the FFI evolved toward a professional association dominated by FB consultants with a background in psychology.

The Emergence of Family Business Studies in Europe

The institutionalization of family business studies in Europe started in 1987–8, with Frank Tilley's appointment to the International Management Institute (IMI) as executive-in-residence (Lank and Thomassen 1991). Tilley was a second-generation owner-CEO of a Canadian luxury leather-goods company. It was he who advised the faculty and administration of the IMI to address the particular concerns of family-controlled enterprises and helped the school to establish contacts with many European family firms, as well as with academics and consultants interested in this topic. According to Alden Lank, the IMI was not interested in family business and was not supportive at all (interviewed June 26, 2009). However, it was Tilley who launched the IMI's first International Program for Family Business (IPFB), choosing its core faculty: John Davis (University of Southern California), Ivan Lansberg (Yale), and John Ward (Loyola). Tilley gathered a small group of Europeans to discuss what could be done to respond effectively to the needs of family firms. The seminar "Leading the Family Business" had 750 participants from about 400 families and 40 countries between 1988 and 2003 (Kaslow 2006: 12).

In 1988–9, Tilley was succeeded as executive-in-residence by Jerry Stempler, a textile manufacturer who had just completed a dissertation on succession in family firms. He established a formal network of Europeans interested in family business, which would evolve into the European Study Group on Family Business, promoting cooperation with the FFI. This cooperation was strengthened by Stempler's successor, George Raymond, the second-generation chairman of Raymond Manufactures and a founding member of the FFI. Raymond decided to start an independent organization, the Family Business Network (FBN), with Lank's assistance. Lank stated that the main aim of the FBN was to play an important part in fostering greater understanding of the vital place of family businesses in the political, social, and economic life of Europe and the world (Lank and Thomassen 1991). The FBN annual conference attracted participants: from 40 attendants in 1990, it reached 500 by 2002, and, by 2006, it had a membership of 1,600 people from 50 different countries (Kaslow 2006: 12).

The headquarters of the FBN were established in Lausanne, the seat of the IMEDE business school (Institut pour l'Enseignement des Méthodes de Direction de l'Entreprise). In the late 1980s, the IMEDE received an endowment of 3 million Swiss francs from the Swiss entrepreneur Stephan Schmidheini to create a Family Business Center and a Family Firm Studies Chair, the first of its kind in Europe. The chair was held by Alden Lank, an American specialist in business strategy. In 1990, the IMI and the IMEDE merged to become IMD (International Institute for Management Development). Lank's first institutional project was the Family Business Network. Its founding board was composed of eight European-based family business experts: Rik Donckels, director of the Small Business Research Institute at UFSAL University (Universitaire Faculteiten Sint-Aloysius), Brussels; Miguel Ángel Gallo, professor of family business at the IESE (Instituto de Estudios Superiores de la Empresa), Barcelona; Johan Giertsen, University of Bergen; Joost van Hamel, partner of Ondernemingsbestuur in Zeist, Netherlands; Bernd A. Klughardt, BK Losingen fuer Familienunternehmen in Kolsaberg, Austria; Anthony W. Travis, partner of Price Waterhouse in Geneva; Alden G. Lank, professor of family enterprises at the IMD in Lausanne; and Albert J. Thomassen, professor of management and organization at University of Groningen, the Netherlands. Thomassen and Lank were elected president and executive director, respectively, of the new institution.

The FBN's first recruiting campaign was quite successful. This allowed it to hold its first annual conference, which took place in 1990 in Lausanne, on the theme "Family Business in Europe: The Challenges to the Oldest and Predominant Form of Enterprise." The second conference was held one year later in Barcelona under the sponsorship of the IESE. It coincided with the establishment of IESE's chair of family business, the second in Europe, under the lead of Miguel Ángel Gallo.

The relationship between the FBN and the IMD has continued to be close. The program launched by Tilley twenty years ago, now called "Leading the Family Business," remains the flagship of the school in family business education, with more than 700 participants according to the school's website. The family-owned private bank Lombard Odier Darier Hentsch & Cie has regularly contributed to the development of the IMD's Family Business Center.

In 2012, the FBN had 5,600 family business members in 56 countries with 26 chapters worldwide.[6] Its focus is on networking and the sharing of knowledge and best practices. Unlike its mentor the FFI, the FBN lacks an academic journal. Its official publication, which began in 1992, is *Families in Business* magazine.

Discussing the influence of the FFI on the FBN, Lank states that it was huge, albeit indirect. Many of the promoters were on the boards of both institutions, and the same people met frequently at their conferences. The FFI provided a small, yet influential, group of European family entrepreneurs with a new awareness of the importance of analyzing, in a theoretical manner, issues such as ownership structure, succession design, and conflict management in family-owned businesses.

Family Business Owners and Scholars Since the 1990s: Going Global?

The available evidence suggests that the knowledge generated in American academic centers by specialists in family-owned businesses in the United States was adapted quite eclectically to large- and medium-sized

---

[6] Available at: http://www.fbn-i.org (Accessed October 5, 2012).

European firms along with the direct assistance of a few family firm owners and consultants. But Lank soon realized that there was a danger of competition, because their goals were similar (education and networking). Even more important was the fact that the FBN was growing slowly, and European business people found the FFI conferences too academic. Consequently, he quite literally expelled academics from its membership (and, later on, from the board) to make the FBN an association for business owners. The focus (and success) of the FBN soon became education and the next generation international program.

The American Family Firm Institute and the European Family Business Network provided the founding group of the Spanish Instituto de la Empresa Familiar (IEF) with the necessary ideas, professionals, and contacts to make their project successful. In contrast with the more educational American experience that underpins the legitimization of family business, the Spanish experience has focused on the tax system. What is interesting here is the impact of the Spanish lobby on other European countries. Many Spanish entrepreneurs had business contacts with other European family firms, and word of the Spanish success spread throughout Europe and in Latin America. In the late 1990s, other European family business interest groups soon tried to imitate the strategies of the Spanish Institute to achieve social and political recognition, and centers and organizations fostering diverse interests connected with this kind of firm blossomed in each national legal context. The national association of family firms adopted similar external strategies, following the Spanish model: the members had to be distinctive and important family firms; websites insisted on educational and social goals; workshops and conferences often dealt with the internal problems faced by large, traditional family firms, and with the investments to be made in a globalized economy. It was in this context that the Groupement Européen des Enterprises Familiales (GEEF) appeared in 1997, with ten national associations (Bulgaria, Finland, France, Germany, Italy, the Netherlands, Norway, Portugal, Spain, and Sweden). The pioneering figures of the new institution were originally two Spaniards, who were also leading figures within the IEF: Marian Puig and Fernando Casado. Spaniards have a more than significant presence in the directorate of the GEEF. In 2008, Marian Puig was the honorary president, Jesús Casado of the IEF Madrid was secretary-general, and Alfonso Líbano of Cobega represented the IEF as one of the GEEF's three vice presidents.[7] The name was changed to EFB-GEEF (European Family

---

[7] Available at: http://www.geef.org/structure.php.

Businesses) in 2009 to reflect the evolution that it has experienced in these twelve years, from being a European group with economic interests to its new identity as a federation of national associations, with the leadership of Philip Aminoff and Jesús Casado, and a permanent representation in Brussels to negotiate with the European Commission. In May 2012, and after a meeting of European vice president Othmar Karas with the new president of the EFB, Roger Pedder, the European Parliament debated – for the first time – two key issues affecting family businesses: taxation, and succession (*IEF Magazine* 2012: 13).

Other countries started to turn their heads toward the U.S. and Spanish models of organization of family business, adapting some of their features to their own particular needs. Thus, in 1997, the year of the creation of the GEEF, the Associazione Italiana delle Aziende Familiari (AIdAF)[8] was created in Italy (now with 26 founding members, and Alberto Falck as chairman from 1997 to 2003). In addition, Latin American and Asian entrepreneurs studying in American and European institutions soon learned of the efficient methods of international networking. Data from the Family Business Network (FBN), with which the European national associations have close contacts, show that national centers and organizations for the promotion and networking of family firms appeared everywhere in the world, except in Africa. Between 1990 and 1998, eight national associations, called chapters, were created and linked to the FBN. Since 1998, national associations to promote the study of the specialized aspects of family firms have also appeared: in the Netherlands (1999); Brazil and France (2000); Japan and the United Kingdom (2001); India, Ireland, and Belgium (2005); Austria, Chile, and Colombia (2006); Australia and Bulgaria (2007); and Denmark and Switzerland (Geneva) (2008). Like the FBN and the IEF, most of these associations lack the academic drive and ambition of the FFI, which promoted the legitimization of family business. Like the FBN and the IEF, these associations have strong links, especially their headquarters, with business schools, for many of which the financial and social support of large local family firms is vital.

THE CREATION OF NEW ACADEMIC KNOWLEDGE ABOUT FAMILY BUSINESS STUDIES IN SPAIN IN THE EARLY 1990S

Following the intense process of networking and association of significant family business leaders in America and the United States, some academic

---

[8] Available at: http://www.aidaf.it.

centers and scholars began work to prepare textbooks and conferences addressing the needs of this kind of firms and their associations. Miguel Ángel Gallo created a school of thought and developed research during three decades, leaving a strong influence in Spanish-speaking scholars of Europe and America specialized in family business studies.

Probably the first person who published a book on family businesses in Spain was Ngô Bá Thành, a former legal assistant to the president of the Southern Republic of Vietnam in the 1960s. She wrote a Ph.D. dissertation in 1961 under the supervision of professor Antonio Polo about the anonymous family firm, which was published as a book two years later (Ngô 1963). This occurred only a few years after the first dissertation on family businesses had been presented at a public university in the world by Grant H. Calder, at the University of Indiana in 1953, and the first book on the subject appeared, written by Stephen Cambien – professor of business administration at the École d'Administration des Affaires des Facultés Catholiques in Lille – in France in 1959 (Forces et faiblesses des enterprises familiales, translated into Spanish in 1960 by the Asociación Católica de Dirigentes y Pylsa S.A.). Cambien taught the first course on family businesses at the private school Instituto de la Empresa Familiar (IESE) of Barcelona, in 1961, the same year that Ngô Bá Thành finished her dissertation on legal and mercantile aspects of the family firms in Spain in an international framework. Joaquín Arquer published a book much later, in 1979, on the manageurial aspects related to these firms (Empresas Familiares, in Universidad de Navarra, Barcelona).

However, family business research and studies gained momentum with the establishment of the chair of Family Business at the private business school IESE, in Barcelona, which, significantly enough, was negotiated in 1986, the year of Spain's adherence to the European Economic Community, and started its activities a year later, in 1987. The IESE invited Miguel Ángel Gallo to be its first chairman, and, until his retirement in 2003, he developed continuous research and used his personal talent to attract family business members as well as students to the activities organized by the chair.

Gallo was able to adapt modern U.S. concepts and methods of management and family business organization to the very different needs of the small- and medium-sized family businesses that dominated backward economies like the Spanish one. He elaborated textbooks, theoretical models, and case studies and actively supported international networking with experts from other European and American countries. Family businesses in Spain, as in other Latin countries in both Europe and

America, had, in those decades, to combine the problems of a changing society with its changing family values, with business problems related to the need to address the challenges involved in the integration in world markets.

In the early 1990s, Gallo combined three uncommon features: (1) experience in the management of a medium-sized family business; (2) close knowledge of pioneering U.S. concepts, methods, centers, associations, and scholars that specifically addressed family business needs; and (3) an excellent supportive local environment in which to teach and publish his ideas about the organization and strategy of family business, in the private business school IESE of Barcelona (Gallo 2008).

Miguel Ángel Gallo Laguna de Rins had worked in his family business for seven years, a business that specialized in screw manufacturing, which employed around 500 employees in the 1950s. The business had been founded by Gallo's maternal great-grandfather and had good connections with Banco Central and with Juan Villalonga, a very influential person in Gallo's life. Miguel Ángel Gallo was also heavily influenced in his ideological education by his membership in the Catholic association Opus Dei from 1953. Gallo was also influenced by his university education in Barcelona, where he obtained a Ph.D. in industrial engineering, and by the seven years that he spent afterward working in the family firm. His life changed when he accepted the proposal of IESE's Antonio Valero for him to work in this private business school in Barcelona in 1966 (with a yearly salary of 240,000 pesetas, approximately a fifth of the income he earned in the family firm). His responsibility would be to teach a course entitled the "Organization of Production" and to write books about organization and corporate social responsibility (CSR). His experience in organization would prove extremely important to understand the kinds of ideas and methods that he developed when he initiated his contact with family business studies in 1988.

Sometime between 1986 and 1987, a "theoretically" anonymous local entrepreneur donated one million U.S. dollars to the IESE to create the first Spanish chair of family firms, the second one in Europe. This entrepreneur was probably Rafael Pich Aguilera, who had kinship ties with the Roca family (of the large family business group Corporación Roca), and who had been one of the first alumni and professors at the IESE business school.[9] In 1989, Gallo organized the first seminar on family firms in

---

[9] When Rafael Pich Aguilera died, Carlos Cavallé of IESE wrote in the *Revista de Antiguos Alumnos* of IESE that the students remembered "his sense of humour and his attractive

Spain with the IESE alumni and professors who specialized in this field who had been invited (such as Peter David, from Wharton). It was a great success and received invitations to continue with a successive conference dealing with taxation issues. Gallo asked for – and obtained from Carlos Cavallé – leave from his teaching duties in 1988 to concentrate his efforts as the family business chair. He was a visiting professor at MIT, where the vice dean asked him to speak to Leon Danco, Gibb Dyer, and John Davis. Gallo realized that the pioneers from whom he had to learn during his stay in the United States in 1989 were Gibb Dyer, John Davis, John Ward, Ernesto Poza, Barbara Hollander, and Ivan Lansberg. He designed a program of networking to obtain direct feedback from these scholars. In this way, he presented a paper at the meeting of the FFI and spent three days at John Ward's home (which was highly influential in helping Gallo to design his own model of family agreement or "protocol"), two days at John Davis' home in Santa Monica, and two days in Massachusetts, where he worked closely with Ivan Lansberg. Gallo has indicated (interview, May 26, 2009) that he felt that, from the point of view of the strategy and organization of firms, the U.S. concepts and methods were not extremely different from those he had seen at the IESE school in Barcelona. For Gallo, the U.S. scholars who specialized in family business whom he met were somewhat obsessed with the issue of conflict, with many influences in the models and ideas coming from psychology and psychiatry. In his view, these U.S. scholars were not contributing in a significant way to the conceptualization of how the process of strategic management could be applied to the family business. This, he saw, was an intellectual niche to develop (Fernández and Puig 2004; Puig and Fernández 2008). The fact that an industrial engineer who was well trained in Organization could combine his knowledge with family business needs was possibly the key factor that helps us understand the peculiarities of the first models, concepts, and ideas developed in the first Spanish chair of family business. They were strongly biased toward the problems of strategy and organization.

Miguel Ángel Gallo returned to Spain and resumed his activities in his chair at the IESE school in the early 1990s with many ideas and much influence from U.S. scholars: the three circles from John Davis, the

realism when he supervised case study discussions," and that Pich-Aguilera "decided, generously, to support the creation of the Cátedra de Empresa Familiar" in 1986. *Antiguos Alumnos IESE*, no. 111, X–XII, 2008, p. 136. Quoted in Carles M. Canals (2009), pp. 194 and 400.

importance of ownership and the life cycle in the transfer of entrepreneur-ship within the family business from John Ward, and the relevance of conflict within families for the business from Hollander, among others. He realized, however, that the Spanish entrepreneurs – many of whom belonged to small- and medium-sized family businesses – were worried, in the late 1980s, not by internal conflicts as was the case among many U.S. family business leaders of multigenerational family firms, but by three dif-ferent issues: taxation; self-esteem in relationship with the standing of the big public corporations of the country owned by the holding INI (Insti-tuto Nacional de Industria); and lack of knowledge of the international markets in which they increasingly had to operate, following Spain's adherence to the European economic institutions in 1986 (Fernández and Puig 2007; Tàpies 2009; Fernández Pérez 2012). Most of the largest fam-ily firms in Spain had been created after the 1940s, and thus, in the 1980s, most of them were not multigenerational. Many were in the transition to the second generation, and their problems were, in a rather aggregated way, the problems that the founders of family firms have to plan for, namely, succession in the context of growing market opportunities, and relatively little tradition or willingness to finance expansion with exter-nal capital or control. In these decades, Spanish family business leaders needed information, trustable local counselors, and experts in tax-saving strategies for their increased profits, the transmission of their wealth to the next generation, and the establishment of a basis for the much-needed internationalization of their business strategies in a changing world econ-omy. They also needed institutions that could train their successors in an appropriate way, in new organizational techniques, new networking skills, and traditional values.

Miguel Ángel Gallo worked in close cooperation with a team of pro-fessors at the IESE who shared his goals. Among them, Mariano Artigas (professor of natural philosophy, a follower of Karl Popper) or Juan Antonio Pérez López (professor of control, an expert in the motivational theory in Organization studies, and supervisor of doctoral dissertations in family business at the IESE). He has written extensively, but there are some key ideas in his work that he has recently developed either alone or with co-authors. Some of them have contributed to improve the definition of what a family firm is, to establish scientific typologies of family busi-nesses, to compare family and non-family firms, and to combine human visions of life with agency theories in family business theory (Gallo and Tomaselli 2006; Gallo 2008; Gallo et al. 2009).

CONCLUSIONS

Family business studies are not newcomers in scientific research. In the early decades of the twentieth century, anthropologists started to study the structures of kinship and how they affected both the society and the economy of distant tribes of the so-called primitive or uncivilized human groups. By the mid-twentieth century, social historians and political historians were curious about studying the relationship among marriage, kinship, and family structures in developed countries from medieval to early modern times. Both anthropologists and historians were attracted by distant places and distant times to conduct research on families and their microeconomic behavior. They usually wrote from a personal distance, trying to remain objective and to apply scientific methods to human groups that were treated in a neutral way. Practitioners of these kinds of studies rarely came together and only exceptionally created their own centers, associations, or journals.

In the 1970s, multigenerational family firms in the United States started to have problems in controlling the transfer of wealth for many reasons, including changes in the economic environment, and in what was supposed to be the traditional American family. The increase in divorce and the frequent migration of family members within the United States broke up the unity and consensus typical of the nineteenth-century Bostonian families. Family business leaders such as the Rockefellers, the Fords, and the newcomers all needed multidisciplinary counselors to help them control the family, the business, and the relationship of both with their society and institutions. In this context, family business scholars flourished and provided support to new centers, associations, and scholarly literature.

In the late twentieth century, Europe had a different situation with regard to external factors that influenced family firms. Some countries had old multigenerational firms in which traditional values were still held in high standing, as in Italy. But other countries, such as the United Kingdom, France, Spain, and the countries of northern Europe, had younger family firms (owing to the high mortality rates, for different national reasons, in the decades after the 1940s). These younger family firms had problems that had little to do with those of their U.S. cousins. The case of Spain, where a group of academic consultants and business owners played a major role in the creative transplantation of American ideas and institutions into European soil, clearly illustrates this point.

References

Interviews

- Miguel Ángel Gallo, May 26, 2009, at the IESE, Barcelona. With P. Fernández
- Miguel Ángel Gallo, November 12, 2009, at the IESE, Barcelona. With P. Fernández
- John Davis (HBS), Boston MA, May 13, 2009. With N. Puig
- Alden G. Lank (FBN), Boston MA, June, 15, 2009. With N. Puig
- Ivan Lansberg (Lansberg Associates), New Haven, CT, July 20, 2009. With N. Puig
- Judy Green (FFI), Boston, MA, July 30, 2009. With N. Puig

Publications

Ariès, Philippe (1960). *L'enfant et la vie familiale sous l'ancien régime.* Paris: Plon.

Ariès, Philippe, and George Duby, eds. (1986). *Histoire de la vie privée.* Paris: Seuil.

Beckhard, Richard, and Gibb Dyer W. Jr. (February 1981). "Challenges and Issues in Managing Family Firms." Working Paper, Alfred P. Sloan School of Management, MIT, pp. 1181–88.

Bird, Barbara, Harold Welsch, Joseph H. Astrachan, and David Pistrui (2002). "Family Business Research: The Evolution of an Academic Field." *Family Business Review,* 15(4): 337–50.

Canals, Carles M. (2009). *Sabiduría práctica. 50 años del IESE.* Barcelona: Planeta.

Casey, James (1989). *The History of the Family.* Oxford: Blackwell.

Casson, Mark (1999). "The Economics of the Family Firm." *Scandinavian Economic History Review,* 47(1): 10–23.

Chacón, Francisco, and Juan Hernández, coord. (2007). *Espacios sociales, universos familiares. La familia en la historiografía española: XXV aniversario del Seminario Familia y élite de poder en el Reino de Murcia siglos XV-XIX.* Murcia: Ediciones Universidad de Murcia.

Chacón, Francisco, Eni Mesquita, Teresa Lozano, and Antonio Irigoyen (2003). *Sin distancias: familia y tendencias historiográficas en el siglo XX.* Murcia: Universidad de Murcia.

Colli, Andrea (2011). "Family firms in European Economic History." In Isabelle Stamm, Peter Breithschmid, and Martin Kohli (eds.), *Doing Succession in Europe. Generational Transfers in Family Businesses in Comparative Perspective.* Zurich: Schulthess Verlag 29–58.

Colli, Andrea, Paloma Fernández Pérez, and Mary B. Rose (2003). "National Determinants of Family Firm Development? Family Firms in Britain, Spain and

Italy in the Nineteenth and Twentieth Centuries." *Enterprise & Society*, 4(1): 28–64.

Collier, Peter, and David Horowitz (1987). *Los Rockefeller*. Barcelona: Tusquets Editores (English original: *The Rockefellers. An American Dynasty*, 1976).

Duby, Georges, and J. Le Goff, eds. (1977). *Famille et parenté dans l'occident medieval*. Rome: École Française de Rome.

Evans-Pritchard, E.E. (1940). *The Nuer: A Description of the Modes of Livelihood and Political Institutions of a Nilotic People*, Oxford: Oxford University Press.

Fagerberg, Jan, David C. Mowery, and Richard Nelson (2005). *The Oxford Handbook of Innovation*. Oxford: Oxford University Press.

Fernández Pérez, Paloma (1997). *El rostro familiar de la metrópoli. Redes de parentesco y lazos mercantiles en Cádiz 1700–1812*. Madrid: Siglo XXI.

Fernández Pérez, Paloma (2003). "Reinstalando la empresa familiar en la Economía y la Historia Económica. Una aproximación a debates teóricos recientes." *Cuadernos de Economía y Dirección de Empresas*, 17: 45–66.

Fernández Pérez, Paloma (2007). "Small Firms and Networks in Capital Intensive Industries. The Case of Spanish Steel Wire Manufacturing." *Business History*, 49(5): 647–77.

Fernández Pérez, Paloma (2012). *La última globalización y el renacer de los grandes negocios familiares en el mundo*. Bogotá: Universidad de los Andes-Cátedra Corona.

Fernández Pérez, Paloma, and Nuria Puig (2004). "Knowledge and Training in Family Firms of the European Periphery. Spain 18th to 20th centuries." *Business History*, 46(1): 79–99.

Fernández Pérez, Paloma, and Núria Puig (2007). "Bonsais in a wild forest. A historical interpretation of the longevity of large Spanish family firms." *Revista de Historia Económica-Journal of Iberian and Latin American Economic History*, XXV(3): 459–97.

Fernández Pérez, Paloma, and Mary B. Rose, eds. (2010). *Innovation and Entrepreneurial Networks in Europe*. New York: Routledge.

Flandrin, Jean Louis (1976). *Familles, parenté, maison, sexualité dans l'ancienne Société*. Paris: Hachette.

Gallo, Miguel Ángel (2008). *Ideas básicas para dirigir la empresa familiar*. Pamplona: Ediciones Universidad de Navarra (EUNSA).

Gallo, Miguel Ángel, Sabine Klein, Daniella Montemerlo, Salvatore Tomaselli, and Kristin Cappuyns (2009). *La empresa familiar multigeneracional*. Pamplona: Ediciones Universidad de Navarra (EUNSA).

Gallo, Miguel Ángel, and Salvatore Tomaselli (2006). *Protocolo familiar: Sus resultados*. Madrid: Fundación Rafael Escolá/Family Business Consulting Group España.

García González Cuenca, Francisco, coord. (2008). *La historia de la familia en la Península Ibérica. Balance regional y perspectivas. Homenaje a Peter Laslett*. Cuenca: Ediciones de la Universidad de Castilla La Mancha.

Gies, Frances, and Joseph Gies (1987). *Marriage and the Family in the Middle Ages*. New York: Harper and Row.

Goody, Jack (1983). *The Development of the Family and Marriage in Europe.* New York: Cambridge University Press.

Hall, Peter Dobkin (1988). "A Historical Overview of Family Firms in the United Status." *Family Business Review*, 1(1): 51–68.

Hall, Peter D., and George E. Marcus (1998). "Why should men leave great fortunes to their children? Class, dynasty and inheritance in America." In Robert K. Miller Jr. and Stephen J. McNamee (eds.), *Inheritance and Wealth in America.* New York: Plenum Press, pp. 139–70.

Hollander, Barbara S., and Nancy S. Elman (1988). "Family-Owned Businesses: An Emerging Field of Inquiry." *Family Business Review*, 1(2): 145–64.

Instituto de la Empresa Familiar (2004). *Actividades y logros de los primeros años del IEF 1992–2004.* Barcelona: IEF.

Jones, Geoffrey, and Mary B. Rose, eds. (1993). Special Issue on Family Capitalism. *Business History*, 35(4).

Kaslow, Florence W. (2006). "Brief History of the Family Firm Institute." In F.W. Kaslow (ed.), *Handbook of Family Business and Family Business Consultation. A Global Perspective* (pp. 3–24). Binghamton, NY: Haworth Press.

Khurana, Rakesh (2007). *From Higher Aims to Hired Hands: The Social Transformation of American Business Schools and the Unfulfilled Promise of Management as a Profession.* Princeton, NJ: Princeton University Press.

Kipping, Matthias (1999). "American Management Consulting Companies in Western Europe, 1920 to 1990: Products, Reputation and Relationships." *Business History Review*, 73(2): 190–220.

Lank, Alden G., and Albert J. Thomassen (1991). "Introducing the Family Business Network." *Family Business Review*, 4(2): 225–30.

Lansberg, Ivan (1988). "Family Business as an Emerging Field." *Family Business Review*, 1(1): 1–8.

Lansberg, Ivan (1993). "Reflections of the Founder: A Conversation with Barbara Hollander." *Family Business Review*, 6(3): 313–25.

Lévi-Strauss, Claude (1947). *Les structures élémentaires de la parenté.* Paris: P.U.F.

Lewin, Linda (1987). *Politics and Parentela in Paraiba: A Case Study of Family-Based Oligarchy.* Princeton, NJ: Princeton University Press.

Marcus, George, and Peter D. Hall (1992). *Lives in Trust. The Fortunes of Dynastic Families in Late Twentieth Century America.* Boulder, CO: Westview Press.

Ngô, Bá Thành (1963). *La sociedad anónima familiarante la ley española de 1951.* Barcelona, Editorial Hispano Europea.

Ozment, Steven (1983). *When Fathers Ruled: Family Life in Reformation Europe.* Cambridge, MA: Harvard University Press.

Poutziouris, Panikkos Z., Cyprus X. Smyrnios, and Sabine B. Klein, eds. (2006). *Handbook of Research on Family Business.* Cheltenham: Edward Elgar Publishing.

Puig Raposo, Nuria, and Paloma Fernández Pérez (2008). "La gran empresa familiar española en el siglo XX: claves de su profesionalización." *Revista de la Historia de la Economía y de la Empresa*, II(2): 93–122.

Radcliffe-Brown, Alfred Reginald, and Cyril Daryll Forde, eds. (1950). *African Systems of Kinship and Marriage*. Oxford: Oxford University Press.

Rey, Marta, and Nuria Puig (2013). "Globalization and the Organization of Family Philanthropy: A Case of Isomorphism?" *Business History*, 55(2): 1–28.

Rodríguez, Pablo, coord. (2004). *La familia en Iberoamérica 1550–1980*. Bogotá: Convenio Andrés Bello-Universidad Externado de Colombia.

Rose, M.B., ed. (1995). *Family Business*. Cheltenham: Edward Elgar Publishing.

Sharma, Pramodita (2004). "An Overview of the Field of Family Business Studies: Current Status and Directions for Future." *Family Business Review*, 17(1): 1–36.

Sharma, Pramodita, J.J. Chrisman, and J.H. Chua (1996). *A Review and Annotated Bibliography of Family Business Studies*. Norwell, MA: Kluwer Academic.

Sharma, Pramodita, J.J. Chrisman, and J.H. Chua (1997). "Strategic Management of the Family Business: Past Research and Future Challenges." *Family Business Review*, 10(1): 1–135.

Sharma, Pramodita, F. Hoy, J.H. Astrachan, and M. Koiranen (2007). "The Practice-driven Evolution of Family Business Education." *Journal of Business Research*, 60(10): 1012–21.

Smith, Tom W. (1999). *The Emerging 21st Century American Family*. GSS Social Change Report no. 42. Chicago: National Opinion Research Center, University of Chicago.

Stone, Lawrence (1977). *The Family, Sex and Marriage in England, 1500–1800*. New York: Harper & Row.

Tàpies, Josep (2009). *Empresa familiar: Ni tan pequeña, ni tan joven. Una renovada aproximación a la edad y el tamaño de la empresa familiar española*. Barcelona: Fundación Jesús Serra/Catalana Occidente.

2

Family Firm Longevity

A Balancing Act between Continuity and Change

Pramodita Sharma and Carlo Salvato*

LONGEVITY

In this chapter, longevity refers to the continuity of a family firm beyond the career span of its founder(s). It is often signified by the year the firm was founded or the number of generations during which the firm has been controlled by a family. For example, SC Johnson of the United States proudly broadcasts its longevity as a family firm with its simple slogan of "SC Johnson, a family company since 1886," while across the globe, Darrell Lea of Australia celebrates its status as a privately held family firm established in 1927 by the Lea family. Against the backdrop of limited human lifespans, changing family structures, wars and natural disasters, and industrial and environmental turbulence, long-lived firms inspire awe: the Japanese guest house Hoshi Onsen has been run by the descendants of Garyo Hoshi for 46 generations spanning more than 1,300 years, and the French wine maker Château de Goulaine goes back more than 1,000 years. They are celebrated in noteworthy lists such as the "World's Oldest Family Businesses" compiled by *Family Business Magazine*.

Although many founders desire longevity for their enterprise, only a fraction of them achieve it. However, those who do come from a wide range of industries, geographical regions, and families of different cultural backgrounds (see Chapter 6 in this volume). This makes the quest for a universal formula for longevity elusive. In her article on the World's Oldest Family Businesses, Leah Kristie speculates that "perhaps the secret

* We gratefully acknowledge the helpful comments received from Andrea Colli, Harold James, and Paloma Fernández Pérez on earlier versions of this chapter.

34

to success lies not in what the companies produce, *but in how they adapt.* In 1697, Folkes Group (#65 *in this list*) began making chain mail and swords. Now, they're in real estate."[1] Although adaptation is critical, it is also important to keep in mind that the very reason that Folkes Group is on this coveted list is because of the continuity provided by the Folkes family to the enterprise. Thus, some combination of continuity and adaptation is at play. To understand the dynamics of this combination, we need to delve deeper into the concept of longevity. At its most basic level, two necessary conditions must be met to guarantee the longevity of a "family firm":

1. The name of the firm must continue; and
2. The family involvement in the firm must continue.

Failure to meet either of these conditions leads to the demise of the family firm. If a firm closes down, is bought by another entity, or legally changes its name, it becomes difficult to recognize and trace it to its founding. Although historical descriptions of a company may provide its genealogy, it soon becomes a distant memory in the minds of people. Woolco is a good example of the importance of the continuity of a firm's name. This discount retailer was launched in the United States in the same year (1962) as Kmart, Wal-Mart, and Target. At its peak, it had hundreds of stores in the United States, Canada, and Europe. However, since its acquisition by Wal-Mart in 1983, it has faded from the public memory. In contrast, Wal-Mart continues to thrive both in name recognition and in the family involvement in the enterprise. Although the company continues to evolve in terms of store configuration, merchandise, logistical innovations, and geographic scope, the continuity of both its name and the family involvement has left it easily traceable to its founder, Sam Walton, and his brother, Bud. In terms of longevity, Wal-Mart is still young, as it is in the second generation of family leadership under Chairman S. Robson Walton, son of Helen and Sam Walton. Time will be the judge of how the largest retailer of the world fares as a family enterprise in terms of longevity. Interestingly, however, Sam and Bud Walton's pre–Wal-Mart entrepreneurial ventures – Ben Franklin stores or Walton's Five & Dime stores – have already faded from memory. This reiterates the importance of the continuity of a firm's name to ensure its longevity both legally as well as in the public mind, whether the name refers to the family or not.

---

[1] Available at: http://www.familybusinessmagazine.com/index.php?/channels/oldest.

When the name of the original firm prevails but the family involvement is lost over time, the firm remains a well-recognized name that celebrates its history and founding year. However, it is no longer a "family firm." One such example is Merck & Company, which traces its origin to Friedrich Jacob Merck of Germany, who purchased a drugstore in 1668. Although the company underwent several significant changes, such as the establishment of a new company in the United States in 1891 by a member of a later generation of the Merck family, the acquisition of Charles E. Frosst in 1965, and, more recently, the merger with Schering-Plough in 2009, the name of the firm has remained largely intact. However, because the founding family no longer controls this publicly traded firm, it does not qualify as a "dynastic family firm."

The cymbal-making company Avedis Zildjian is evidence of the dual importance of both the family name and the continuous involvement of the family in a firm. It was started in 1623 by Avedis Zildjian and is currently led by the fourteenth generation of the Zildjian family. Though founded in Turkey, this is the oldest family firm active in the United States. Continuity of family involvement and the name of the firm enable this family to trace and celebrate its historical roots. Flexibility and adaptation are also evident in this company, which has persisted through the untimely deaths of family members, the move across the Atlantic, wars, fires, political turmoil, and the Great Depression to invent new models of cymbals for use in religious feasts, prayers, royal weddings, military bands, and symphonies – all while "sticking together" as the Zildjian "cymbal" family. Beyond survival and persistence, however, there are no restrictions on the tasks, products/services, or markets that a firm engages in, or how it is organized, controlled, managed, or governed. Nor is there any restriction on the boundary conditions of a "family," that is, how a family is defined by the controlling group. Theoretically, therefore, there are several degrees of freedom in the composition of a family and in the pursuits of the firm. However, in most instances, family firm leaders, scholars, and advisors tend to assume (inadvertently, perhaps) restrictive definitions of family, as well as what a firm can and must pursue. These are based on normative and cultural forces, past experiences, and the perception of the resources available. Let us delve a little deeper into the definitional issues of a family firm.

INTRODUCTION

Family firms are a central feature of both emerging and less dynamic market economies (Fernández Pérez and Colli, Introduction to this volume;

see also Chapter 3 in this volume). What do long-lived family firms around the globe have in common? Do they persist because they are uniquely blessed with no family troubles and ruptures across generations of family life? Or, is it because they chose an industry or business model that is uniquely rare and nonreplicable over generations of business leaders? We contend that it is neither of these. Although the dynamics of organizational endurance may vary cross-culturally (see Chapter 6 in this volume), we argue that it is the underlying *assumptions* held by the controlling family, with regard to the boundaries of the family and of the business, that influence or determine the longevity of a family enterprise. Families that believe in and follow dynamic and flexible boundaries for both "family" and "business" are more likely to survive over longer periods of time than others who adhere to impermeable boundaries anchored in the "components-of-involvement," as opposed to the "essence," approach. In other words, families with rigid assumptions and beliefs regarding *what a family is* and/or *what business we are in* are less likely to prevail over generations. The core rationale is that flexibility enables adaptability to the changing internal and external environment. In turn, adaptability is a necessity for longevity.

Research has highlighted the importance of both *continuity* (Miller and Le Breton-Miller 2005) and *adaptation* (Hatum 2007; Fernández Pérez 2010) in ensuring the longevity of family enterprises. High-performing family firms in the United States that have thrived over generations have been found to pursue relentlessly a meaningful substantive mission, highlighting the critical importance of continuity for longevity (Miller and Le Breton-Miller 2005). For example, the enduring purpose of the New York Times Company for more than 150 years has been to "enhance society by creating, collecting and distributing high quality news, information and entertainment" (http://www.nytco.com/company/) while "creativity, innovation, quality and caring" have been guiding Hallmark, the greeting cards company, for more than a century. Continual pursuit of these anchoring missions has kept both of these family firms at the forefront of their respective industries for more than a century. Other studies of family dynasties such as Argentina's Aceitera General Deheza (Hatum and Pettigrew 2006) or Italy's Falck Group (Salvato, Chirico, and Sharma 2010) suggest the critical role of "adaptation" as the basis of the longevity of enterprises. Innovative dynasties (Bergfeld and Weber 2011) whose leaders embrace organizational flexibility and adaptability have been found to thrive in the face of economic and political turbulence, whereas those who rigidly stick to their core markets, products, and industries dissipate.

Although both continuity and adaptability are integral to longevity, the thorny question for organizational leaders and scholars is: What must be preserved and what must be changed? Flexibility without stability results in chaos (Volberda 1996). On the other hand, lack of flexibility leads to rigidities that eventually cause the demise of family firms (Hatum 2007). Thus, to preserve an enterprise the degree, pace, and process of change must be carefully managed. Commenting on the impact of the transformational change of Italy's Falck Group from the steel industry, which it had dominated for several decades from its inception in 1906 to the renewable energy business in mid-1990s, the president of the advisory board of this dynastic family enterprise stated:

Closing an activity of that size is obviously something which leaves a mark. However, the Falcks are so active, so inclined to the entrepreneurial sense of life.... Throughout all these years, after the decision to shut down steel activities, nobody has ever mentioned steel, other than in a technical sense, when discussing about the few remaining activities.... I believe the Falck family has always had an entrepreneurial vision which went beyond steel, the specific business in which they had been active since the beginning.... It's in their blood, in their DNA; it's the bloodline which prevails – they just don't surrender. You can feel the activism, the resolution to persist, always struggling to improve.... It's the family's entrepreneurial spirit. (Filippo Tamborini, President of Falck's Advisory Board from 1976 in Salvato et al. 2010:337–8)

At times, even the dynastic families that intuitively embrace continuity and adaptability seem uncertain of the factors that lead to their success. For example, the director of Aceitera General Deheza (AGD), a highly flexible family dynasty in the edible oils business in Argentina, noted that:

... if you compared our business now and ten years ago, you would think we were a different company ... however, if you ask an employee whether they have felt the changes, they would say that they had not noticed internal turmoil. They did not feel threatened by the changes. I do not know how or why this has happened. (Hatum and Pettigrew 2006: 130)

The important, yet puzzling, questions are: If longevity is the objective, what aspects of the family enterprise must be continued? And what might be adapted? In other words, *to ensure the longevity of a family firm, where must the line between continuity and flexibility be drawn?* Reflecting on and understanding these perplexing questions and their possible answers is likely to be helpful to leaders who seek the longevity of their firms, to scholars who devote their lives to understanding the unique dynamics and issues of these enterprises, and to the advisors who are called on to guide family firm leaders in their pursuit of the endurance and longevity

[handwritten marginal note: The ability to change without huge turnover/turmoil?]

of their family firms. These questions are addressed in this chapter using the definitional perspective of the controlling family.

The following section reflects on the meaning and basics of longevity. If the leaders of a family firm wish for longevity, which aspects of the enterprise must remain constant and which can change? Section 3 highlights the two approaches to defining family business – components and essence approaches – that are useful to tease out the dimensions of longevity. Although the original conceptualization of these definitional approaches has focused on the organizational unit of the "family business," to begin to understand "what must be preserved" versus "what must be discarded" over time for the sustainability of a family firm, we need to understand the components and essence of the two subsystems of family and business separately. Building from this base, this section provides separate definitions of the "components-of-involvement" and the "essence" of both a family and a business. Section 4 builds arguments related to the longevity of the family or of the business or of the family business, depending on the fundamental beliefs of the controlling family. We suggest that family firms guided by the prominence of "essence" definitions for *both* the family *and* the business systems are more likely to enjoy sustainability over the long term compared to other family firms. Section 5 provides examples of some of the strategies used by long-lived family firms to retain the focus of their internal and external stakeholders on the essence of the family and of the business, rather than becoming entrapped by the limiting component definitions in their mind-set and decision making. The chapter concludes with some practical and research implications.

DEFINING A FAMILY FIRM

Definitional issues have always been central to the emergence of family business studies (see Chapter 1 in this volume). After a review of 250 articles, Chua et al. listed twenty-one definitions of the term "family business" in use by researchers (Chua, Chrisman, and Sharma 1999). These authors observed a need to differentiate between theoretical and operational definitions. They proposed doing this by distinguishing between the "components-of-involvement" and the "essence" approaches to defining family firms. Since the publication of their article more than ten years ago in 1999, scholars have embraced these ideas. Whereas the "essence"-based definition of family business is commonly accepted as the theoretical definition in family business studies, "components" are generally specified and used to differentiate family from non-family firms in empirical research. More recently, the components definition has been used to distinguish between various categories of family firms both conceptually (Sharma and Nordqvist 2008) and empirically (García-Castro and Sharma forthcoming; Sciascia and Mazzola 2008). Each approach is discussed in the following sections.

The Components-of-Involvement Approach

The components-of-involvement approach defines family firms based on the extent and nature of the family involvement in business. The focus is on the "who and what" questions, such as the following: What is the extent of family involvement in the ownership, management, or governance of the business? Who are the family members currently involved in the business? Will the next-generation family members be involved in the business? If so, what roles will they play? Three dimensions researchers generally use to distinguish family firms from their non-family counterparts both in privately and publicly held firms are ownership, management, and governance. Different combinations of these factors determine the varying levels of professionalization that can be observed across family firms (see Chapter 11 in this volume).

For example, Sciascia and Mazzola (2008) define family firms as those in which a family controls the business through its involvement in ownership and management positions. Family involvement in ownership (FIO) was measured as the *percentage of equity held by family members*. Family involvement in management (FIM) was calculated as the *percentage of a firm's managers who are also family members*. In their study of randomly selected privately held Italian firms, the average family involvement in ownership was 77.24 percent, while family involvement in management was 63.22 percent.

Other authors (e.g., McConaughy, Walker, Henderson, and Mishra, 2008) consider publicly held firms to be family enterprises if their CEO is either a founder or a member of the founding family. However, this notion of including "lone" founders – (if no other member of the family is involved in the business – in the category of family firms has been challenged in recent research by a scholarly team led by Danny Miller (see, e.g., Miller, Le-Breton Miller, Lester, and Cannella 2007). Along these lines, other authors (e.g., Gomez-Mejia, Larraza-Kintana, and Makri 2003) maintain that before businesses can be considered publicly held family firms, multiple members of a family must, in addition to having an equity stake, be involved in the company's management or governance.

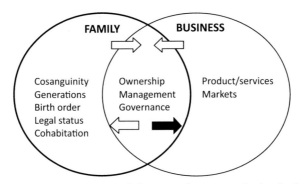

FIGURE 2.1. Components of the two subsystems of a family firm.

Block (2010) categorized firms as family managed if a member of the founding family was the CEO or chairman of the board. He also used the percentage of ownership held by the controlling family in his study of the 500 largest family firms in the United States. The ownership fraction that a family must hold before it is considered a family firm varies significantly, ranging from 5 to 50 percent of the voting stock (Miller et al. 2007).

The underlying assumption of the components approach is that family involvement in a given business is a sufficient condition for an enterprise to be categorized as a family firm. Researchers and practitioners alike tend to hold strong beliefs on the combination of family involvement in ownership, governance, and management, which serve to differentiate family enterprises from non-family enterprises. However, although the extreme anchors of family involvement in a business are relatively easy to recognize, there is no agreement as to where, in the continuum of family and non-family enterprises, the demarcation lies. Sampling difficulties arise when firms with the same degree of family involvement in ownership or management disagree as to whether they are family or non-family firms, thus leaving another decision point open for researchers. In combination, these factors have led to mixed and nonsignificant findings with regard to the impact of family involvement on firm performance (Garcia-Castro and Sharma 2011; Miller et al. 2007).

Two core issues of interest to family business scholars are (1) understanding the factors that distinguish family from non-family firms and (2) understanding the heterogeneity within family firms. This has led to a focus on the components of family involvement in business, that is, the overlap areas between family and business (see Figure 2.1).

More specifically, scholarly attention has been devoted to understanding how the family involvement in ownership, management, and governance influences the dynamics of the business system (see solid right pointing arrow in Figure 2.1). However, to date, much less attention has been paid to the reverse questions of how the components of the business or of the family influence the overlap area of family involvement in the business or how the components of the overlap area influence the family system (James, Jennings, and Breitkruz 2012; Litz, Pearson, and Litchfield 2012). The open arrows in Figure 2.1 indicate these exciting areas for future research. Although it is beyond the scope of this chapter to elaborate on the many nuanced relationships broadly depicted by these arrows, when one reflects on the longevity of a family firm (the whole system), it becomes essential to think not only of the components of involvement in the overlap area, but also of the two subsystems of the family and the business. Thus, we briefly discuss the components of the family and the business subsystems.

The business subsystem has received significant attention by scholars in many functional areas of business schools, such as marketing, finance, and supply chain management, whereas the family subsystem has been relegated to the family science fields (James et al. 2012; Litz et al. 2012). Although several outcome variables of business, such as its size and performance, have received attention in the literature, two components that lie at the heart of "what business are we in" are determined by its:

- Products/services
- Markets

Frequently, business enterprises derive their identity from these two components. For example, Cargill Inc., the largest privately held firm in the United States, describes itself as follows, anchoring itself by the scope of its geographic markets and product/services in four different industries:

Cargill is an international producer and marketer of food, agricultural, financial and industrial products and services. Founded in 1865, our privately-held company employs 131,000 people in 66 countries. We help customers succeed through collaboration and innovation, and are committed to sharing our global knowledge and experience to help meet economic, environmental and social challenges. (http://www.cargill.com.cn/en/index.jsp)

For Cargill, this breadth of scope is combined with innovation to meet societal needs. With the continuous evolution in the products/services as well as the global markets, adaptability and flexibility become necessities for survival and longevity even for companies such as Mittal Steel that anchor themselves to one core product. We return to this point in the next section, but first let us briefly discuss the family system.

It is interesting to note that there has been no discussion, in the family business literature, about the operationalization of the "family." Lacking an explicit assessment of what the "family" is, and how it is measured in questionnaire-based studies, the issue of whether respondents actually belong to the same family, and how such a family is defined, is left implicit and unspecified. No questions have been asked to ascertain whether the respondents from family firms use the same or different definitions of the "family." For example, even in scales such as F-PEC (Klein, Astrachan, and Smyrnios 2005; Holt, Rutherford, and Kuratko 2010), which aim to measure the family influence on the business through its Power, Experience, and Culture (PEC), or others that aim to understand the prevailing processes in a family, such as the Family Climate scales (Björnberg and Nicholson 2007), the definition of the "family" is left to the respondents.

Does it matter if the family members are of the same gene pool or not, or whether it is a nuclear, extended, or blended family? Is the gender or generation mix of the family important? Does it make a difference whether the focal couple is legally married or not, or cohabiting or not? Today, there are a myriad of possible variations of the concept of the "family." With one notable exception regarding the number of generations involved, which is occasionally used in research studies, the current literature seems to assume that such finer distinctions of the "family" are not really pertinent to our understanding of either the performance or other dynamics of family firms. But we contend that it is pertinent, especially if the interest is in understanding factors that have an impact on the longevity of a family firm. This is because the continuity of the family's involvement in the firm is a necessary condition for the longevity of the family firm in question. If there are no family members available, interested, or able to continue the involvement in the ownership, management, or governance of the firm in question, it is virtually impossible for such an entity to continue as the family firm controlled by the founding family. Thus, we must not only understand and delineate the components of the family involvement in the business (products/services, markets) and in the overlap areas between the family and the business systems (ownership, management, governance), but we must also direct our attention to the components of the family as well.

Unconsciously, familial norms become an unchallenged part of everyday life as each generation learns from the previous generation the acceptable modes of behavior, while the evolutionary forces of change work quietly in the background (Nicholson 2008). Although most families do not sit down to define where they are drawing the boundaries of their family unit, their key decisions and forms of behavior are guided by these unstated assumptions. For example, when it comes to family involvement in business, some families draw the boundary at blood relatives, leaving little room for in-laws or adopted family members to contribute to the enterprise (Santiago 2011). Those who follow primogeniture as the norm restrict the leadership of the firm to the oldest male of the family. But, for others with more permeable boundaries and egalitarian mind-sets, the best and brightest from within their extended family or even network family are encouraged to assume the leadership roles of the enterprise (Fan, Wiwattanakantang, and Bunkanwanicha 2008; Mehrotra et al. 2010). Thus, at any point in time, each family holds sacrosanct beliefs about the composition and boundaries of a family when it comes to acceptability in terms of involvement in the ownership, management, or governance of an enterprise. Family science scholars note the protean nature of the family in both time and place (Bengtson et al. 2005). Although the family has remained a basic unit of human organization biologically, socially, and economically since prehistoric times, the concept of the "family" can refer to disparate phenomenon in society (Bernandes 1985; Hill 1995; Davis and Daly 1997). Some dimensions that determine variations in what is meant by the term "family" across different cultures include the following:

- Consanguinity – Can nonbiological relatives own, manage, or govern a family firm?
- Gender – Is involvement in the business open to family members of one or both genders?
- Birth order – Are there any distinctions or expectations from older or younger family members in terms of their involvement in the family firm?
- Generations – How many generations can own, manage, or govern the firm at any point in time?
- Legal status – What rights and responsibilities do the children of a previous marriage have? Must an individual be legally married or adopted in a family before he or she can own, manage, or govern the family firm?
- Cohabitation – What is the status of individuals who are cohabitating with a biological relative of the controlling family? Can they own, manage, or govern a family firm?

Each controlling family has underlying beliefs with regard to these components that define the norm for family involvement in business. These prevailing assumptions are put to the test at defining moments for the family firm and often determine key strategic decisions at times, which can lead to conflict (Sharma and Manikutty 2005). Although research is needed to understand the relationships between the different defining components of the family and the outcome variables of interest, this chapter takes the first step by highlighting these components separately for the business and family subsystems of a family firm.

The Essence Approach

The essence approach aims to understand the behavioral distinctiveness of family firms from their non-family counterparts. From this perspective, the components of the family involvement in the business are considered a necessary but insufficient condition by which to define a family firm. Instead, it is the combination of family involvement in the business with distinctive forms of behavior, such as the intention to continue a firm across generations of family control, or create financial, social, or emotional wealth for the controlling family, that distinguishes family firms from others. Thus, this approach draws attention to the "why" question: the purpose for which an organizational system such as a family business exists. The most frequently used "essence"-based definition of family business is the one suggested by Chua, Chrisman, and Sharma:

The family business is a business governed and/or managed with the intention to shape and/or pursue the vision of the business held by a dominant coalition controlled by members of the same family or a small number of families in a manner that is potentially sustainable across generations of the family or families. (Chua, Chrisman, and Sharma 1999: 25)

Although the longevity of the family business is in built in this definition, aimed toward the transgenerational sustainability of the enterprise, it is silent on the essence of the two subsystems of business or family. To understand the core question of this chapter, that is, what to continue versus what to adapt toward the goal of the longevity of a family firm, it is necessary to understand the essence, or core beliefs, and the prevailing assumptions of the controlling family with regard to its "family" and its "business."

It is interesting to find that most dictionary meanings of "family" focus on components of this system. For example, the *Oxford English Dictionary* describes a family "as a group consisting of two parents and their children living together as a unit,"[2] whereas *Webster's Dictionary* uses a broader definition that includes "other social units differing from but regarded as equivalent to the traditional family of two parents and their children; individuals living under one roof; from the same ancestry."[3] Thus, the dictionary definitions of the word "family" follow the components approach.

In the family science literature, the growing variations in the family structures are widely recognized and studied from different perspectives (Bengtson et al. 2005; McGoldrick, Carter, and Garcia-Preto 2011). For example, scholars aim to understand the purpose of the family in society (functional perspective); why family relationships form or endure (the social exchange perspective); changes in the concept of the family over time (the family development or life-course perspective); and why gender inequality exists (the feminist perspective). However, the term "family" is left undefined. Earlier, we noted a similar silence regarding the definition of the "family" in the family business literature. However, recently, Hoy and Sharma (2010: 17) offered the following "essence"-based definition of family, which is the definition that we have adopted in this chapter:

Family is a group of people affiliated through bonds of shared history and a commitment to share a future together while supporting the development and well-being of individual members.

Turning to the "business," dictionaries explain it as a commercial activity engaged in as a means of livelihood, whereas textbooks describe business as "an organization engaged in the trade of goods, services, or both to consumers"[4] – thereby remaining close to the components approach. But scholars who have studied dynastic enterprises note that the essence lies in the core values and purpose of the organization. This is evident in the following statement made in 1992 by John Young, a former CEO of Hewlett-Packard (HP) and shared by Collins and Porras in their book, *Built to Last: Successful Habits of Visionary Companies*:

Our basic principles have endured intact since our founders conceived them. We distinguish between core values and practices; the core values don't change, but the practices might. We've also remained clear that profit – as important as it is – is not why the Hewlett-Packard Company exists; it exists for more fundamental reasons. (Collins and Porras 2002: 46)

Even today, as this company operates in virtually every nation worldwide and has evolved in terms of its products and services several times,

[2] Available at: http://oxforddictionaries.com/definition/family.
[3] Available at: http://www.merriam-webster.com/dictionary/family.
[4] Available at: http://en.wikipedia.org/wiki/Business.

it is guided by the Corporate Objectives of HP, which were written more than fifty years ago in 1957 by its co-founders Bill Hewlett and Dave Packard. A commitment to serve their customers by providing the highest quality and value through useful innovative products to meet their needs lies at the center of these objectives. The essence lies in identifying and serving human needs and is achieved through the components of the business and the family's overlap on the business. If we look back at the purpose of New York Times Company or Hallmark, serving customer needs in different ways lies at their core. Based on these observations, we propose the following "essence"-based definition of business: Business is an enterprise that brings together resources to provide products and services that serve the identified societal needs.

As these needs evolve, so must the business. Thus, by its very definition, the essence of a business is dynamic. Although some founders such as Dave Packard and Bill Hewlett articulate their core values, most do not. Even persons such as Fred DeLuca and Pete Buck of Subway restaurants, who have expanded their enterprise from one store in 1965 to almost 35,000 stores across 98 countries in 2011, did not put their core values down in writing. Instead, when they launched their firm, they followed a "numbers dream" of setting the goal of having 32 stores in the first 10 years. Although they clearly understand the importance of quality products, excellent customer service, and low costs, the driving force in this American success story seems to be market expansion while retaining the focus on one product line. Whether this remarkable enterprise will continue to thrive beyond the careers of its founders or not remains to be seen.

In this section, we have discussed two approaches to defining a family enterprise – the essence and components approaches. In addition to the essence- and components-based definitions of a family firm, we suggest that these two perspectives be kept in mind for each of the subsystems of the family and the business as well. With this foundation of the definitions based on the components and the essence of the "family," the "business," and the "family business," we are now ready to reflect on the longevity of family enterprises.

THE ESSENCE OF LONGEVITY

Earlier, we described "longevity" as the continuity of a firm beyond the career span of its founder(s). Longevity is a desirable objective for many, albeit not all, organizational founders. As an example, a recent study of the 100 largest Australian family firms confirms that survival or longevity is the single most prevalent goal expressed by these large companies on their websites and in the media (McKenny et al. 2012). It therefore comes as no surprise that the quest to understand the reasons for longevity continues. Both scholars and entrepreneurs are attracted to the pursuit of strategies that will enable them to understand the survival of a firm beyond the current generation's tenure. The success of books such as *Built to Last: Successful Habits of Visionary Companies* (Collins and Porras 2002), *Managing for the Long Run: Lessons in Competitive Advantage from Great Family Businesses* (Miller and Le Breton-Miller 2005), and *Perpetuating the Family Business* (Ward 2004) written by reflective scholars and practitioners attests to the widespread desirability of achieving this objective, and this book is further evidence of the continued interest in it. In this section, we have proposed that the longevity of a family firm needs *both* the continuity of the firm's name *and* of the family's involvement in the firm. Let us discuss each of these in turn.

The Longevity of a Firm

It is no secret that, for a firm to continue, it must adapt and regenerate itself to meet the ever-changing needs of society. If the demand for the products or services provided by a firm dries up and the firm does not renew itself to offer new options needed in the market, it expires. But, as argued by the authors in several revered books, such as *The Innovators Dilemma: When New Technologies Cause Great Firms to Fail* (Christensen 1997), *The Icarus Paradox: How Exceptional Companies Bring About Their Own Downfall* (Miller 1992), and *How the Mighty Fall: And Why Some Companies Never Give In* (Collins 2009), it is extremely challenging for successful firms to renew themselves. Flexibility and adaptability have been found to be key to survival in the face of changes both within and outside an organization (Volberda 1996; Hatum 2007; Bergfeld and Weber 2011). Perhaps this is most succinctly summarized by James March (1995: 435) as follows:

> Stories of rapid environmental change invite a prediction that future environments will favor organizations that are able to be flexible and to adapt quickly to change. Organizations that fail to adapt seem destined to expire as the world around them changes.

Flexibility, in turn, flourishes in a firm in which the top leadership has a variety of experience and backgrounds. In addition, the structures and processes adopted by them encourage the permeability of boundaries, which leads to an easy inflow and outflow of ideas. Based on an in-depth comparative study of two highly flexible and two nonflexible firms in Argentina, Hatum and Pettigrew (2006: 132) note that "The main difference between highly flexible and less-flexible firms is in the way their identity – through their organizational values – helped them to change or trapped them in inertial forces."

We suggest that a focus on the components of a business – the existing products/services and markets – is likely to encourage a past orientation of the firm with a reluctance to change what has worked well. On the other hand, firms with dynamism in their essence, such as the entrepreneurial vision of the Falck family, which went beyond steel, or the enduring desire of the New York Times Company to enhance society, are likely to prevail over time.

[handwritten in margin: Broader goals are key.]

For a family firm to continue, not only must the business entity prevail over time, but so must the engagement of the family members in it. Two related factors are involved in the second condition – first, the involvement of family members in the business, and second, an adequate number of family members in the following generations. But what factors actually support the longevity of a family? And, what factors attract capable next-generation members toward the family firm? In the next section, we turn to these questions.

The Longevity of a Family

Family studies scholars note the tenacity of the "family" as a unit of organization. Its resilience has been suggested to be a consequence of its ability to transform itself over time and space, mirroring the societal changes and meshing with it (Cigoli and Scabini 2006). In his *A Treatise on the Family*, Gary Becker (1991) noted that family firms persist because they are highly efficient at adaptation to satisfy societal needs. For example, in the last century, paralleling the dominant forms of economic activity – preindustrial, industrial, postindustrial – family structures have changed from extended multigenerational, to nuclear, to the heterogeneous family structures of today that satisfy the diversity and fluid movement of society.

Reflecting on the families of our time, Elizabeth Markson observed the "beanpole" structure of today's families, with an increasing height caused by the coexistence of multiple generations but with a lack of width owing to fewer siblings (Markson 2007). This structural change has profound implications for family firms who wish for longevity. Although the career spans of successive generations are longer, the number of available candidates to lead a family firm is lower than in the previous ones. Against this backdrop of societal context, families with extremely rigid or overly diffuse boundaries find it hard to persist. Instead, it is the families with permeable boundaries that retain their core essence but allow some movement of individuals into and out of the family system that seem to prevail. Based on these observations, we propose that, in comparison to those families anchored in the essence approach, those that inherently adopt the components approach to defining their familial boundaries have a lesser chance of prevailing as a family, as well as of supporting an enterprise. Essence-focused families are more receptive to the entries and exits of the members from its system, while supporting the development of all its members (Hoy and Sharma 2010).

The Longevity of a Family Firm

The preceding discussion suggests that the prevailing norms regarding the underlying definition of the family and of the business, in the controlling family of a business, can vary depending on whether the components approach or the essence approach governs the core assumptions and beliefs of the family. As depicted in Table 2.1, broadly speaking, four alternatives are available to the leadership of a family firm: the components approach based on the implicit or stated definitions of the family and/or of the business; or the essence approach based on the definitions of one or both systems. We propose that family firms guided predominantly by an "essence" approach for *both* the family and the business systems are more likely to enjoy sustainability over the long term when compared to other family firms.

Adaptation is the key to longevity because the focus on essence enables flexibility of the components of each system. Flexibility, in turn, supports adaptation, making the system resilient to the changing internal and external environments. In the next section, we discuss a few strategies found to be useful by long-lived family firms to retain their focus on the essence of their family and of their business, rather than being anchored to the more limiting components definitions in their mind-set and in their decision making.

TOWARD THE PURSUIT OF LONGEVITY

In this chapter, we have argued that family firms that survive over generations of family and business life cycles are adept at retaining their core focus on the *essence* of the family and of the business, while

TABLE 2.1. *Components of Involvement versus Essence of Family and of Business*

		DEFINITION OF FAMILY	
		Components of family involvement	Essence of family
		Who/what of family? Gender, generation, marital status	*Forms of Behavior* Development and well-being of all members
DEFINITION OF BUSINESS	**Components of business** *Who/what of business?* Ownership, management, governance, products, markets	*Rigid family and business boundaries*	*Flexible family boundaries; rigid business boundaries*
	Essence of the business *Mission* Entrepreneurial spirit, regeneration through innovation, serving societal needs	*Rigid family boundaries; flexible business boundaries*	*Flexible family and business boundaries: long-lived family firms*

embracing change with regard to the *components-of-involvement* in the two subsystems. In other words, they are simultaneously pliable and flexible regarding the components involved in both the family and the business, while being tenacious and resilient with regard to the core essence of each of these. Although different trends in the family composition – such as marriages, divorce, and birth rates – across countries may significantly affect the meaning and relevance of longevity to entrepreneurial families (Aldrich and Cliff 2003), we contend that the essence-components dialectic is key to all family firms. How might a focus on essence and flexibility be achieved in both family and business systems? A few strategies found to be useful by long-lived family enterprises are listed in Section 5.1.

The Flexible-Family System

In addition to the extended family of preindustrial times and the nuclear family of industrial times, several different forms of family are found in today's postindustrial society. These include the growing numbers of single households, single-parent families, blended families in which the children from previous relationships of one or both parents combine to form the new family unit, and several others. Given the relative newness of these different familial forms, many enterprising families are still establishing the norms for the degree and mode of the family involvement in the business. As stated earlier in the chapter, each component of the family leads to several possible alternatives for the family's involvement in the business, which are generally addressed at defining moments in the life of a family and its business. Scholars have observed three strategies used by dynastic families to continue their family firm over generations: a belief in the continuing importance of the institution of the family, expanding the qualified "family" labor pool, and selecting the best talent to lead the enterprise.

Values are the essence of a family business' spirit (see Chapter 10 in this volume). Dynastic families nurture the critical role of the institution of the "family" amidst the changing external environment. Often, the senior members of the family take on an active role in imbuing the junior generations with the core familial values. As with all families, there continue to be exits and entries from the family system, but the turbulence caused by these changes in the components is not deep enough to rupture the essence of the family. The focus is on supporting the diverse needs of all individuals in a family so that the full potential of each family member can be developed.

Although some families continue to follow the restrictive norm of primogeniture, in which the eldest male must lead the family enterprise, progressive dynastic families around the globe strategically expand their labor pools by encouraging the most capable and interested members of the next generation to lead the enterprise (Chrisman et al. 1998; Sharma and Rao 2000), by engaging capable in-laws in leadership roles (Fan et al. 2008), or by employing capable non-family adults (Mehotra et al. 2010) to lead the enterprise. Although the access of women to power in family firms brings a change in the traditional roles in the family and creates significant challenges for themselves and their environment (see Chapter 9 in this volume), examples of primogeniture giving way to women leaders of enterprising families include Craigie Zildjian's leading The Avedis Zildjian Company, breaking three generations of family tradition, and Stephanie Sonnabend's becoming the CEO and president of Sonesta Hotels, working alongside her other siblings and cousins. Engagement of capable in-laws in long-lived family firms can be found in Laurent Beaudoin's taking charge of Bombardier Inc., a global enterprise founded by his father-in-law, Joseph-Armand Bombardier. The employment of capable non-family adult sons is a tradition in Japan aimed at simultaneously mitigating the threat of deadening the ambitions or talents of biological sons while ensuring the continuity of both the family name and its leadership in capable family hands, be they genetic or adopted. This strategy has helped global empires such as the Suzuki and Toyota motor companies (Fan et al. 2008).

The Flexible-Business System

To ensure the continuity of their enterprises both in name and in substance, dynastic families ensure that their firm follows a dynamic essence. Satisfying a societal need is the moving target that is tenaciously pursued. As needs change, so, too, do their key components of products, services, and markets.

The leaders of such dynastic firms stay connected with their users and their environment but are not enmeshed in it (Hatum and Pettigrew 2006). This enables them to serve current customer needs and continue their expansion of the markets with their current products and services and an exploration of new ones. The task of full exploitation of current product/service mix through incremental innovations is generally left to capable non-family executives. Simultaneously, however, family members devote their efforts to the exploration of new opportunities that not only require radical innovation but are also likely to ensure the continuity of the enterprise in both the medium and long terms (Bergfeld and Weber 2011).

These firms encourage the heterogeneity of the backgrounds and experience of leaders. Research has revealed the synergistic roles played by both family and non-family executives in long-lived firms. Not only does this strategy allow for simultaneous exploitation of the current options and exploration of new ones, but it also provides the firms with opportunities to build the human capital of all its members. This in turn leads to stronger engagement of the most talented family and non-family employees, which is a prerequisite for the well-being of the family enterprise (Salvato et al. 2010). A high level of development of human capital leads to satisfying productive careers for individuals and growth for their employers (Salvato, Minichilli, and Piccarreta 2012).

In other words, changes in the components of family or business systems stimulate progress. The institution of the family is preserved by embracing the flexibility of the components while ensuring that the potential of each member is developed and nurtured by the family unit. At the same time, the essence of serving society's needs lies at the core of their enterprise. In closing, dynastic family firms are a living example that follow Collins and Porras' credo in *Built to Last*:

If you are involved in building and managing an organization, the single most important point to take away from this book is the critical importance of creating tangible mechanisms aligned to preserve the core and stimulate progress. This is the essence of clock building. (Collins and Porras 2002: 89)

References

Aldrich, Howard E., and Jennifer E. Cliff (2003). "The Pervasive Effects of Family on Entrepreneurship: Toward a Family Embeddedness Perspective." *Journal of Business Venturing*, 18: 573–96.

Becker, Gary S. (1991). *A Treatise on the Family*. Boston: Harvard University Press.

Bengtson, Vern L., Alan C. Acock, Katherine R. Allen, Peggye Dilworth-Anderson, and David M. Klein (2005). *Sourcebook of Family Theory & Research*. Thousand Oaks, CA: SAGE.

Bergfeld, Marc-Michael H., and Felix-Michael Weber (2011). "Dynasties of Innovation: Highly Performing German Family Firms and the Owners' Role for Innovation." *International Journal of Entrepreneurship and Innovation Management*, 13(1): 80–94.

Bernardes, Jon (1985). "Do We Really Know What 'the Family' Is?" In P. Close and R. Collins (eds.), *Family and Economy in Modern Society* (pp. 192–227). London: Macmillan.

Björnberg, Åsa, and Nigel Nicholson (2007). "The Family Climate Scales – Development of a New Measure for Use in Family Business Research." *Family Business Review*, 20(3): 229–46.

Block, Joern. (2010). "Family Management, Family Ownership, and Downsizing: Evidence from S&P 500 Firms." *Family Business Review*, 23(2): 109–30.

Chrisman, James J., Jess H. Chua, and Pramodita Sharma (1998). "Important Attributes of Successors in Family Businesses: An Exploratory Study." *Family Business Review*, 11(1): 19–34.

Christensen, Clayton M. (1997). *The Innovator's Dilemma: When New Technologies Cause Great Firms to Fail*. Boston: Harvard Business School Press.

Chua, Jess H., James J. Chrisman, and Pramodita Sharma (1999). "Defining the Family Business by Behavior." *Entrepreneurship Theory and Practice*, 23(4): 19–39.

Cigoli, Vittorio, and Eugenia Scabini (2006). *Family Identity: Ties, Symbols, and Traditions*. Mahwah NJ: Lawrence Erlbaum.

Collins, James C. (2009). *How the Mighty Fall: And Why Some Companies Never Give In*. New York: Harper Collins.

Collins, James C., and Jerry I. Porras (2002). *Built to Last: Successful Habits of Visionary Companies*. New York: Harper Business Essentials.

Davis, Jennifer N., and Martin Daly (1997). "Evolutionary Theory and the Human Family." *Quarterly Review of Biology*, 72: 407–25.

Fan, Joseph P.H., Yupana Wiwattanakantang, and Pramuan Bunkanwanicha (2008). "Why Do Shareholders Value Marriage?" ECGI Working Paper in Finance no. 227/2008.

Fernández Pérez, Paloma (2010). "Uncovering the Bottom of the Iceberg: Innovation and Large Family Firms in Spanish Metal Manufacturing." In Paloma Fernández Pérez and Mary B. Rose (eds.), *Innovation and Entrepreneurial Networks in Europe* (pp. 81–98). New York: Routledge.

García-Castro, Roberto, and Pramodita Sharma (2011). "Family Involvement-Firm Performance Link: Winning Configurations Revealed by Set-theoretic Methods." *Universia Business Review*, 4: 54–68.

Gomez-Mejia, Luis R., Martin Larraza-Kintana, and Marianna Makri (2003). "The Determinants of Executive Compensation in Family-controlled Public Corporations." *Academy of Management Journal*, 46(2): 226–37.

Hatum, Andres (2007). *Adaptation or Expiration in Family Firms: Organizational Flexibility in Emerging Economies*. Northampton, MA: Edward Elgar.

Hatum, Andres, and Andrew M. Pettigrew (2006). "Determinants of Organizational Flexibility: A Study in an Emerging Economy." *British Journal of Management*, 17: 115–37.

Hill, Mark (1995). "When Is Family Not Family?" *Journal of Family and Economic Issues*, 16(1): 55–82.

Holt, Daniel T., Matthew W. Rutherford, and Donald F. Kuratko (2010). "Advancing the Field of Family Business Research: Further Testing the Measurement Properties of the F-PEC." *Family Business Review*, 23(1): 76–88.

Hoy, Frank, and Pramodita Sharma (2010). *Entrepreneurial Family Firms*. New York: Pearson Prentice Hall.

James, Albert E, Jennifer E. Jennings, and Ronda Breitkruz (2012). "Worlds Apart? Re-bridging the Distance between Family Science and Family Business Research." *Family Business Review*, 25(1): 87–108.

Klein, Sabine B., Joe H. Astrachan, and Kosmas X. Smyrnios (2005). "The F-PEC Scale of Family Influence: Construction, Validation, and Further Implication for Theory." *Entrepreneurship Theory & Practice*, 29: 321–39.

Litz, Reginald A., Allison Pearson, and Shanan Litchfield (2012). "Charting the Future of Family Business Research: Perspectives from the Field." *Family Business Review*, 25(1): 16–32.

March, James G. (1995). "The Future, Disposable Organizations and the Rigidities of Imagination." *Organization*, 2(3–4): 427–40.

Markson, Elisabeth W. (2007). *Social Gerontology Today: An Introduction*. New York: Oxford University Press.

McConaughy, Daniel L., Michael C. Walker, Glenn V. Henderson, Jr., and Chandra S. Mishra (2008). "Founding Family Controlled Firms: Efficiency and Value." *Review of Financial Economics*, 7: 1–19.

McGoldrick, Monica, Betty Carter, and Nidia Garcia-Preto (2011). *The Expanded Family Life Cycle: Individual, Family, and Community Perspectives*, 4th ed. New York: Pearson.

McKenny, Aaron F., Jeremy C. Short, Miles A. Zachary, and G. Tyge Payne (2012). "Assessing Espoused Goals in Private Family Firms Using Content Analysis." *Family Business Review*, 25(3): 298–317.

Mehrotra, Vikas, Randall Morck, Shim Jungwook, and Yupana Wiwattanakantang (2010). "Adoptive Expectations: Rising Sons in Japanese Family Firms."
University of Alberta School of Business working paper.

Miller, Danny (1992). *The Icarus Paradox: How Exceptional Companies Bring
about Their Own Downfall.* New York: Harper Collins.

Miller, Danny, and Isabelle Le Breton-Miller (2005). *Managing for the Long
Run: Lessons in Competitive Advantage from Great Family Businesses.* Boston:
Harvard Business School Press.

Miller, Danny, Isabelle Le-Breton Miller, Richard H. Lester, and Albert A. Cannella Jr. (2007). "Are Family Firms Really Superior Performers?" *Journal of
Corporate Finance*, 13: 829–58.

Nicholson, Nigel (2008). "Evolutionary Psychology and Family Business: A New
Synthesis for Theory, Research and Practice." *Family Business Review*, 21(1):
103–18.

Salvato, Carlo, Francesco Chirico, and Pramodita Sharma (2010). "A Farewell
to the Business: Championing Exit and Continuity in Entrepreneurial Family
Firms." *Entrepreneurship and Regional Development*, 22(3–4): 321–48.

Salvato, Carlo, Alessandro Minichilli, and Raffaella Piccarreta. (2012). "Faster
Route to the CEO Suite: Nepotism or Managerial Proficiency?" *Family Business
Review*, 5(2): 206–24.

Santiago, Andrea L. (2011). "The Family in Family Business: Case of the In-laws
in Philippine Businesses." *Family Business Review*, 24(4): 343–61.

Sciascia, Salvatore, and Pietro Mazzola (2008). "Family Involvement in Ownership and Management: Exploring Nonlinear Effects on Performance." *Family
Business Review*, 21(4): 331–45.

Sharma, Pramodita, and Sankaran Manikutty (2005). "Strategic Divestments
in Family Firms: Role of Family Structure and Community Culture."
Entrepreneurship Theory and Practice, 29(3): 293–312.

Sharma, Pramodita, and Mattias Nordqvist (2008). "A Classification Scheme for
Family Firms: From Family Values to Effective Governance to Firm Performance." In J. Tàpies and J.L. Ward (eds.), *Family Values and Value Creation:
The Fostering of Enduring Values within Family-owned Businesses* (pp. 71–
101). New York: Palgrave Macmillan.

Sharma, Pramodita, and Sankaran A. Rao (2000). "Successor Attributes in Indian
and Canadian Family Firms: A Comparative Study." *Family Business Review*,
13(4): 313–30.

Volberda, Henk W. (1996). "Toward the Flexible Form: How to Remain Vital
in Hypercompetitive Environments." *Organization Science*, 7(4): 359–74.

Ward, John L. (2004). *Perpetuating the Family Business: 50 Lessons Learned
from Long-lasting, Successful Families in Business.* New York: Palgrave
Macmillan.

3

Family Values or Crony Capitalism?

Harold James

INTRODUCTION

There exists today an increasing interest in the role that family businesses play in economic development and in the stimulation of entrepreneurial values. The interest stems from two interconnected sources: a more general reassessment of the political economy of development, in which institutional strength is seen as a critical determinant of the possibility of successful economic emergence; and second, from the empirical perception that family firms are a central feature of most successful emerging market economies, whether in Asia, the Middle East, or Latin America. But does the proliferation of family firms necessarily mean that they are successful; or do they rather account for the retardation of these economies? Family firms are also in abundant evidence in some very undynamic economies. Two streams of academic literature focus on this problem: analyses of political economy, on the one hand, and of corporate governance, on the other. Political scientists, economists, and lawyers all have something to add to the debate, but mostly their interventions either lack a deeper historical background or rely on largely untenable historical assumptions.

The debate about the durability and efficiency of family firms is sometimes cast as an aspect of an institutional transatlantic divide, and sometime as a competition between the United States (with the United Kingdom) and the rest of the world. Sometimes, the story is told as one of the continental European perpetuation of family capitalism as a form of European exceptionalism, or of a political and institutional reluctance to follow the U.S. path of "modern capitalism." Alternately, it can also be thought of as a case of American exceptionalism, in which the rest of the world operates on a different model, one based more on the family.

Academic interpretations respond very easily to contemporary events. In the first half of the 1990s, a great deal of the literature emphasized trust and the capacity that families held out of cooperation with political instances to achieve a long-term plan for growth. After the 1997–8 Asia crisis, the "crony capitalism" view prevailed. As the effects of the Asia crisis proved to be rather short lived and the dynamic of success inherently quite powerful, the beneficial interpretation was revived. In the twenty-first century, some big Asian family firms, some old (such as the Tata dynasty), and some new (such as the Mittals), extended the principles of family business internationally and started to buy up iconic firms in the mature industrial world.

The outbreak of the Euro-crisis after 2010 has produced a dynamic similar to that of the Asia crisis, with large and apparently successful family firms in the crisis countries (such as large Greek shipping dynasties or the Italian textile dynasty of the Marzottos) being treated as a source of corruption and criminality and other family firms hit by financial strains (Schaeffler in Germany) or disintegrating (Merckle).

This chapter briefly reviews the historical evidence on family firms and then investigates the debate on the efficiency and effectiveness of the family enterprise before briefly examining the lessons of Europe's long and continuing history of family capitalism. We then turn to an explanation of the strength of family capitalism, before reaching some general conclusions on why family firms are especially likely to be viable and prominent in times of turbulence and transformation.

THE EMPIRICAL EVIDENCE

A great deal of recent research powerfully documents the significance and the extent of the phenomenon of family capitalism. La Porta, Lopez-de-Silanes, and Shleifer (1999) documented the extent to which the ten and twenty largest companies in their study were family controlled, but their sample of countries was heavily focused on Europe and hence on quite prosperous economies. The evidence was used to derive conclusions about the superiority of Anglo-Saxon capitalism.

Faccio and Lang extended the picture (2002). According to their calculation, in Germany seventeen of the hundred largest companies are in family hands; in France, twenty-six; and in Italy, forty-three. France and Italy still consider themselves to be the "champions of family capitalism."

In France at the beginning of the twenty-first century, 33.8 percent of the total market value of listed corporate assets was controlled by just fifteen families (and 22.0 percent by five families). For Italy, the equivalent figures are 21.9 percent and 16.8 percent, and for Germany 25.0 percent and 15.7 percent. By contrast, in the United Kingdom, the equivalent figures are just 6.6 percent and 4.1 percent.

After the 1997 Asia financial crisis, a new academic focus on emerging markets as plagued by endemic bad governance began. In the aftermath of the crisis, Claessens, Djankov, and Lang (2000) looked in detail at 2,980 publicly traded companies in nine East Asian countries and documented the prevalence of pyramid control schemes that allowed families to control large conglomerates with relatively little capital. The ten largest families in Indonesia controlled 57.7 percent of corporate assets and in the Philippines 52.5 percent. Thailand (46.2 percent), Korea (29.7 percent), and Hong Kong (32.1 percent) also had very powerful and concentrated family control, whereas Taiwan, with a much larger small enterprise sector, had a much lower ratio (18.4 percent).

The European and Asian streams of literature sit uneasily together. Some European countries demonstrate similar or comparable degrees of dominance by family firms. The most striking are some of the most successful and prosperous small European economies, Sweden and Switzerland, societies that generally rate highly as being agreeable to live in, and that are not considered to be corrupt. At the turn of the millennium, one family in Sweden, the Wallenbergs, managed to control an industrial empire that accounted for about half of Sweden's stock market capitalization, in part with shares with a 1:1000 voting differential (Högfeldt 2005). There may have been a gradual relinquishing of control, but there is still an acceptance of voting arrangements that perpetuate the pyramid system. In 2004, the Wallenberg sphere and another major owner agreed, for instance, to replace the 1:1000 arrangement in Ericsson with a more modest 1:10 class of special share.

More recently, Fogel (2005), as well as Morck and Yeung (2004) and Morck, Wolfenzon, and Yeung (2005), have tried to join the debates on European and emerging market family capitalism together to demonstrate with panel regressions that there is an association between the increased prominence of family business and bad governance, corruption, and inefficiency. One problem with this analysis is that highly family-dominated countries such as Sweden seem to be in a different world than that of the crony capitalism of Malaysia or Indonesia, and the question arises of whether the cases really belong in the same type of analysis. It might be tempting on the basis of the correlation of family capitalism and corruption (Figure 3.1) to think more in terms of different continental characteristics, but, even then, countries such as Singapore, with good governance and a prominent family sector, will appear as an interesting and challenging test of the theories of the macroeconomic and macropolitical impact of different corporate governance mechanisms.

THE DEBATE ON THE EFFICIENCY OF FAMILY FIRMS

The political economy literature points tantalizingly in two opposing directions. On the one hand, it sees families, particularly with extended kinship patterns, as creating trust. This is the positive side of family capitalism. The centrality of trust was popularized by Francis Fukuyama (1995). But the opposite picture is intractably bound up with the interpretation of the advantages of family capitalism. It is as if it were simply the obverse of the coin. Superior levels of trust or connectedness mean "insider" relationships, which breed corruption. In this view, family capitalism can easily be redescribed as crony capitalism.

The law and finance literature pioneered by Andrei Shleifer and others (La Porta et al. 1998; La Porta, Lopez-de-Silanes, and Shleifer 1999) interprets legal structures that inhibit financial openness as a key source of economic inefficiency and backwardness. In an extreme version of the negative hypothesis, the argument suggests that powerful and dominant family firms cannot rely on achieving economic viability in a straightforward competitive struggle. Instead, they systematically tend toward a limitation of competition as a way of perpetuating their dominance. They need to preserve their influence by limiting the rights of capital owners generally, so that they can continue to hold onto dominant positions with a relatively modest capital basis, often through pyramid holding companies or through stock with preferred or special voting rights. They become "entrenched." To secure their positions firmly, they need to intervene in property rights or to weaken legal and political guarantees of property rights. Such intervention requires political action, with the consequence that the action of the families can be reinterpreted as capturing political rents. The controlling families also oppose international opening, as foreign competition in trade and foreign investment would both lead to an erosion of their dominant position. In consequence, in poorer countries, there is an intertwining of politics and business life, and both are dominated by "oligarchs." Though the term is used most frequently to explain Russian developments in the 1990s, in particular, the conspiracy by six

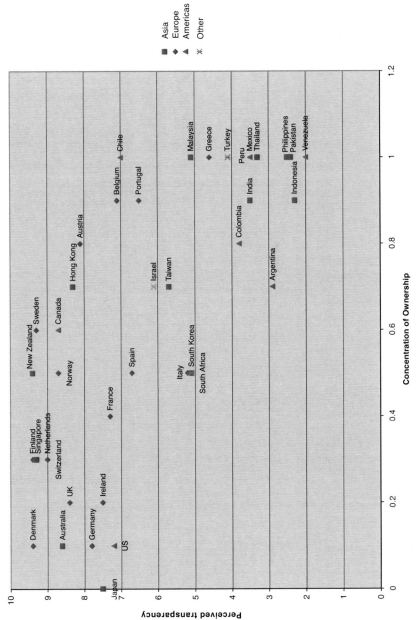

FIGURE 3.1. Perceived transparency and concentration of ownership. (Data on ownership concentration from Fogel (2005), and Transparency International, Corruption Perceptions Index 2007.)

or seven (accounts vary on the numbers) "oligarchs" to reelect President Vladimir Putin in 1996, it is now applied very elastically, to East Asia, the Middle East, and South America. Morck and Yeung (2004) observe a strong correlation between corruption and family control of businesses.

An extension of this approach even suggests that the phenomenon of oligarchical capitalism is causally related to the increasing precariousness on a global level of democratic institutions and to the resurgence of authoritarianism in the new millennium. Rich oligarchical élites are likely to be afraid of democratic political outcomes because a majority-directed government would be inclined to reward its supporters by expropriating the rents that have been seized by the oligarchs (Boix 2003).

This negative hypothesis has had enormous resonance in policy circles, and, in particular, with the major international financial institutions. The diagnosis of rent-seeking as the fundamental malaise of developing countries was pioneered by Anne Krueger as Chief Economist of the World Bank in the 1980s (Krueger 1974; see also Krueger 2002). The diagnosis of crony capitalism as the illness of the developing economies was then developed by the World Bank and also by the International Monetary Fund (IMF) in the 1990s. Governance reform was then seen as the key to a longer-term solution of emerging market crises. Especially after the outbreak of the Asian crisis of 1997–8, the IMF, in public and private statements, tried to root out "crony capitalism." In a remarkable reorientation of its traditional mission, the IMF ceased having distinguished macroeconomists as its chief economist, and instead appointed successively two academic microeconomists, whose best known work was concerned with the analysis of corporate governance issues. Ragu Rajan had long been concerned with insiders and outsiders in corporate finance (Rajan and Zingales 2003). One of Simon Johnson's most influential papers, appearing in the wake of the Asia crisis, was an examination of the way in which capital and exchange controls in Malaysia strengthened those businesses that were well connected (Johnson and Mitton 2003).

The modern discussion of governance, driven by developments in emerging markets, has been paralleled by a much older debate about the role of the family firm in continental European development. Unfortunately, the literature on European business history has been cast almost entirely in national terms, with the result that peculiar theses are put forward that usually bear little comparative analysis. In each case, the family firm is linked to every negative development. Particularly for France and for Italy, the family firm is blamed for relatively poor performance.

Many of these national European debates are also influenced by a particular vision stemming from a quite unique U.S. structure, in which older family firms play a much less important role than anywhere else, and where much of the second half of the twentieth century was dominated by the large managerial corporation with a widely dispersed ownership. Most American academics and analysts have, in consequence, assumed, following the work of Alfred Chandler, that there is a simple one-way trajectory that leads from the infantile stage of the family firm to the mature managed corporation with a widely dispersed ownership. This is still the model that is taught in most American business schools.

In consequence, for almost every country (with the exception of the United States), and whether or not it is experiencing above-average economic growth, the contribution of family capitalism to economic performance is assessed critically. Because there is usually some comparative disadvantage, and economic growth is often poorer than it might be, the family business arguments come in handy surprisingly frequently as a quick description of an economic malaise. Thus, even in Sweden, which is often seen from the outside as a model of good labor relations and strong economic performance, it is frequently claimed that family capitalism became entrenched and consequently dedicated itself to pushing "an old, established, large-scale industrial structure . . . to its limits" (Högfeldt 2005: 564; see also Lindbeck 1997). The outcome is then claimed to be more responsible for poor performance than the overexpansion of the state sector and inappropriately high levels of taxation are.

Those who see the United Kingdom as part of an American model of capitalism are surprised by the extent of the literature that shows how the deleterious consequences of family firms linger long after they ceased to play a major role in economic life. Since the early twentieth century, there have been fewer large family firms in comparison with continental Europe, but there is still a powerful tradition in explaining the longevity of a long "tail" of very poorly managed and poorly performing firms in terms of family ownership. Alfred Chandler, in *Scale and Scope*, portrays Britain as still being in thrall to "personal capitalism" in which family relations played a big part (1994). The term refers to a style of management, and not exclusively to the actual structure of ownership. William Lazonick uses a similar diagnosis for the ills of British capitalism (1986).

In France, the academic literature on family capitalism as a source of backwardness goes back at least to a seminal article by David Landes (1949), but Landes was simply pricking up and explaining a widespread postwar feeling that the Third Republic's industrial performance had been

stymied by the family. Charles Kindleberger repeated the accusation that
the French family firm "sinned against economic efficiency" (1964).

Pavan (1973) extended the Landes thesis to Italian business and found
family firms replete with low degrees of diversification, poor management, and general conservatism. In Italy, the same sense of frustration
already existed after the First World War, when it helped to fuel fascist
experiments in industrial reorganization and the imposition of a new cor-
poratism; but it surfaced again in the thinking about industrial structure
after the Second World War.

In the Indian takeoff after 1991, a prominent role has been played by
family firms and family groups; in some cases older and well-established
industrial giants such as the Tatas, which have also moved into new
growth areas such as software (Wipro, TCS or Tata Consultancy Services,
and Satyam), are all linked to family-owned business groups. There are
also much newer family groups. Yet, the family firms were also blamed for
sluggish growth in the colonial period, and the post-independence governments favored a socialist and state-centered pattern of development.

It is easy, in the abstract, to see why family firms might be thought of as
inefficient. Their family-based entrepreneurs might try to exercise control
functions for much longer than they were really effective. The handover
to the next generation of the family is always problematical as it does not
necessarily involve entrepreneurial talent. There may be disputes between
brothers and sisters, and divided ownership might have a negative impact
on the effectiveness of management.

Recently, these prevailing assumptions have received quite sophisticated empirical support. Bloom and Van Reenen (2006) have presented
evidence based on the evaluation of survey data on management practice, which uncovered major differences in management performance and
effectiveness between the United States and Europe. They also looked at
family firms and discovered that family-owned firms that employed professional managers demonstrated a mildly positive association with good
managerial practice. By contrast, family-owned firms in which the CEO
was chosen simply by primogeniture, in other words, a strict law of succession, performed very poorly. Such primogeniture inheritance tended
to be most pronounced in France and the United Kingdom, and, in these
cases, it accounted for the long tail of very poorly managed firms and a
significant part of the "management gap" with the United States.

Equally, family firms have particular advantages. In an atmosphere in
which there is a great deal of uncertainty and suspicion, and in which
the political framework and property rights are uncertain, they generate

reputational advantages. Critics from Karl Marx and Friedrich Engels onward have attacked the family as an economic, rather than an emotional, construct: the bourgeois family was kept in place by a sense of property rather than by romantic love or tender paternal and maternal feelings. The intangible assets and networks of the family thus became quite material and tangible. But, in this tradition, material advantages balance out the psychological dysfunctionality of the family enterprise. Pierre Bourdieu and Monique de Saint Martin (1978, in an article illustrated by a photograph of members of the French Wendel family lined up at the family funeral of the dynastic patriarch), concluded that

The family spirit and even the affection which creates family cohesion are transfigured and sublimated forms of the interest specifically attached to the membership in a family group, or the participation in a capital whose integrity is guaranteed by family integration. . . . The membership in an integrated family assures every individual the symbolic profits corresponding to the cumulative connections of all members of the group.

Families can be a powerful way of transmitting particular skills: the craft traditions of the *Ancien Régime*, particular approaches to labor relations, and skills in dealing with customers are all aspects of business conduct requiring a practical wisdom that is not simply or easily taught.

Old companies do not necessarily have to be spectacularly successful. A recent study indeed pointed out that the overwhelming majority of the eighteen U.S. companies from the first Forbes listing of the hundred largest American corporations in 1917 that survived to 1987 had underperformed the market as a whole, and that the group's average returns were 20 percent below the compound growth rate of the market as a whole (Foster and Kaplan 2001). Long life thus does not necessarily mean continuous outperformance. Family firms, if they are old, are thus more likely to be slower growing, not because they are family firms but simply because of the logic of age. Families, however, are likely to keep businesses alive longer than non-family owners, who may be tempted to react to slower growth by selling out or (if the problems are more acute) by closing down the business.

Even while family capitalism is so prevalent, in consequence of the intellectual popularity of an alternative model, its major figures feel hesitant and self-critical. The modern owners of many family firms, especially in advanced industrial countries, are often skeptical or ironical about their family's achievements in a way that goes beyond conventional mild self-deprecation. The influential Haniel dynasty in Germany likes to celebrate its "modesty." Ernest-Antoine Seillière, until recently the CEO of the family holding group, Wendel Investissment, sometimes refers to these large family enterprises as rare species that really belong in a zoo of quaint entrepreneurship (*Financial Times* 2002). When I spoke to the head of the Italian equivalent of Wendel, the former steel producer Falck, the family patriarch told me that "We are a rich family. We can afford to lose a lot of money." For a long time in the twentieth century, the families hid behind anonymous sounding initials, CGIP for Wendel, GHH for Haniel, or AFL for Falck. The GHH's official histories did not even mention the Haniel family ownership and control.

In fact, because of its long history, the European case of family capitalism supplies an important insight into the dynamic of the political, social, and economic role of family firms, in both the way in which the social strength and depth of family ties can compensate for weaknesses and instabilities in political and constitutional development and also, consequently, the way in which family intrusions into politics spark off a controversial debate about influence. The following observations are made on the basis of an admittedly subjective assessment of some prominent and powerful European family firms.

THE EUROPEAN MODEL

There is great diversity among European family firms: some are very large, some are small, some have concentrated on one product for very long periods of time, and others have diversified to the point when they are more like conglomerates. Nevertheless, there are some common features, family resemblances as it were, that make for something on an ideal type of the European family business.

Entrepreneurship

Characteristically, the great European dynasties began with an entrepreneur. Concrete achievements laid a basis for a future. The fortunes of the great European family firms began with tremendous technical breakthroughs and real entrepreneurial innovation. In France at the end of the eighteenth century, Ignace de Wendel was a scientist who helped to develop new techniques of large-scale iron smelting. In Germany, in the 1840s and 1850s, Franz Haniel worked out how to extract coal from under the water-laden marl layers that covered most of the great Ruhr coal basin. Giorgio Enrico Falck, at the beginning of the twentieth century, applied hydroelectric power to scrap iron to overcome Italy's resource under-endowment in a crucial technology for Europe's industrialization.

A Motivating Story

An entrepreneurial past, particularly if it was a long time ago, seems as if it might be of only antiquarian interest. Initial entrepreneurial profits are often quickly competed away. But there is also a question of how the past can be used. The modern families in great family firms can also all tell beautiful stories about their dynamic and buccaneering ancestors, who lived in turbulent and exciting times. François de Wendel bought back the family firm from the French state after the Revolution had confiscated the assets of his émigré father Ignace, who had ended up seeking shelter at the court of Saxe-Weimar with the poet Goethe. Franz Haniel built up a fortune smuggling coffee and wine past the Napoleonic armies that occupied Germany, conspired with General Bernadotte (the future King of Sweden), and danced at balls with the future Queen Louise of Prussia (nineteenth-century Germany's equivalent of Lady Diana). Giorgio Enrico Falck was driven out of Italy after the failed revolution of 1848 by the Austrian occupiers. Members of the FIAT dynasty of Agnelli are widely regarded as the "uncrowned kings of Italy."

These stories told about the families are often what gives them cultural power.

A Brand

In the twentieth century, and with the rise of a consumer culture, branding became more and more vital to business success. One of the reasons for the resurgence of family identities in business on a much broader scale in the second half of the twentieth century is that the family became a brand asset. In sectors where consumer appeal is critical, even fictional characters have power as a brand (Ann Taylor or Thomas Pink in clothing; Jean Louis David in hair-styling). Families have a special appeal as a truthful brand, in which the name stands for a commitment.

Family continuity gives a guarantee of quality and dependability, as in Wilkin & Sons marmalades and jams in Britain or Dr. Oetker's puddings and pie fillings in Germany. It is most characteristic of luxury brands, such as the eighth-generation German-Luxembourg tableware producer Villeroy & Boch. The most iconic family brands emerged in the Italian clothing and textile business: from fabric makers such as Loro Piana, to textile manufacturers who made the transition to clothing such as

Ermenegildo Zegna (founded in 1910, but still only a second generation firm), or to shoes and leather goods (Prada, Gucci).

But even the older families saw more use in their name than they had when their heavy industrial output was the driver of their business interests. The Haniel dynasty in Germany, which moved into wholesale pharmacies, office products, logistics, and wholesale marketing, kept its distinctive green Rhine barges on the river as a public sign long after they had ceased to be a major element of the business group's profitability. The Wendels in France, who had hidden behind anonymous acronyms such as CGIP, restyled their holding group as Wendel Investissement and then (from 2007) simply as Wendel.

A Network

The most enduring organizational feature of family businesses was their networking capacity. Some types of activity were grouped in industrial districts, in which patterns of relationships between suppliers, manufacturers of equipment, and distributors were established. The most famous of these industrial districts are the concentrations of engineering firms in Baden-Württemberg in Germany, where the bulk of employment in machinery is still in enterprises employing fewer than a thousand workers (Herrigel 1996: 165), and the Italian concentrations of textile producers in the Biella and Valsesia areas of Piedmont (home to Ermenegildo Zegna and Loro Piana) or the Valdagno in the Veneto (Marzotto). But there are also districts where optical products and eyewear, shoes and leather goods, and furniture are prevalent, all with concentrated areas of specialized artisan skill. The family character of this business, ranging from large to quite small-scale, made long-term commitments and business alliances easier. Since the 1980s, this Italian sector has been powerfully internationalized, with global marketing and distribution, so that commentators now speak of Italy's "fourth capitalism" (Colli 2005).

Political Networks

Such networks inevitably extended to politics. As the role of the state expanded in the course of the twentieth century, the rents to be captured from political activity increased. But this activity had been there from the beginning. The French and the Italian cases are probably the most striking examples, and their notoriety accounts for a great deal of the ambiguity with which French and Italian analysts view the issue of family capitalism.

Can use human capital to get edge @ point in time?

The Wendels already cultivated close relations with the state under France's *Ancien Régime* monarchy. The only customer of the de Wendel forge for most of the eighteenth century was the royal artillery works in Thionville. Ignace de Wendel built up a naval yard as well as new foundry in central France at Le Creusot. After the second Restoration in 1815, his son François went into politics and saw his business and personal careers as mutually enhancing. In business, he would need to "perfect manufacture so that we can produce at low prices; and accustom the workers here to produce all detailed products" (Gille 1968, 71). Politically and personally, he saw two major objectives: "to establish my fortune on a solid base, and leave a good reputation to my children, as the best of all inheritances"; and secondly, "to derive from my political position the goal that I must reasonably expect, the peerage." He concluded this optimistic assessment:

Why, with things arranged like this, with good ancestors, real services given to the state, descendants who are nobly established, some means which I can spend, why cannot I get to a peerage which so many others have achieved only by low intrigues and cowardly compliance. It seems to me that I am well placed to deserve the good will of a just government." (Gille 1968: 70–2)

Subsequent Wendels also sought parliamentary careers, and François' great grandson, another François de Wendel, who was first a deputy and then a senator, as well as a regent of the *Banque de France*, was widely seen as the embodiment of the nefarious "two hundred families" whom the political left imagined controlling France. The economic historian Bertrand Gille speaks of the "permanence of the large owners in the political life of the nation" (Gille 1968: 31).

The intertwining of politics and business life was equally dramatic and equally controversial in Italy. The postwar Christian Democratic Party was launched in the Milan house of Enrico Falck, and Falck quickly withdrew from business practice to promote his political career.

Such close connections with the world of politics have helped to generate the "black legend" of family business' malign grip on politics. The analysis of capture is present from beginning to end in the European story. It is, perhaps not surprisingly, in those countries most characterized by persistent and long-lived family capitalism that this diagnosis is most frequently made.

In the French Revolution, many firms well connected to the *Ancien Régime* were expropriated. By the twentieth century, the story of family capitalism was often presented as that of "bourgeois dynasties," a concept popularized in France in Beau de Loménie's work on the Second World War, entitled *Les responsabilités des dynasties bourgeoises*, which set out to unmask the sinister behind-the-scenes influences that had weakened the France of the Orleanist monarchy and of the Third Republic, and had, in consequence, led to repeated national defeat and humiliation.

The major families whose descendants are today at the head of our financial and industrial general staff, established the base of their fortunes and power and official influence in the economic sectors which depend on the state and where political relations have shielded them from the main risks. (Beau de Loménie 1943: 163–4)

In the course of the turbulent interwar years, hostile attention focused "two hundred families" (the families of shareholders of the central bank, the *Banque de France*, which was alleged to be in cahoots with big business).

This focus, however, creates a vicious circle of instability and suspicion. First, the remedy for the prominence of destructive or parasitical family firms is seen as lying in greater state control of the economy. The accusations against family business in the French interwar Third Republic were hurled even more ferociously after the Second World War: their conservatism had led to underinvestment, which had contributed not only to a general economic stagnation but had also made France vulnerable to the superior economic and military power of Germany. The involvement of family firms in political networks provided the basis for a powerful reaction against their influence in a democratic framework.

The only response to this attack was to build relations with organized labor. This provided the basis for the sustained relationship between the prominence of family firms in dynamic and stable economies such as Sweden, in which concentrated ownership and political social democracy are in a tight embrace (Roe 2003).

EXPLANATION

Five sorts of explanation can be given for the prevalence of family firms in many countries: as a response to weaker legal protection of owner rights; as a consequence of political manipulation ("entrenchment"); as an outcome of differing degrees of regulatory competition; as a consequence of inheritance law and inheritance practices; and, finally, as a reaction to inherent advantages in assessing prospects from a long-term perspective. These are examined in turn. But, at the outset, it is important to note that each of these explanations, with the exception of the last, focuses on a particular historical epoch and its political and legal institutions as generating the divergence of country experiences of corporate governance.

Law and Finance

The most influential approach has recently been the new orthodoxy, which asserts that common law societies have produced more successful firms than the largely continental European Roman law traditions because owner or shareholder rewards and remuneration are more closely aligned with those of the company. Shareholders are more powerful and influential because they can litigate more easily. The long-term consequence is that there is more information about company behavior and results available in the public domain. It is therefore possible for owners to make more informed and thus more rational or better decisions on the allocation of capital. Most of this discussion has focused on the consequences of different degrees of legal shareholder protection for the investment strategy of enterprises. But the issue of common law versus continental codified law is also central to the particular issue of governance in family-owned and family-controlled companies (La Porta et al. 1998; La Porta, Lopez-de-Silanes, and Shleifer 1999).

This interpretation is open to objection on a number of counts. First, it explains a phenomenon of the late twentieth century, from which the supporting evidence is drawn. U.S. shareholder class-action suits, which have been a critical driver of the new enforcement of property rights, are a recent and, perhaps, quite transitory, phenomenon. By contrast, for much of the nineteenth century, the antiquated British system of Chancery law made for the famously long drawn out and convoluted court cases described in Charles Dickens' novel *Bleak House* and afforded an inferior degree of protection to French administrative law, which strongly protected owners' and creditors' rights. Second, the arrangements described tend to weaken owners relative to managers, rather than simply weakening minority owners. They thus have made firms on a U.S. model with widely dispersed ownership and a strong management prone to manipulate the strategy of the firm in a way that does not benefit the owners. Management is interested in fast growth, in increased size of the enterprise, and in short-term profitability, but it is hard to devise incentives to align managers with the longer-run interests of the owner of the company. The bias not only produces short-termism but also increases managerial instability and a rapid turnover of CEOs. In an extreme version, it leads to

the direct expropriation of shareholders because of exaggerated managerial compensation, with an estimated 10 percent of market value being
simply diverted to managers (Bebchuk and Fried 2006; Monks 2007).
This argument has become increasingly influential as a critique of U.S. or
Anglo-Saxon style capitalism.

Tax Incentives

Perhaps the divergence of corporate governance paths lies further back
than is suggested by the law and finance literature. Morck (2003) argues
that the divergence of institutional paths between the United States
and the United Kingdom, on the one hand, and the rest of the world,
on the other, was largely established in the interwar period because of the
introduction of a new corporate tax regime. Roosevelt's New Deal and
analogous legislation in the United Kingdom did not allow the tax deduction of dividend payments, with the result that multiple and pyramided
complex holding-company systems became tax inefficient. By contrast,
other governments saw the formation of large industrial structures as
desirable from the public policy viewpoint (perhaps indicating that they
had been "captured"). Germany, for instance, had a *Schachtelprivileg*,
which gave tax exemptions for holdings greater than 25 percent until the
law was watered down in a reform of 1977.

But the 1930s are relatively late in the story of the ending of family
capitalism in the United States and Britain, and a great deal of the shift had
already taken place. Roosevelt's government was, in this sense, fighting a
battle against the trusts and the families that controlled them, but it was
a battle that had already been won.

Voting Privileges and Law

Many continental European countries had a strong equity culture
throughout the late nineteenth century. But they then experienced a strong
political reaction against the stock market and speculative activity, which,
in turn, transformed corporate finance. Germany and Austria experienced
a speculative bubble and then a collapse in 1873, which gave rise to
calls for greater regulation. In 1884, the size of the minimum share was
increased dramatically. A stock exchange law of 1896 almost completely
restricted futures speculation (*Termingeschäfte*). At the same time as continental European law became stricter, U.S. legislation was liberalized.
Initially, most U.S. states had so-called prudent-mean voting rights that

aimed at stopping the exercise of large concentrations of voting power (Dunlavy 2004). By the 1880s, this restriction had largely disappeared and set off a new dynamism on stock markets that became very pronounced at the turn of the century. In the merger wave of the early 1900s, many large family firms disappeared. Dunlavy and Welskopp (2007) explain the U.S. outcome in terms of a regulatory competition between states, in which each wanted to offer a more favorable framework: a regulatory race that was first won by New Jersey, which was then superseded by Delaware.

The merger wave of the early 1900s is a central step in the divergence of the U.S. and the continental European corporate paths. The more restrictive European approach compared with a more liberal law in the United States, and this helped make the family-dominated big company vulnerable to mergers. Some analysts, however, offer a different story, in which the disappearance of the American family firm in the merger wave of the 1900s simply reflects the "vast appetite for capital" or the "frenzied finance" generated by the geography of a "large country with a large single market" (Becht and DeLong: 621).

Both of these mechanisms can be seen at work in early twenty-first century Europe. The single currency and more integrated capital market have produced a greater mobility of companies. There is more pressure for a reduction in the level of shareholder protection, generated by competitive, rather than legal, concerns. Thus, at the same time, many U.S. corporations regard some form of dual voting rights as important to protect the company against outsiders, and the number of dual class firms with at least one class listed on the stock exchange rose from 100 in 1994 to 215 in 2001 (Becht and DeLong: 653). The very well-publicized IPO of Yahoo! was on the basis of dual voting shares. There is thus an increasing transatlantic convergence after the century long divergence.

Family Structure and Inheritance Law

An alternative explanation sees the divergence as lying further back, in the early nineteenth century, as a consequence of different inheritance laws in continental Europe. The *Code Napoleon* of 1802 influenced law not just in France, but also in other reforming European polities, notably in Italy and western parts of Germany. The *Code* was Napoleon's attempt to distill the essence of the French Revolution. The crucial provision with regard to inheritance was the requirement that each child should inherit a minimum fair share of his or her parents' estates. It abolished the custom of primogeniture under which titles and property passed to the eldest son.

Only a very small part of property could be freely left by will. The result was that the family business was divided among an increasingly large number of family members. By contrast, British firms were usually left to the oldest son in an exact analogy of the way an aristocrat passed on his title.

The requirement that all children have a stake in their parents' firm made for a unique development, in which firms that lasted over several generations had successively ever large numbers of owners. This arrangement was unpopular with many business owners and caused frequent and distressing family feuds and legal cases. There were struggles over which son should take over management functions, as well as difficulties with family members who wanted to withdraw their capital share from the business and thus weaken it. This mechanism, incidentally, as much as the decreasing entrepreneurial aptitude of successive generations, is what led to the demise of Thomas Mann's fictional family firm, the *Buddenbrooks*. (The younger siblings, Clara and Christopher, make disastrous marriages that lead to a loss of the capital of Thomas' enterprise.) The continental inheritance pattern required very tight and skillful management not just of the company, but also of the family. The wealth of the family was the capital deployed in its business, and any loss resulting from the inappropriate behavior of one member of the family would have repercussions on the whole unit. In many crafts and commercial activities, there were also business secrets that would be damaging if they left the family circle. Not surprisingly, this simple economic fact spawned a culture of control over nuptial behavior. Marriages were often used as a way of making strategic business alliances (for instance, between the German Haniels and the Belgian – originally British – Cockerills). There is still, in the twenty-first century, evidence that stock markets positively value strategic marriage alliances by family-controlled firms.

Family values meshed especially well with craft traditions in manufacturing. Iron-working or textiles abounded in all sorts of arcane techniques and secret tricks that needed to be carefully guarded from competitors. Businesses were continually prying and trying to lure skilled workers away from their rivals, and industrial espionage evolved into a major *Ancien Régime* activity. The best defense mechanism against defecting craftsmen was to restrict the most important secrets to sons or even daughters: the sons would be locked into the business, and the daughters would be a useful bargaining chip in the strategic game of dynastic marriage.

The importance of the right marriage choice receded somewhat in the later nineteenth century as a consequence of the increased availability of the legal form of the joint stock company. The result of the availability of tradable shares meant that a withdrawal of capital by a family member was less catastrophic. Although it might lead to a dilution of ownership, this issue could be tackled by measures such as the institution of share classes with stronger voting rights. At this time, in fact, many family firms adopted the form of a joint stock company.

The Inherent Characteristics of the Family Firm

Family firms have some endogenous advantages, which are relatively long-lived and long-lasting, in solving commitment problems. The fact of the family's existence – especially if it has a history of past success – is a guarantee of a continued presence. It can make for a high degree of flexibility in the face of new challenges.

TURBULENCE AND THE FAMILY FIRM

The eighteenth and nineteenth century origins of Europe's long-lived enterprises are now quite far removed in time; and the twentieth and twenty-first century story of survival has to be explained in a very different way. For France, Germany, and Italy, in the past century, strong family firms were a way of dealing with the problem of preserving business continuity in a very turbulent political and economic environment. A test of the family firm as a social institution is its capacity to change and modify itself in response to changing political and market circumstances.

In fascist Italy, the Falcks started to assert their family identity as a reaction against the state and its claims. In 1931, the firm changed its name from the rather anonymous "Lombard Iron and Steel Company" to include the name Falck, and it started to present itself as a family company. The annual report of that year introduced the notion of a new corporate identity in the following way, with a personal note from the president:

While I express my gratitude allow me to say that for me the most satisfying sense of such an event lies in the will to express the unity and unanimity with which our great family has always marched toward ever greater goals. For twenty-five years I have identified myself with this work of construction, to which I have devoted every fire and every passion. (Acciaierie e Ferriere Lombarde Falck 1931)

In Germany after the Second World War, the Allies tried to impose a "de-cartelization" and broke up the big steel trusts of the Rhine-Ruhr industrial area. But because many of the broken up companies had the same family owners, they were able to recombine quite easily and painlessly. The Haniels revived a transport company, France Haniel et Cie., as a vehicle to control their old steel and engineering interests. It was exactly in this period, in the 1950s, that the Haniels first became really conscious of their history, and began to organize family reunions, historical explorations, lectures, and orientation for young members of the family. The great era of family capitalism in Germany came after 1945, in part when some old firms – often controlled by bitterly divided families – remade themselves, and took on a new entrepreneurial dynamism; in part, with new dynasties such as the Quandts or the Burdas. There are obvious analogies in Japan, where, after 1945, the U.S. occupation dissolved the *zaibatsu*, or financial clique, and purged fifty-six members of *zaibatsu* families, but, within ten years, the family groupings had effectively reconstituted themselves.

After the Second World War, large steel and engineering businesses in Europe were subjected to increasing political control, to directed investment, obligations to develop poorer parts of the countries in which they were located, as well as to price controls. The families needed to respond to a problem of rapidly changing technology in the industry at the core of their entrepreneurial history, iron and steel, which required investments on a scale that seemed impossible for a family enterprise that did not want to lose control. But this required a dramatic break with the entrepreneurial past, which was enormously difficult for the men who had grown up in the world of particular technologies as well as particular values.

The secret for family success was moving out of steel, and of the three national cases in a comparison of long-lived large steel and engineering firms (James 2006), the firm that moved out of steel and engineering first, Haniel, which already started to diversify its investment in the 1960s, did best. The precipitating event for the Haniel family was the discussion that erupted in 1967 about the need to increase the capital of the steel and engineering concern GHH. From 1970 to 1982, the Haniel family reduced its holding in the GHH to a modest 9.6 percent. Wendel started the discussion somewhat later, when the energy crisis of the 1970s had already made the steel sector very problematical; in successive reorganizations from 1975 to 1979, the family exchanged some steel holdings to acquire another steel company (Marine) that had a diversity of industrial participations. The last to exit from steel, Falck, which made the decisive move only in the first half of the 1990s, and extensively reorganized between 1994 and 2002, lost the most, and was radically reduced in size.

It was easiest to handle the move if the external challenge coincided with a generational transition; but even in this case, enormous psychological skill – one might also say personal charisma – was involved. One of the problems that emerged for the Falcks, in particular, was that the withdrawal from steel (which had given the firm its identity) seemed to be a betrayal of its origins. Haniel, on the other hand, could point to its origins as a trading house in the eighteenth century. The story of the original firm made the recent adaptation seem more natural. As a result, it occurred earlier, more painlessly, less divisively, and much more profitably.

All three family businesses became diversified holding companies, with Haniel having interests in retail (Metro), wholesale and retail pharmacies (Celesio, which owns the British Lloydspharmacy), treatment of catastrophic fire and water damage (Belfor), professional laundry and clothing (CWS), ELG (recycling of specialty steel materials); Falck in renewable energy and a stake in the Aeroporti di Roma; and Wendel in information technology (Cap Gemini), medical products (Bio Merieux Alliance), abrasives (Wheelabrator), publishing (Editis), automobile parts (Valeo), certification, and risk management (Bureau Veritas). *diversification*

Modern family businesses thus do not usually resemble very closely the traditional images that they sometimes like to celebrate, and they are not the companies mired in antiquated techniques and primitive or nonexistent marketing. The successful cases have to be innovative and flexible and depend on three kinds of novelty.

First, there is less of a financial constraint on the family firm than existed in the past. When banks were the major or only source of external finance, especially in continental Europe, the family firms often worried about putting themselves into a situation in which they were dependent on banks. The availability of the capital market since the 1980s means that many firms can go to financial markets without experiencing a loss of family control. Iconic companies such as Ermenegildo Zegna in consequence have gone to the stock market (in this case, in 1990), but without surrendering family control. They have often, like the Wendel group, cultivated relations with large U.S. financial institutions, pension funds, and mutual funds. Again, personal continuities or commitments play a substantial part of the attractions of the package offered.

Second, the successful cases have engaged in a wide-ranging internationalization. Since the 1990s, Haniel, for instance, has sold more abroad than in Germany because the majority of its workforce has not been in Germany.

Third, they focus on niche products, and, in some cases, a quite diverse range of niches. It is then a technical dominance, rather than a grip on politics, that produces the capacity to draw entrepreneurial profits.

For these reasons, internationalized niche-product family firms, or "pocket multinationals" as they are often referred to in Italian and German debates, are the antithesis to the rent-collecting enterprise that is at the heart of much of the analysis of a malaise in emerging markets. They are likely to flourish most in small open economies, which, in consequence, retain good governance institutions while maintaining family dominance (see Figure 3.1). They are widely used to explain the recent success of the German export economy, where 1,307 companies have been identified as "hidden champions" (Simon 2012). European family firms have an undoubted history of "entrenchment," and the result was reflected in bitter national debates about "family capitalism." But they also offer an alternative, in which family ownership appears to generate an enhancement of reputation.

CONCLUSION

Families are not simply unchanging realities: they also reflect very concrete historical circumstances. Their behavior is shaped by a legal framework that recognized the family, and they will be vulnerable in a setting when the legal respect for the family changes or wanes. If there is a modern crisis of the family in Europe, then family firms will be vulnerable, too – with deleterious consequences. In the past, but also today, family firms are vulnerable to bad legal and tax regimes applied by governments at the insistence of analysts who wrongly argue that family firms are a sign of economic backwardness.

In each country where family business has been prominent, the fact of this prominence alone is sufficient to make for a contentious debate about the extent to which the family has restricted growth and development. These debates are classic instances of an attempt to use analysis to split complicated social phenomena. Maybe it would be better to see the family as a biological facilitator in which some aspects are at some times dysfunctional. Complaints about the family and its influence are analogous to the sentiment that, at times, some biological organs malfunction; however, although this is true, the analysis does little to acknowledge the role of the organs at other times.

Internationalization offers a way for family firms to break out of the political economy traps that national political cultures set for them: the temptation, on the one hand, for firms to look to capture rents and to "entrench" themselves and, on the other, the populist retort of campaigning against the oligarchs. Once the extended family firm or pocket multinational globalizes, it escapes from the national market and faces global financial opportunities and competitive market pressures. The scope for rent-seeking is then reduced, and a whole series of new forces molds a new business approach.

The joint stock company is now a less attractive model than it was in the nineteenth century. Nineteenth-century legislation that enabled the creation of joint stock companies was very clear in asserting that a company existed for a very particular purpose that needed to be closely defined in the company's statutes. The twenty-first century environment can be much more diffused and less focused – what some would call more postmodern.

The strength of modern capital markets makes it possible for companies – private as well as public – to borrow on dynamic corporate bond markets. Banks are no longer needed as lenders or intermediaries. By the early twenty-first century, there is little surprise when even major companies want to "go private." Family companies are very well poised to take advantage of the new opportunities, and Wendel has started to redescribe itself as a "private equity company," in other words, one of those companies at the forefront of what the French see as "Anglo-Saxon" financial techniques.

The lesson of the European story is that family capitalism has been particularly important in countries and societies with profound shocks and discontinuities. The Euro-crisis is currently producing a new episode in the long story of European shocks. The coherence of a family firm is a way of managing risk in a high-risk environment, whether that risk is political (as in the first half of the twentieth century) or economic (as in the early twenty-first century's globally transformed markets).

The family is also important as a brand or a guarantee of quality. The older family firms examined in this chapter were concerned mostly with mass products in the nineteenth and early-twentieth century, where quality issues do not arise very immediately or directly. The family character of the enterprise consequently remained very much in the background. When, however, they moved out of steel and into areas where service and reliability play a more vital role, it also became much more important to emphasize the family character of the enterprise. Indeed, the very visible family has become the calling card of the most successful Italian family firms in fashion and textiles.

The family historically provided networks of relationships, which could expand as time passed. The information gains provided by such networks can be described as a social capital that complemented financial capital. They contribute to the efficiency of the firm by lowering transaction costs.

At one level, then, the family seems to offer an alternative pole of loyalty to political allegiances – in other words, to the state. At another level, it can substitute for the anonymous abstractions of the market. This is a function that companies in general have: they are – following the classical analysis of Ronald Coase – ways of substituting control for market operations in a climate of information uncertainty. Family firms offer a particularly clear logic of control. The story of economic development is thus best understood as the narrative of the interplay of families, states, and markets, and of the differing ways in which they understood themselves and each other.

Family ownership has the advantage of being visible and identifiable, in contrast to the anonymous capitalism of large numbers of individual investors or the facelessness of institutional investors. If ownership is an important, or even the defining, feature of the capitalist process, it may be desirable that it is transparent. The greater difficulties that arise when disposing of ownership, in consequence, offer a guarantee of continuity, and make property part of a stakeholding and relatively permanent pattern of institutional arrangements, in which there are higher levels of commitment. This means that it may be easier to motivate managers and workers than in a setting in which they do not know whether tomorrow the (faceless) owners will walk away. Families in business recently responded to this sort of analysis by developing a concept of "professional ownership." The family and its long-term vision thus offered a striking and reassuring alternative to the emphasis on "shareholder value" that had been so fashionable in the 1990s and had been linked with the "Americanization" of business conduct.

This historical role of the family firm is confirmed by recent academic work suggesting that, in developing countries undergoing economic transition, family firms play a major role. They can generate a better access to market capital, because they create a degree of trust that offers a response to market failure. They provide a higher degree of human or social capital. Such institutions hold out an attractive path for many emerging economies. With the liberalization of the Indian economy since 1991, family groups (which many predicted would disappear over the course of development) have become more important. The Tatas very explicitly saw themselves as filling in a gap left by the inadequacies of state-centered growth (Khanna and Palepu 2005: 300), but the Tatas and the Mittals have internationalized themselves very quickly. Family groupings are also at the core of most of recent Chinese economic growth. Chinese and Indian patriarchs should be accumulating fascinating tales of entrepreneurial derring-do that they can pass on to their descendants as the inspiring myths that lie at the core of successful corporate images. When Asian economies look around for models of successful performance, they look not so much to the large Anglo-American corporation – that was the model of the last century – but to the dynamic and entrepreneurial family firm. This, indeed, may be the model of the future.

References

Acciaierie e Ferriere Lombarde Falck (1931). *Relazioni del consiglio d'amministrazione e del collegio sindacale.*

Acemoglu, Daron, Simon Johnson, and James Robinson (2005). "Institutions as the Fundamental Cause of Long-Run Growth." NBER Working Paper no. 10481. In Philippe Aghion and Steve Durlauf (eds.), *The Handbook of Economic Growth*. Amsterdam: North Holland, pp. 385–472.

Anderson, Ronald, and David Reed (2003). "Founding Family Ownership and Firm Performance: Evidence from the S&P 500." *Journal of Finance*, 58(3): 1301–29.

Attig, Najah, Yoser Gadhoum, and Larry H.P. Lang (2003). "Bid-Ask Spread, Asymmetric Information and Ultimate Ownership." EFMA 2003 Helsinki. Available at: SSRN: http://ssrn.com/abstract=332020 or http://dx.doi.org/10.2139/ssrn.332020, accessed 1/31/2012.

Barca, Fabrizio, and Marco Becht (2001). *The Control of Corporate Europe*. Oxford: Oxford University Press.

Beau de Loménie, E. (1943). *La responsabilité des dynasties bourgeoises*. Paris: Denoel.

Bebchuk, Lucian (1999). "A Rent-Protection Theory of Corporate Ownership and Control." NBER Working Paper 7203.

Bebchuk, Lucian, and Jesse Fried (2006). *Pay Without Performance: The Unfulfilled Promise of Executive Compensation*. Cambridge, MA: Harvard University Press.

Becht, Marco, and J. Bradford DeLong (2005). "Why Has There Been So Little Block Holding in America." In Randall K. Morck (ed.), *A History of Corporate Governance around the World: Family Business Groups to Professional Managers* (pp. 613–60). Chicago: University of Chicago Press.

Ben-Porath, Yoram (1980). "The F-Connection, Families, Friends and the Organization of Exchange." *Population Development Review*, 6(1): 1–30.

Boix, Carles (2003). *Democracy and Redistribution*. Cambridge: Cambridge University Press.

Bourdieu, Pierre, and Monique de Saint Martin (1978). "Le patronat." *Actes de la Recherche en Sciences Sociales*, 20–21: 3–82.

Burkart, Mike, Fausto Panunzi, and Andrei Shleifer (2003). "Family Firms." NBER Working Paper 8776. *Journal of Finance*, 58(5): 2167–201.

Chandler, Alfred D., Jr. (1977). *The Visible Hand: The Managerial Revolution in American Business*. Cambridge, MA: Belknap Press of Harvard University Press.

Chandler, Alfred (1994). *Scale & Scope: The Dynamics of Industrial Capitalism*. Cambridge, MA: Harvard University Press.

Claessens, Stijn, Simeon Djankov, and Larry H.P. Lang (2000). "The Separation of Ownership and Control in East Asian Corporations." *Journal of Financial Economics*, 58(1): 81–112.

Colli, Andrea (2003). *The History of Family Business 1850–2000*. Cambridge: Cambridge University Press.

Colli, Andrea (2005). "Il quarto capitalismo." *L'industria: Rivista di Economia e Politica Industriale*, 2: 219–36.

Colli, Andrea, Paloma Fernández Pérez, and Mary B. Rose (2003). "National Determinants of Family Firm Development? Family Firms in Britain, Spain, and Italy in the Nineteenth and Twentieth Centuries." *Enterprise and Society*, 4(1): 28–64.

Dunlavy, Colleen (2004). "From Citizens to Plutocrats: 19th-Century Shareholder Voting Rights and Theories of the Corporation." In eds. Kenneth Lipartito and David Sicilia, *Constructing Corporate America: History, Politics, Culture*. Oxford: Oxford University Press, pp. 66–93.

Dunlavy, Colleen, and Thomas Welskopp (2007). "Peculiarities and Myths: Comparing U.S. and German Capitalism." *Bulletin of the German Historical Institute, Washington DC*, 41: 33–64.

Faccio, Mara, and Larry Lang (2002). "The Ultimate Ownership in Western European Corporations." *Journal of Financial Economics*, 65(3): 365–95.

Fear, Jeffrey (1997). "August Thyssen and German Steel." In Thomas K. McCraw (ed.), *Creating Modern Capitalism: How Entrepreneurs, Companies, and Countries triumphed in Three Industrial Revolutions* (pp. 185–226). Cambridge, MA: Harvard University Press.

Financial Times (2002). "Rare Animals Take First Steps into Outside World." February 28.

Fogel, Kathy (2005). "Oligarchic Family Control, Social Economic Outcomes, and the Quality of Government," *Journal of International Business Studies*, Vol. 37, No. 5. (September 2006), pp. 603–622.

Foster, Richard, and Sarah Kaplan (2001). *Creative Destruction: Why Companies That Are Built to Last Underperform the Market – and How to Successfully Transform Them*. London: Crown Business.

Fukuyama, Francis (1995). *Trust: Social Virtues and the Creation of Prosperity*. New York: Free Press.

Gille, Bretrand (1968). *La Sidérurgie française au XIXe siècle. Recherches historiques*. Genève: Droz.

Herrigel, Gary (1996). *Industrial Constructions: The Sources of German Industrial Power.* Cambridge: Cambridge University Press.

Högfeldt, Peter (2005). "The History and Politics of Corporate Ownership in Sweden." In Randall K. Morck (ed.), *A History of Corporate Governance around the World: Family Business Groups to Professional Managers* (pp. 517–79). Chicago: University of Chicago Press.

James, Harold (2006). *Family Capitalism: Wendels, Haniels, Falcks and the Continental European Model.* Cambridge, MA: Harvard University Press.

Johnson, Simon, and Todd Mitton (2003). "Cronyism and Capital Controls: Evidence from Malaysia." *Journal of Financial Economics,* 67(2): 351–82.

Khanna, Tarun, and Krishna Palepu (1997). "Why Focused Strategies May Be Wrong for Emerging Markets." *Harvard Business Review,* 75(4): 41–51.

Khanna, Tarun, and Krishna Palepu (1999). "Policy Shocks, Market Intermediaries, and Corporate Strategy: The Evolution of Business Groups in Chile and India." *Journal of Economics and Management Strategy,* 8(2): 271–310.

Khanna, Tarun, and Krishna Palepu (2000). "Emerging Market Business Groups, Foreign Investors, and Corporate Governance." In R. Morck (ed.), *Concentrated Corporate Ownership,* National Bureau of Economic Research Conference Volume. Chicago: University of Chicago Press, pp. 265–294.

Khanna, Tarun, and Krishna Palepu (2005). "The Evolution of Concentrated Ownership in India. Broad Patterns and a History of the Indian Software Industry." In Randall K. Morck (ed.), *A History of Corporate Governance around the World: Family Business Groups to Professional Managers* (pp. 283–320). Chicago: University of Chicago Press.

Kindleberger, Charles P. (1964). *Economic Growth in France and Britain 1851–1950.* Oxford: Oxford University Press.

Krueger, Anne (1974). "The Political Economy of the Rent-Seeking Society." *American Economic Review,* 64(3): 291–303.

Krueger, Anne (2002). "Why Crony Capitalism Is Bad for Economic Growth." In Stephen Haber (ed.), *Crony Capitalism and Economic Growth in Latin America: Theory and Evidence.* Stanford, CA: Hoover Institution Press.

Landes, David S. (1949). "French Entrepreneurship and Industrial Growth in the Nineteenth Century." *Journal of Economic History,* 9(1): 45–61.

La Porta, Rafael, Florencio Lopez-de-Silanes, and Andrei Shleifer (1999). "Corporate Ownership around the World." *Journal of Finance,* 54(2): 471–517.

La Porta, Rafael, Florencio Lopez-de-Silanes, and Andrei Shleifer (2000). "Investor Protection and Corporate Governance." *Journal of Financial Economics,* 58(1–2): 3–27.

La Porta, Rafael, Florencio López-de-Silanes, Andrei Shleifer, and Robert Vishny (1997). "Trust in Large Organizations." *American Economic Review,* 87(2): 333–9.

Lazonick, William (1986). "The Cotton Industry." In Bernard Elbaum and William Lazonick (eds.), *The Decline of the British Economy* (pp. 18–50). Oxford: Oxford University Press.

Lindbeck, Assar (1997). "The Swedish Experiment." *Journal of Economic Literature,* 35(3): 1273–1319.

Mauro, Paolo (1995). "Corruption and Growth." *Quarterly Journal of Economics*, 110(3): 681–712.

Miller, Sandra K. (1997). "Minority Shareholder Oppression in the Private Company in the European Community: A Comparative Analysis of the German, United Kingdom, and French 'close corporation problem'." *Cornell International Law Journal*, 30: 381–427.

Monks, Robert A.G. (2007). *Corpocracy: How CEOs and the Business Roundtable Hijacked the World's Greatest Wealth Machine – And How to Get It Back*. New York: John Wiley & Sons.

Morck, Randall (2003). "Why Some Double Taxation Might Make Sense: The Special Case of Inter-Corporate Dividends." NBER WP 9651.

Morck, Randall, David A. Stangeland, and Bernard Yeung (2000). "Inherited Wealth, Corporate Control, and Economic Growth: The Canadian Disease." In R. Morck (ed.), *Concentrated Corporate Ownership*, National Bureau of Economic Research Conference Volume. Chicago: University of Chicago Press, pp. 319–72.

Morck, Randall, Daniel Wolfenzon, and Bernard Yeung (2005). "Corporate Governance, Economic Entrenchment, and Growth." *Journal of Economic Literature*, XLIII: 657–722.

Morck, Randall, and Bernard Yeung (2004). "Family Control and the Rent-Seeking Society." *Entrepreneurship Theory and Practice*, 28(4): 391–409.

Pavan, Robert (1973). *Strategy and Structure of Italian Enterprise*. Ann Arbor, MI: University Microfilms.

Rajan, Raghuram G., and Luigi Zingales (2003). *Saving Capitalism from the Capitalists: Unleashing the Power of Financial Markets to Create Wealth and Spread Democracy*. New York: Crown.

Roe, Mark (1994). *Strong Managers, Weak Owners: The Political Roots of American Corporate Finance*. Princeton, NJ: Princeton University Press.

Roe, Mark (2003). *Political Determinants of Corporate Governance*. New York: Oxford University Press.

Simon, Hermann (2012). *Hidden Champions – Aufbruch nach Globalia: Die Erfolgsstrategien unbekannter Weltmarktführer*. Frankfurt: Campus Verlag.

World Bank (1994). *Bureaucrats in Business: The Economics and Politics of Government Ownership*. World Bank Policy Research Report. New York: Oxford University Press.

4

Risk, Uncertainty, and Family Ownership

Andrea Colli

INTRODUCTION

One of the common refrains in family business studies concerns the relationship between the involvement of relatives and family members in the business activity and uncertainty and risk. In family business literature, family ownership (whatever its definition[1]) is generally considered as a device that is useful in uncertain environments that are characterized by

---

[1] The issue of defining family ownership is basically a never-ending one and has its own history. Restrictive and inclusive definitions have been employed across space and time and still are in research published on the topic. The European Commission has recently proposed a definition for family business, published in a report with the title "Overview of Family-Business-Relevant Issues: Research, Networks, Policy Measures and Existing Studies," November 2009, in which it provides the following definition of the subject:

"A firm, of any size, is a family business, if:

(1) The majority of decision-making rights is in the possession of the natural person(s) who established the firm, or in the possession of the natural person(s) who has/have acquired the share capital of the firm, or in the possession of their spouses, parents, child or children's direct heirs.
(2) The majority of decision-making rights are indirect or direct.
(3) At least one representative of the family or kin is formally involved in the governance of the firm.
(4) Listed companies meet the definition of family enterprise if the person who established or acquired the firm (share capital) or their families or descendants possess 25 per cent of the decision-making rights mandated by their share capital.

This definition includes family firms which have not yet gone through the first generational transfer. It also covers sole proprietors and the self-employed (providing there is a legal entity which can be transferred)."

Available at: http://ec.europa.eu/enterprise/policies/sme/promoting-entrepreneurship/family-business/#h2-2 (Accessed March 26, 2011).

high transaction costs. This has been widely recognized by historians, particularly business historians, who have analyzed family firms from both historical and comparative perspectives. The studies concerning both the period before the European industrialization process and those dealing with the phase of the First Industrial Revolution (Pollard 1965; Kirby and Rose 1994) implicitly and explicitly stress the relevance of the family dimension in those aspects of the business characterized by high uncertainty and risk. Berghoff (2006) has been moving along the same lines, stressing the positive role played by familiness among German *Mittelstand* firms in general, in particular, in periods of crisis, instability, and transition (Berghoff 2006). The current family business literature deals with the same topic extensively, stressing the positive role played by family ownership not only in the reduction of risk, but also in the improvement of flexibility in the decision-making process in conditions of uncertainty and in the consolidation and transmission of competencies and knowledge.

From another point of view, albeit with a smaller audience and lesser appeal, critics of family capitalism stress how family ownership may be, and, in some cases, actually is, a relevant obstacle to the firm's ability to survive, grow, and compete. Economic historians have frequently discussed in depth, on the basis of uncontestable evidence, the problems and hazards (i.e., risks) inherent in family ownership and control. The widely held opinion is that, far from being a positive element, family ownership actually becomes a continuous source of tensions and danger. According to the most critical views of family capitalism, deterioration and decline are almost inevitable; it is only a question of time. Maybe well after the third generation (the threshold of the well-known *Buddenbrooks* syndrome), but inevitably, sooner or later, the intergenerational transmission of the business activity and of the entrepreneurial *élan vital* is going to fail, and this failure will damage the business itself. Other pessimistic perspectives emphasize the problems arising from the interaction

The definition is extremely detailed; however, from the point of view of scientific research (and especially of those with a longitudinal and comparative perspective), it poses some problems. As far as historical studies are considered, for instance, the requirements of the definition can often hardly be met given the lack of information available about voting rights or decision-making rights. From another point of view, the historical evidence provides several examples of situations in which the criteria of the definitions are not met, even if the family control is out of question. This is, for instance, the case of the Japanese *Zaibatsu* before World War II, in which families – both directly and indirectly – controlled the large conglomerates, managed by professionals linked to the family itself by close ties of loyalty and commitment, common in the Japanese culture.

between the two spheres, that of the family and that of the business activity, stressing how tensions inside the family are going to affect the management of the business enterprise.

In sum, family firms deal with the issue of uncertainty and risk in different ways. According to some observers, uncertainty stems from the self-interest of economic actors (strategic uncertainty), from the contingent assessment of the characteristics (and value) of a certain good or service, from asymmetric information, and from the obvious consideration that future events are frequently unpredictable or unknown to economic actors.

Even if it has not been defined in detail, risk can be seen as the probability of failure and economic damage generated by an uncertain situation. To reduce uncertainty means to lower the probability of damage or failure, that is, to reduce (but not to eliminate) the level of risk. On the contrary, increasing uncertainty in the absence of other correctives results in a higher risk level. Moving the argument a step forward, it is possible to argue the existence of a positive relationship between risk and disequilibrium. In the framework of this chapter, disequilibrium is basically considered as a status in which economic organizations face a loss of stability that results in further damage, for instance, financial loss versus profit, or also in terms of the ability of the organization to formulate and carry out effective and successful competitive strategies. In the rest of this chapter, I apply this conceptual framework to the analysis of family firms. The basic argument goes as follows: family firms are not, per se, devices that reduce or increase uncertainty, risk, and/or disequilibrium; they tend, by their nature, to do both and hence both viewpoints discussed earlier are true. *Inside* the firm, the coexistence of family ties and business activity can result not only in a reduction of uncertainty levels (e.g., by allowing a smooth and flexible decision-making process), but also in an increase of organizational "entropy," and thus greater uncertainty (e.g., the complex issue of governance among family members). The final result can be, alternatively, an *internal* equilibrium or disequilibrium. *Outside* the firm, in its relationship with the external environment, a similar scheme applies. The uncertainties in the external environment, owing to transaction, information, and control costs and asymmetric information imply, for its economic organization, policies and forms of behavior (strategies) that rely on family ties to lower uncertainty. Family firms will, from this perspective, have an advantage over non-family firms in terms of flexibility and the effectiveness of their competitive strategies, as frequently noted in the literature. At the same time, according to other observers,

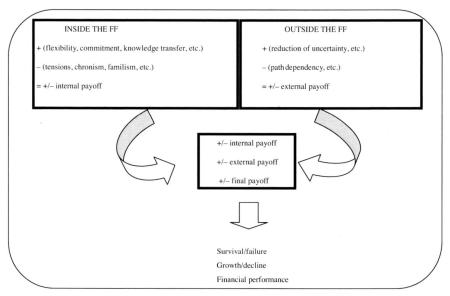

FIGURE 4.1. The family-firm payoffs.

the presence of family ties and kinship relations drives the behavior of economic organizations toward rather conservative approaches in terms of both strategies and structures. On the other hand, while aiming at reducing uncertainty and risk, the presence of kinship relations and family ties in economic organizations can thus result not only in more effective strategies, but also in more risk-averse attitudes and suboptimal equilibriums, for instance, those implied by path dependency. To put it trivially, the pros and cons also balance here.

If the final outcome of the internal and external payoffs is positive, the family firm enhances its probability of success, at least in terms of survival (see Figure 4.1).

In a provocative and seminal article, the psychoanalyst Manfred F.R. Kets de Vries (de Vries 1993) listed the "good" and the "bad" news for family business. Even though the article's *incipit* is an instructive story of a family-run pottery that goes from rags to rags in three generations, de Vries focuses, in the rest of the article, on the internal dynamics of family firms, basically from a static point of view. The list of the pros and cons in family firms that he provides has become famous and widely cited. In synthesis, the advantages include long-term orientation, independence of action, pride, identification and commitment, financial commitment, continuity in leadership, flexibility and easier knowledge transmission. The disadvantages – on which the author focuses at length – include unwillingness to grow, messy organizations, nepotism, successors' frustration, autocracy, financial strain, and succession troubles. De Vries' perspective is right. However, it is, in my opinion, a partial one, focused on what I consider to be the *internal* dynamics of family firms and from a static point of view, that is, one that does not take the dimension of change into account.

The longitudinal perspective that characterizes business history not only allows us to find a large amount of evidence about risk and uncertainty management in family firms, but also gives us the possibility to put this relationship into a dynamic framework. For instance, as is widely recognized, during the life cycle of a single family business, the role of family ties can transform and evolve considerably, enhancing the equilibrium up to a certain point in time or phase of its development, and then undermining it; conservatism and path dependency can emerge after a period in which family ties play a positive role in enhancing the competitive strategies of a firm. Changes in the general context in which the economic activity takes place (market dynamism, technology, institutional and legal settings) can emphasize either the positive role of family ties and trust creation or the negative effects of excessive familism.

The following sections review and discuss the evidence provided by family business studies, in the fields of both management and business history, about the pros and the cons of family firms facing uncertainty and risk. However, even though it is of central relevance, owing to space constraints the chapter only partially addresses the role played by the institutional framework and the dynamic evolution in the conditions that link family firms and uncertainty and risk.

INSIDE THE BLACK BOX: RISK, UNCERTAINTY, AND THE FAMILY FIRM

The "*Buddenbrooks* syndrome," from Thomas Mann's famous novel describing the saga of a merchant family in Lübeck over three generations from rags to riches and then to failure, is a good starting point. Business historians and management scholars make extensive use of this stereotype, which usually refers to the basic life cycle of the family firm and to the fact that the intergenerational transmission of leadership is per se a humble process, in which a number of variables increase uncertainty: the selection of the leader, the conflicting interests both between generations and within the new generation, and the tensions generated by the process of growth (e.g., in terms of additional financial resources needed). This pessimistic (maybe realistic) view stresses how, sooner or later and in the absence of a planned and careful management of the situation – of the leadership succession, for instance, or simply the end of the family leadership in favor of professional managers – uncertainty will prevail and will result in a loss of efficiency, and, ultimately, in the failure of the company.

The life-cycle model is based largely on a mixture of variables ranging from human nature, to biology, and even technology and markets. The main point is that family firms are intrinsically weak, given the mixture of the two spheres (that of the kin and that of the business); the fact that entrepreneurial attitudes cannot be transmitted biologically; and also that delegation, the hiring of professionals, and the decision to go public cannot be avoided if efficiency and growth are to be pursued. In this framework, technology and markets matter, especially when their combined force provides a strong push toward the expansion of the business activity, something that questions the capability of a family to provide enough entrepreneurial and financial resources and determines the recourse to professional managers. Family business literature is full of paradigmatic stories in this regard. The case of Thyssen, as described by the U.S. business historian Jeffrey Fear (Fear 1995), is both an interesting and problematical example. Started as a small family firm (a sibling partnership) in 1871, Thyssen and Co. quickly became one of the most dynamic German corporations. August Thyssen not only was technically able, but also had good relationships with the powerful German banks and with competitors in cartels. It was also competent in designing strategies of growth and in adapting organizational structures, based on cohorts of salaried managers rewarded according to the results that they brought to the company. Paradoxically, the negative relationships ("not as solid as his business' ones") with his family (three sons and one daughter) were, for Thyssen, the main justification for successfully and completely detaching the family dimension from that of the business. This was a fundamental advantage that allowed the German entrepreneur to create one of the most effective organizations of the Second Industrial Revolution.

Family Hindrances

This pessimistic vision is as much diffused as the enthusiastic and "idealistic" ones. One very good example is this review of a recent book by the economic historian David Landes, dedicated to the history of thirteen dynasties (of at least three generations) in family business (Landes 2006). To be honest, this is not Landes's best book, at least not at the level of *Unbound Prometheus* or *The Wealth and Poverty of Nations*. It is a descriptive work, which deals with some more or less good histories but nonetheless lacks the interpretative strength for which he is known and read worldwide. However, this is not the main reason why the reviewer of the prestigious U.K. newspaper *The Independent* criticizes Landes's book. In his own words,

[In Britain], a couple of generations ago (. . .) family-run businesses were prominent in every industry, from retailing to textiles, to shipbuilding, brewing and arms production. But no more. In the period 1960 to 1980, 'family' came to equal old-fashioned and inefficient, and one by one the great dynasties disappeared, taking their paternalism, eccentricities and cruelties with them. Entire industries disappeared as Britain lost its manufacturing base in a single generation. They have been replaced by faceless corporations, run by professional managers who are (. . .) interested in short-term performance only. With their passing, we all lost something in terms of colour, character and stability. But, on the other hand, we gained better labour practices, prosperity, global competitiveness (the City of London has again replaced Wall Street as the world's most important financial centre) stability – and full employment. Which do you prefer? There used to be an old adage in the City, which ran 'Rags to rags in three generations'. It is as true today as it ever was. Big family businesses simply cannot hack it in the modern, global world of hedge funds, private equity funds and short-termism. A good thing? I'm not sure. (Fallon 2007)

Apart from the last sentence, the review gives a clear account of the widespread pessimistic view of the sustainability of family business–based capitalism, especially when large firms are considered.

With greater analytical rigor, the same position is shared by Alfred Chandler, the "founding father" of business history (Chandler 1990). In his opinion, the family firm simply could no longer exist (apart from in some traditional, labor-intensive industries) with the advent of the large corporation, in both scale and capital, during the Second Industrial Revolution. Family firms, especially when ownership also meant the presence of family members in top management positions, were not the best form for industries in which huge amounts of capital were needed, and in which the management increasingly became a specialized, knowledge-intensive activity, to be run by professionals fully in charge of their responsibilities. In line with what Berle and Means noted among the largest U.S. listed corporations at the beginning of the 1930s (Berle and Means 1932), Chandler was also basically making sense of the increasing separation between ownership and control in the U.S. modern corporation in the first half of the nineteenth century (for a general review, see Fligstein 2001). Even though Chandler never expressed this explicitly, family control was fundamentally a danger and a risk for the corporation. Family ownership would normally impose obstacles and constraints on a "natural" process of growth *in that particular industry*, while it could persist in others in which growth and scale were, and still are today, no longer necessary. The aforementioned story of Thyssen is emblematic in this regard.

From a dynamic point of view, the process of growth of the modern firm tends to amplify all the problems inherent in family ownership, which, in their turn, may bring additional risk to the uncertainty surrounding entrepreneurial activity. Basically, family ownership may threaten the process of growth in four main areas. The first is the financial area. Even if it is not clear whether there is a "family effect" (be it positive or negative) on the cost of capital for family-controlled and publicly owned firms (McConaughy 1999; Claessens et al. 2002), the real problem may arise from the unwillingness of the family to find new capital, via either debt or equity, to maintain close control over the company, by relying on self-financing for the necessities of growth. Historically, in many countries (e.g., in Continental Europe), family firms have shown a marked tendency to avoid Initial Public Offerings (IPOs) on the stock market, preferring other means of financing to maintain strict control over the company itself, even when new investments are needed. Hundreds of examples illustrate the idea of limiting investments so as to maintain family control of the assets; a telling example is provided by the history of Lancia, one of Italy's most renowned automobile manufacturers, famous for its high-quality sports cars. After the Second World War and the death of the founder, Vincenzo Lancia, Lancia was run by Adele, his widow, and Vincenzo's only son, Gianni. Notwithstanding the fact that it was clear that the postwar years were increasingly offering the possibility of increasing production to cope with the growing demand, Lancia refused to undertake the necessary steps, for instance, foregoing the possibility of modernizing its plants through the Marshall Plan financing programs to maintain family control. This reduced its competitive advantage and soon, because of other entrepreneurial mistakes, led to its sale in 1956 (Amatori 1996).

The second area is, broadly speaking, the organizational area. One reason for which family ownership is considered as basically unstable is that not only is leadership succession a (quite obvious) risky process, but also, even in the case of success, the family may not have enough human capital to be deployed in the top management positions – or, maybe worse, it may have too much of it, but of low quality. Family firms are thus associated in the literature with the tendency to adopt flat organizational structures with a high degree of centralization, as the U-form or the holding (Whittington and Mayer 2000), which delays the introduction of other organizational architectures that are considered to be more efficient, especially when associated with large overall size and diversification strategies. This means an increasing level of risk that can endanger the survival of the firm itself, especially if unexpected events occur. The early story of Fiat, the Italian automobile manufacturer, is an extremely good example. Founded in 1899 by a creative and vision-ary entrepreneur, Giovanni Agnelli, Fiat soon became the market leader, much bigger and much more integrated than its competitors. The founder was able to create an effective organization, surrounding himself with a cohort of managers. The organizational structure was, however, quite flat, and the founder had close control over all the main firm's opera-tions. The shared belief was that the leadership was going to pass to the founder's son, Edoardo, but he died in a plane crash in 1935, leaving three young sons and five daughters. Fiat was run again for some years by the founder, and, when he died in 1945, it was a strong manager, Vittorio Valletta, who took over the leadership in a very centralized way, albeit – as he used to say – "in *loco parentis*" (in place of the father), to stress his loyalty toward the family. The five daughters were totally excluded from the business, and one of the sons was completely unable to participate because of a permanent illness. Only in 1966 were Gianni and Umberto, in their early forties, ready to take over the management of the company. Fiat's family control was thus able to survive thanks to a combination of professional management loyal to the family and self-selection of family leadership.

The third area is, also broadly speaking, the "entrepreneurial" area. The process of growth, especially if it lasts for generations, sooner or later requires the adaptation of the entrepreneurial formula to avoid danger-ous path dependencies. Family ownership may undermine this necessary adaptation from two points of view: (1) the resistance of the founder to change (Zahra 2005) and (2) the tendency of new leaders to adhere to consolidated strategies instead of searching for new ones, also owing to the involvement in the business of the previous generation (Davis and Harveston 1993). The economic historian Harold James published a book about the history of three European dynasties in the steel industry in 2006

(James 2006). The book reviews a couple of hundred years of steelmaking through the stories of the Italian Falcks, the French Wendels, and the German Haniels. The book is full of fascinating hints about the internal dynamics of family firms – especially multigenerational ones. However, the broad message emerging from the whole book is that, in the cases of both the Wendels and the Haniels, the decision to exit from the steel market to engage in other activities – financial services and distribution – was taken at the right time, and the family was able to take the steps required to achieve the necessary turnaround. In the case of the Falcks, however, the decision was, for a long time, to stay with their traditional field, and, when the decision to diversify was finally taken, it was probably too late. Today, the three families have a very different weight in their respective countries' industrial scenario. The role of cultural patterns in shaping the entrepreneurial vitality of family firms is still under analysis by scholars, who stress not only the positive side of having a strong cultural identity, but also the risks inherent in the dominance of a given cultural pattern or its imprinting over the new generations of leaders (Hall, Melin, and Nordqvist 2001). In these cases, the reproduction of the existing entrepreneurial culture may have serious consequences on stability, especially in rapidly changing competitive scenarios.

The fourth area in which the presence of the family may result in increasing instability and uncertainty is that of governance. Agency issues may arise not only between managers and family members, but also among family members (when some are involved in the management of the company and others not) and, more importantly, between family owner-managers and other shareholders, both in privately held and in listed companies (Morck and Yeung 2003), especially where control-enhancing mechanisms allow a high degree of control in the presence of a small degree of ownership (and, hence, direct financial involvement), which may lead to the expropriation of the firm's resources by family members. In many cases, this very peculiar agency problem has also been tolerated owing to a favorable institutional environment. However, when this starts to change, governance problems emerge, increasingly questioning the way in which the family's control was achieved and maintained. A good example of this is the story of the Swede Wallenberg's empire during the last twenty years. The Swedish dynasty was traditionally able to control a vast portion of the country's big business through a mixture of direct ownership and control-enhancing mechanisms such as dual class shares and pyramids, with the blessing of the governing parties and of the Swedish business community as a whole. More recently, however, evolution in the political and economic scenario has increasingly challenged this equilibrium, considerably endangering the ability of the Swedish family to exert close control over the country's largest firms (Eriksson 2011).

What it is important to stress here is that these potential areas of instability in family firms may expand during the process of growth, adding further turbulence to other more intuitive elements besides those put forward by Kets de Vries (1993: exhib. 1, p. 61) and extensively analyzed in the literature on family firms.

Family Matters

The same Kets de Vries, however, stresses that, if this intrinsic instability of family firms, from both a static and a dynamic perspective, is a matter of fact, the persistence of the firms, not only those of small and medium sizes, but also the largest ones, is also true. This phenomenon is widely confirmed in the existing literature and by comparative analysis (La Porta et al. 1999; Faccio and Lang 2002), which stresses the diffusion of family ownership and control, even with high threshold size, among the world's largest corporations.

A (wide) portion of the literature (especially in the field of finance and governance) endeavors to explain this situation by emphasizing the role of the legal and institutional frameworks. The diffusion of large family firms and concentrated ownership in general is thus to be seen as the response to poor legal protection of shareholders and/or the consequence of high rent-seeking possibilities and incentives (Bebchuck and Roe 1999; La Porta et al. 1999). Many commentators, however, stress that the persistence of family ownership in large firms is basically due to the fact that it brings superior advantages, which, in the end, result in superior performances. This, for instance, is the position of Miller and Le Breton-Miller (2006), who focus on large, publicly traded family-controlled firms (with a threshold of at least 20 percent), and try to explain why, in many cases, they achieve superior performances compared to non-family firms. Their discussion essentially is based on stewardship theory, developed in the literature on family firms, which points out how executives are often not acting on the basis of personal self-interest, but for the benefit of the organization and of its stakeholders (Davis, Schoorman, and Donaldson 1997). Above-average performances are obtained when the equilibrium inside the organization is high. This condition is to be found, comparatively, in firms in which family ownership is neither too high (which results in higher agency costs) nor too low (which lowers incentives to stewardship), when a strong family CEO is surrounded by family members committed to independent, but accountable, directors.

Stewardship is clearly one of the elements that allows family firms to lower transaction costs, while gaining stability over time. Looking at the four critical areas mentioned above, in which the presence of family control may result in a high and increasing level of risk (finance, organization, entrepreneurship and governance), it is clear how the presence of a controlling family can result in the improvement of the equilibrium in all these areas, and thus in a lower level of risk.

From a financial point of view, family control may constitute a positive element when it results in the presence of what is called "patient capital" that is, investment decisions are taken with a long-term orientation and with less emphasis on short-term returns, as in the case of non-family firms in which the executives are constantly under the pressure of the market. Patient capital also means that families may accept lower (than the average) returns from the capital invested, and, hence, managers can run the business with a wider choice of opportunities without the pressure of delivering results in the short term. What is more, this argument may serve to stress how, in some cases, family executives may be willing to accept a higher degree of risk in strategic decisions and business diversification, given the possibility that they have of delivering lower returns to the other family members. One good example of this is provided by the history of another famous Italian firm, the department store La Rinascente, which started its activity in Milan in 1917 under the leadership of two relatives, Senatore Borletti (who provided the financial resources and the support of the Milanese financial community) and Cesare Brustio (a skilled manager able to build the necessary human capital and capabilities from scratch). During the first years of its activity, the leadership of the company heavily re-invested all the resources generated in order to grant the management sufficient freedom to develop its ambitious plans of expansion and consolidation. Borletti had not only to be patient himself, but also to fight hard with the other shareholders (namely, the banks) which were demanding increasing returns on their investments.

As far as organizational structures are concerned, the advantages of centralization and a lower degree of bureaucracy, as well as that of the presence of family members in the top management positions enhances, according to many observers, the flexibility of the decision-making process, which turns out to be an advantage in situations which are characterized by a high degree of uncertainty (Hatum and Pettigrew 2004). If this is a widely recognized advantage of family firms over bureaucratic organizations, the role played by family ownership in new organizational structures, for instance, those based upon networks of firms, remains less explored by the literature. A good exemplification of this issue can be found in the industrial districts literature, which stresses how one relevant characteristic of this peculiar form of production based upon networks of producers, which resembles a "dispersed factory," is that business relationships among small firms in the same value chain are based upon informal agreements which are often strengthened by personal and kinship relations. Some years ago, Michael Piore and Charles Sabel mentioned the so-called *Systéme Motte*," named after the French entrepreneur Alfred Motte, who imagined a system in which each family member who came of age was paired with a skilled technician and provided with the necessary capital to start-up a firm in some of the phases of production that were considered to be necessary for the mother firm The result was a network of independent producers, in which transaction costs were naturally reduced by kinship relations; a system that can still be found today in Italian industrial districts and business community in south Germany (Piore and Sabel 1984; Lessem 1998).

When not degenerating into path dependence, the presence of the family can play a relevant role from the perspective of entrepreneurial creativity. The literature highlights some important areas in which this is particularly evident. One, quite relevant, area is the fact that not only does the family provide strong identity to the business, but it also allows careful on-the-job training for family members, which results in strong stability in terms of leadership, another element that is considered to be proactive in risk and uncertainty reduction. Another version of this role played by the family in enhancing entrepreneurial capabilities is the fact that family ties and networks generated by kinship ties provide a further reduction of uncertainty, especially in the first phases of the activity, thereby allowing access to critical resources (Anderson, Jack, and Drakopoulou-Dodd 2005).

If, as stated earlier, there is a large amount of literature and empirical evidence that associates family firms with poor corporate governance, there are also many commentators who stress how the presence of a ruling family can offset agency costs and tensions through commitment and loyalty. The aforementioned stewardship theory goes precisely in this direction. Stewardship is the way in which the presence of a strong and committed family lowers the tensions and risks implied in the governance process, thereby reducing the governance problems mentioned earlier. More recently, some authors have suggested how a combination of stewardship, specific capacities for knowledge management, and a family-based brand identity results in an improvement of the firm's market orientation – defined as a "set of superior capabilities of understanding and satisfying a firm's customers" (Cabrera-Suarez et al. 2011).

Summarizing the previous sections, it is clear how the internal equilibrium of a family firm is both enhanced and threatened by the presence of kinship and family relationships within the organization. Thus, family relationships simultaneously not only play a relevant role in the reduction of risk and uncertainty and facilitate processes and decisions within the organization, but can also create serious problems that amplify the internal turbulence. These two opposing views have been widely addressed by the literature on family firms, which alternatively takes the positive and the negative view. For instance, in business history, there has recently been a clear shift from a basically negative vision of family ownership to a definitely more positive attitude that takes the relative efficiency of family firms in particular timeframes and institutional and cultural contexts into account (Colli 2006). On the other hand, there is wide consensus that the advantages of family ownership in terms of uncertainty reduction overshadow the potential threats in the first phases of the life cycle of an enterprise, while the process of growth may enhance the tensions generated by the nexus between the sphere of the family and that of business. Clearly, what is not clear is the division between the two phases, nor why, as stated earlier, so many family firms are to be found among the largest companies around the world.

Looking only at the internal dynamics to understand the way in which family firms deal with risk and uncertainty may be misleading. To have a more complete perspective, it is worth turning to the influence of family ownership on the relationship between the firm and the external environment.

OUTSIDE THE BLACK BOX: FAMILY FIRMS AND THE EXTERNAL ENVIRONMENT

The second critical area in which to test the relationship between family firms and the issues of uncertainty and risk is that of the relationships between the company itself and the external environment. This is a very broad concept, containing several aspects that range from competitive policies and strategies to the relations with the local community in which the firm itself is embedded. In this section, I exemplify both the opportunities and the threats that family firms face in their relationships with the external environment by focusing on three critical aspects: cooperation, internationalization, and corporate social responsibility (CSR). All three elements involve a high level of risk and potential instability. In the first case, uncertainty is related to the relationships with other firms; in the second, to a lack of information; and in the third, to the variegated constituency of the firm's stakeholders.

The literature examining the relationship between family firms and risk-taking is neither abundant nor homogeneous in its findings. Recent empirical research (Naldi et al. 2007) has suggested a negative relationship between family ownership and willingness to take risks (especially in the case of long-tenured CEOs; Zahra 2005), and a consequent negative impact on the performance of firms (Zellweger 2006). This is in line with the rest of the literature on agency theory, which points out how identification between ownership and control, and thus a high degree of family ownerships, is negatively related to the propensity to engage in risky activities (Fama and Jensen 1983). Family leaders may have little or no incentive to take risky strategic decisions for fear of putting the family wealth at stake; family firms are thus considered to be more risk averse than non-family firms.

There are, however, some reasons that support a more equilibrated view of the advantages and disadvantages of family ownership in terms of risk and uncertainty management.

Cooperation can be defined as the agreement between two or more economic actors to undertake some common actions, the outcome of which will be known in the future. Another relevant characteristic of cooperation is the fact that it involves – to a certain extent – the necessity for the participants to share resources (material and/or immaterial) that are often highly strategic. This makes cooperation a form of behavior that is characterized by a high level of risk and uncertainty for the economic actors engaging in it, even if, at the basis of the decision of cooperate, there is always the necessity to reduce uncertainty and risk, for instance, by sharing the costs of developing new technologies and new products or of entering new markets. Examples of cooperation range from informal gentlemen's agreements to joint ventures, cartels, and, more recently, networks. In principle, there should be no difference between family firms and non-family firms in terms of their attitude toward cooperation.

However, in reality, there are aspects of cooperation in which the presence of the family proves to be determinant in the decision to engage (or not engage) in cooperative activity (Roessl 2005).

Family firms may be unwilling to accept the risk of cooperation for many reasons, which are related to their own nature. Cooperation means, as already stated, giving up – to a greater or lesser extent – control over strategic resources, and accepting a partial loss of independence in business decisions. Path dependency also means unwillingness to engage in new initiatives and an adherence to business-as-usual. Moreover, family firms are very often characterized by a strong identity that may hinder their propensity to cooperate with other organizations, and by a culture of secrecy and scarce disclosure, which may create problems when co-operative initiatives make it necessary to disclose information that is normally kept within the family. Finally, cooperation, to a certain extent, entails the necessity of sharing not only resources but also corporate culture and orientations, which are normally extremely strong in firms that have been led by the same family for generations (Hedberg, Nystorm, and Starbuck 1976). Incidentally, it should also be noted that cooperation, like other policies and strategies, is a knowledge-based process, which implies the accumulation of competences that are expensive to create. The existence of negative attitudes toward cooperation in addition to this burden may hinder the propensity toward cooperation in family firms.

Notwithstanding all this, family firms may have a number of positive elements that contribute to stimulate a positive attitude toward joint initiatives and cooperation, and that help reduce the uncertainty connected with these activities. The first aspect is long-term orientation, which is an often-recognized basic feature of family firms and is positively correlated with cooperation, which, as stated earlier, is a process that delivers results basically in the long run. The second aspect is commitment and trust, a second characteristic of family firms, which is based on personal relationships among individuals – and that explains the propensity of family firms to engage in cooperative initiatives with other family firms (Fink 2010).

Evidence shows that informal cooperation between family firms is a process that repeats itself, in the sense that it rarely takes place only once and tends to reinforce itself over time when the partners have learned to trust each other. If, in this case, too, there should, in principle, be no difference between family and non-family firms, the latter provide a better chance of self-reinforcement, given the long-term orientation and the multigenerational transmission of the business. An interesting example of the cooperative attitude between family firms (actually potential competitors) is provided by two of the main European leaders in publishing and media, the Spanish firm Grupo Planeta (led by the second generation of the Lara Hérnandez family) and the Italian firm De Agostini (under the control of the third generation of two families, Boroli and Drago). In both cases, long-term orientation proved to be a successful component of the process, especially with regard to international expansion. Family capital and profit reinvestment allowed the top management to pursue effective strategies of growth, and the two companies show more similarities than differences. The main similarity has been the use of alliances and networking to foster expansion into new fields, the acquisition of new capabilities, and last, but not least, the process of internationalization. The two groups engaged in a number of collaborative ventures from the mid-1980s onward, in other words, during the process of their international expansion. The most interesting case is the agreement that they signed in 1985, which led to the creation of a joint venture that focused on installment publications, interactive products, and comics. The collaboration between the two companies has been a long-lasting one; in 2003, they invested jointly in the media and audiovisual industries by promoting a new company, Grupo Planeta De Agostini, which now owns around 40 percent of the Spanish network Antena 3, a media group that comprises a leading TV station in Spain and a radio station named Onda Cero, among other companies. The close relationship between the two families and the fact that they share the same vision and long-term orientation explains the survival of the cooperative initiatives between the two companies.

A second controversial area is internationalization, which is another process characterized by a high degree of risk. According to an extensive part of the existing literature on internationalization, family firms are, in general, less inclined toward internationalization than non-family firms, given the high uncertainty level of a process of geographical diversification (for a review of studies about family firms and internationalization, see Claver, Rienda, and Quer 2008). One of the basic assumptions is that the greater the degree of family ownership, the greater the perception of risk in the internationalization process, given the tendency of family firms to maintain close control of assets and the consequent unwillingness to engage in diversification strategies, especially those of a geographical nature. Moreover, according to other studies, the risk perception increases after the first generation, when the successors feel that it is more important to pursue harmony and to avoid unnecessary risks. Family firms pursue stability and direct control, often have neither access to adequate managerial resources nor the competence to handle the internationalization process, and have limited financial resources to invest in a time-consuming and expensive internationalization process that requires a high level of resource commitment (for a summary, see Fernández and Nieto 2005, 2006).

However, even at a superficial glance, the risky process of internationalization is one of the interesting and relatively new features of, for instance, small- and medium-sized enterprises (SMEs) in the present global economy (see, e.g., Guillén and Canal 2010, who concentrate on the Spanish case). Examples of family firms that have successfully internationalized can be found both in the emerging and in the mature economies. In the case of many Italian family medium-sized firms, the process of internationalization takes place after a successful transition in the leadership and as a consequence of a process not only of growth and expansion, but also of the willingness of the new leaders to start their own entrepreneurial initiative by building on the existing business (Graves and Thomas 2008). The process of the internationalization of SMEs has often resulted in the creation of "pocket multinationals," which specialize in market niches of a global dimension. In these cases, it is possible to talk of a successful process of internationalization of family firms, which often do engage in sophisticated strategies of expansion through direct investments abroad. Disentangling the determinants of this successful internationalization process, it becomes clear that, alongside the presence of a consistent competitive advantage, family ownership plays a relevant role in many aspects. First, successors can deploy sufficient resources to start an internationalization process, which would have been unthinkable for the founder, with a long-term orientation (even under the financial point of view) and with a commitment that is often lacking in non-family firms. The availability of successors willing to transfer the management of new subsidiaries abroad (exactly as in the past when international merchants reduced agency problems through the presence of close relatives) provides the family firm with a valuable risk-reducing asset that is not always available for non-family firms. Finally, the internationalization of SMEs often occurs through the intelligent use of networking and cooperation with partners both at home and abroad, an activity in which – as seen in the preceding section – the family can play an important role, thereby strengthening the advantages of cooperation.

A third area in which family firms deal with the uncertainty and risk in relation to the external environment concerns their relationships with the stakeholders. This relationship, and, in particular, that with employees and local communities, can often be problematical for a company, which in cases of conflict (especially if they are repeated) may suffer significant efficiency losses. The ability to "fit" into the local community is as relevant an element today as it was in the past to explain the success of an organization, and this proves to be true also for family firms, for which the local community is not only the seedbed in which the founder finds the support to create his or her activity, but also often the place in which he or she and his or her respective family both live and are educated (a current perspective on this issue is provided in Gallo 2004; Niehm, Swinney, and Miller 2008). Family firms have historically managed the issue of the relationship with their employees and the local community through something distinctive and unique, which, in the past, was labeled – often with negative connotation – *paternalism*, which has a lot in common with the much more positive, contemporary concept of *corporate social responsibility* (CSR) as a component of corporate social performance, or CSP (Wood 1991). Despite the fact that the concept of CSR has come into use only fairly recently (first in the United States and post-WWII; Carroll and Shabana 2010), entrepreneurs in the early days of industrialization learned almost immediately that it was necessary to share some of the benefits and values created by industrial activity with the local community in which the said activity was taking place. Especially in backward and agricultural societies, the tensions created by the industrialization process could constitute a serious threat. To share some benefits was thus a way of safeguarding the survival of the company, as well as of enhancing the standing of the family within the community in which it lived. Examples of family firms making efforts and deploying resources to strengthen their role and position within the local community are abundant almost everywhere in Europe and in the industrialized world in general. The quality of local embeddedness was considered a relevant indicator of both standing and performance by entrepreneurs, and something that had much to do with the "reputation" of their company and of their name, in a word, of their "house." It must be noted how afterward, CSR and the largest conceptual category (CSP) have taken on many of the intrinsic aspects of the social embeddedness of entrepreneurial families, explicitly incorporating it into its performance goals and often rendered explicit in "social" balance sheets and balanced scorecards. Looking through the filter of history at the most authoritative definition of CSR as "the social responsibility of business [which] encompasses the economic, legal, ethical, and discretionary [later referred to as philanthropic] expectations that society has of organizations at a given point in time" (Carroll and Shabana 2010: 89), it becomes apparent how the promotion of public interest and welfare in search of some kind of return for the company itself is based on the same values that entrepreneurial dynasties historically tried to build on in their local contexts, and results in a reduction of the tensions between the firm and its stakeholders.

Local embeddedness as a measure of corporate value was extremely clear to those who were trying to weaken these linkages, that is, to trade unions and leftist movements, which thought it necessary to weaken the paternalist grip over the workforce. There are multitudes of examples: one very telling example is provided by Michelin's history (Tesi 2010). The multigenerational French tire maker was so intertwined with the local community in Clermont-Ferrand through a number of social initiatives that the first goal that Communist organizations immediately (and unsuccessfully) undertook after the Second World War was to try to break these linkages, which strictly bound the workers to the Michelin family. The Michelin case shows that the social embeddedness of family companies worked extremely well even for large companies. The main point was to "enlarge" the family concept sufficiently, and also for it to include, or embrace, the workers, who often lived together with the owners in the same "factory villages" so diffused in Europe during the first stages of the industrialization. The concept of the "enlarged" family still remains quite strong and diffused today. Family firms still make wide use of the concept of the enlarged family today, especially when the identification with the local community is so strict that it is not easy to see the borders between the latter and the family itself. For instance, in many Italian family firms, even in the most globalized, this is still a common form of behavior, which results in close identification between the management/family and the employees/local community, a low level of conflict with the workforce, and reciprocal commitment. In the cases of Luxottica, Benetton, Ferrero, and Barilla, the global dimension has not meant a weakening of the relationships with the local context in which they originated and prospered and that granted them relatively low conflicts and tensions.

CONCLUDING REMARKS

This chapter has dealt with the relationship among risk, uncertainty, and family firms. The perspective adopted has been deliberately problematical.

Structure

Familiness, family culture, family ownership, and values are examined both as internal features and as elements that interface the firm with its external environment. In both cases, the nature of the family firm is analyzed not only in its positive contribution to the reduction of risk and uncertainty, but also as a negative element that can increase the level of turbulence and uncertainty both within the organization and in its relationships with other firms, the market, and the local community. The final balance of these two aspects may be positive or negative, with relevant effects on the performances and ultimately the survival of the family firm (both in general and as a firm under family control).

Limitations and Research Implications

What this chapter does not address in depth is the contribution of general institutional conditions (in terms of the legal and financial system, of shared values and culture) in the creation of frameworks that are more or less favorable for family firms, with an additional effect on their ability of controlling uncertainty. A second relevant element not addressed by this chapter is the dynamic perspective. As stressed at the beginning, the positive/negative role played by the family nature can change both over time and during the life cycle of the firm itself. The adoption of a dynamic perspective will allow a better understanding of the relationship among family firms, risk, and uncertainty.

References

Amatori, Franco (1996). *Impresa e mercato. Lancia 1986–1969*. Bologna: Il Mulino.

Anderson, Alistair R., Sarah L. Jack, and Sarah Drakopoulou-Dodd (2005). "The Role of Family Members in Entrepreneurial Networks: Beyond the Boundaries of the Family Firm." *Family Business Review*, 18(1): 135–54.

Bebchuk, Lucian, and Mark Roe (1999). "A Theory of Path Dependence in Corporate Ownership and Governance." *Stanford Law Review*, 52(1): 127–70. Available at: SSRN: http://ssrn.com/abstract=202748 or doi:10.2139/ssrn.202748. (Accessed February 8, 2013)

Berghoff, Hartmut (2006). "The End of Family Business? The Mittelstand and Family Capitalism in Transition, 1946–2000." *Business History Review*, 80(2): 263–95.

Berle, Adolf A., and Gardiner C. Means (1932). *The Modern Corporation and Private Property*. New York: Harcourt, Brace & World.

Cabrera-Suarez, M. Katiuska, M. de la Cruz Deniz-Deniz, and Josefa D. Martın-Santana (2011). "Familiness and Market Orientation: A Stakeholder Approach." *Journal of Family Business Strategy*, 2(1): 34–42.

Carroll, Archie B., and Kareen M. Shabana (2010). "The Business Case for Corporate Social Responsibility: A Review of Concepts, Research and Practice." *International Journal of Management Reviews*, 12(1): 85–105.

Chandler, Alfred D. (1990). *Scale and Scope. The Dynamics of Industrial Capitalism*. Boston: Harvard University Press.

Claessens, Stijn, Simeon Djankov, Joseph P.H. Fan, and Larry H.P. Lang (2002). "Disentangling the Incentive and Entrenchment Effects of Large Shareholdings." *Journal of Finance*, 57(6): 2741–71.

Claver, Enrique, Laura Rienda, and Diego Quer (2008). "Family Firms' Risk Perception: Empirical Evidence on the Internationalization Process." *Journal of Small Business and Enterprise Development*, 15(3): 457–71.

Colli, Andrea (2006). *The History of Family Business, 1850–2000*. Cambridge: Cambridge University Press.

Davis, Peter S., and Paula D. Harveston (1999). "In the Founder's Shadow: Conflict in the Family Firm." *Family Business Review*, 12(4): 311–23.

Davis, James, David Schoorman, and Lex Donaldson (1997). "Towards a Stewardship Theory of Management." *Academy of Management Review*, 22(1): 20–47.

De Vries, Manfred F.R. (1993). "The Dynamics of Family Controlled Firms: The Good and the Bad News." *Organizational Dynamics*, 22(4): 5–71.

Eriksson, Emma (2011). Enhancing Blockholders' Power in Sweden: The Wallenberg Case. MSc. Diss., Bocconi University.

Faccio, Mara, and Larry P. Lang (2002). "The Ultimate Ownership of Western European Corporations" (with Larry H.P. Lang). *Journal of Financial Economics*, 65(3): 365–95.

Fallon, Ivan. "Dynasties. By David Landes. The Perils of a Family Affair." *The Independent*, February 9, 2007.

Fama, Eugene F., and Michael C. Jensen (1983). "Separation of Ownership and Control." *Journal of Law and Economics*, 26(2): 301–25.

Fear, Jeffrey (1995). "August Thyssen and German Steel." In T. McCraw (ed.), *Creating Modern Capitalism. How Entrepreneurs, Companies and Countries Triumphed in the Three Industrial Revolutions* (pp. 183–226). Cambridge, MA: Harvard University Press.

Fernandez, Zulima, and Maria Nieto (2005). "Internationalization Strategy of Small and Medium-sized Family Businesses: Some Influential Factors." *Family Business Review*, 18(1): 77–89.

Fernandez, Zulima, and Maria Nieto (2006). "Impact of Ownership on the International Involvement of SMEs." *Journal of International Business Studies*, 37(3): 340–51.

Fink, Matthias (2010). "Trust-based Cooperation Relationships between SMEs – Are Family Firms Any Different?" *International Journal of Entrepreneurial Venturing*, 4(1): 382–97.

Fligstein, Neil (2001). *The Architecture of Markets: An Economic Sociology of Twenty-First-Century Capitalist Societies.* Princeton, NJ: Princeton University Press.

Gallo, Miguel Á. (2004). "The Family Business and Its Social Responsibilities." *Family Business Review*, 17(2): 135–49.

Graves, Chris, and Jill Thomas (2008). "Determinants of the Internationalization Pathways of Family Firms: An Examination of Family Influence." *Family Business Review*, 21(2): 151–67.

Guillén, Mauro, and Esteban Garcia-Canal (2010). *The New Multinationals: Spanish Firms in a Global Context.* Cambridge: Cambridge University Press.

Hall, Annika, Leif Melin, and Mattias Nordqvist (2001). "Entrepreneurship as Radical Change in the Family Business: Exploring the Role of Cultural Patterns." *Family Business Review*, 14(3): 193–208.

Hatum, Andrés, and Andrew Pettigrew (2004). "Adaptation Under Environmental Turmoil: Organizational Flexibility in Family-owned Firms." *Family Business Review*, 17(3): 237–58.

Hedberg, Bo T., Paul C. Nystrom, and William Starbuck (1976). "Camping on Seesaws: Prescription for a Self-designing Organization." *Administrative Science Quarterly*, 21(1): 41–65.

James, Harold (2006). *Family Capitalism. Wendels, Haniels, Falcks and the Continental Model of Capitalism.* Cambridge, MA: Belknap Press.

Kirby, Maurice W., and Mary B. Rose (1994). *Business Enterprise in Modern Britain. From the Eighteenth to the Twentieth Century.* London: Routledge.

Landes, David S. (2006). *Dynasties: Fortunes and Misfortunes of the World's Great Family Businesses.* New York: Viking Press.

La Porta, Rafael, Florencio Lopez-de-Silanes, and Andrei Shleifer (1999). "Corporate Ownership around the World." *Journal of Finance*, 54(2): 471–517.

Lessem, Ronnie (1998). *Managing Development through Cultural Diversity.* London: Routledge.

McConaughy, Daniel L. (1999). "Is the Cost of Capital Different for Family Firms?" *Family Business Review*, 12(4): 353–60.

Miller, Danny, and Isabelle Le Breton-Miller (2006). "Family Governance and Firm Performance: Agency, Stewardship, and Capabilities." *Family Business Review*, 19(1): 73–87.

Morck, Randall, and Bernard Yeung (2003). "Agency Problems in Large Business Groups." *Entrepreneurship, Theory and Practice*, 27(4): 367–82.

Naldi, Lucia, Mattias Nordqvist, Karin Sjöberg, and Johan Wiklund (2007). "Entrepreneurial Orientation, Risk Taking, and Performance in Family Firms." *Family Business Review*, 20(1): 33–47.

Niehm, Linda, Jane Swinney, and Nancy J. Miller (2008). "Community Social Responsibility and Its Consequences for Family Business Performance." *Journal of Small Business Management*, 46(3): 331–50.

Piore, Michael, and Charles Sabel (1984). *The Second Industrial Divide.* New York: Basic Books.

Pollard, Sidney (1965). *The Genesis of Modern Management.* Harmondsworth: Pelican.

Roessl, Dieter (2005). "Family Business and Interfirm Cooperation." *Family Business Review*, 18(3): 203–14.

Tesi, Francesca (2010). "From Paternalism to the Michelin Performance and Responsibility Charter: Aspects of the Non-Profit Activities of a Family Firm." Paper presented at the European Business History Association Conference, Glasgow, August 26–28, 2010.

Whittington, Richard, and Michael Mayer (2000). *The European Corporation. Strategy, Structure and Social Science*. Oxford: Oxford University Press.

Wood, Donna J. (1991). "Corporate Social Performance Revisited." *Academy of Management Review*, 16(4): 691–718.

Zahra, Shaker A. (2005). "Entrepreneurial Risk Taking in Family Firms." *Family Business Review*, 18(1): 23–40.

Zellweger, Thomas (2006). *Risk, Return and Value in the Fmily Firm*. Phd. Diss., St. Gallen University.

PART TWO

EXOGENOUS FACTORS

The Environment

5

Families Breaking the Business Logic

The Entrepreneurial Spirit in the Evolution of Swedish Family Dynasties

Hans Sjögren

The world abounds with dynasties, many of them in the economic sphere. Familiar names such as Rockefeller, Rothschild, Morgan, Ford, Porsche, Agnelli (Fiat), Toyoda (Toyota), and Bombardier are to be found among the international financial and industrial dynasties. Many started as merchant houses, banks, and investment firms. Others accumulated their fortunes through the exploitation of natural resources during the industrial breakthrough, such as the Rockefellers in petroleum. In addition, several family dynasties have their roots in the rapidly expanding production of vehicles during the twentieth century (e.g., Colli 2003; James 2006; Landes 2007). There are even examples of dynasties that, after many splendid decades, expired or were reduced to passive ownership in socially beneficial foundations.

It is characteristic of a dynasty that a family or a group of relatives has, over the generations, succeeded in first obtaining and then maintaining a dominant position in some regard. In the political sphere, there are royal families and princely and ducal houses within which political power has been inherited from one generation to the next. Sometimes the word "dynasty" is used synonymously with an entire period in a nation's history – an era – when a particular king or emperor held political power. The epic novel *Buddenbrooks* by the German author Thomas Mann describes a supposedly typical life cycle of a family firm – sometimes referred to as *the Buddenbrooks syndrome*. It consists of three stages or generations: creation, maintenance, and decline. The founder builds up his enterprise, often on the basis of a clever innovation; the second generation administers the firm without further innovations; and the third generation concentrates on interests other than those of the founder, including cutting corners, self-indulgent luxurious living, and the fortune is thus dissipated.[1]

Given this negative stereotype of family entrepreneurship, it is important to determine objective criteria for defining a family dynasty in the business world. To be considered a dynasty, a firm must have been owned by a particular family for at least four generations. This criterion eliminates those firms that have strictly followed Thomas Mann's posited life cycle, despite that model's firm hold on the public's perception ("Shirt sleeves to shirt sleeves in three generations"). In addition, at least one of the companies controlled by the family must be of sufficient size to be considered a worldwide leader in its business. Family control, however, need not be concentrated in a single type of business but can be spread over various economic activities as long as the total market value of the holdings amounts to a substantial sum. Third, it is necessary that the family has sufficient influence both politically and socially in their country in their country for the government to be influenced by the family's views on important national economic questions, and thus that it can impact the rules of the game in the business world. Such influence can take the form of family representatives having access to government ministers, being regularly consulted concerning government studies and reports, as well as being able to use lobbyists successfully to protect and advance the family's interests when government decision makers act.

The chapter deals with the largest family firms in Sweden. Among them, the Bonniers, the Johnsons, and the Wallenberg sphere are fully mature dynasties, while Kamprad, Lundberg, Stena, Persson, Rausing and Stenbeck are family firms that might develop into mature dynasties in the future. Currently, however, they remain as emerging dynasties. For the sake of convenience, all of these firms are referred to as dynasties even though they fall into two separate groups: *emerging* and *fully mature* dynasties. This distinction is based on the demand for a minimum of four generations of extensive family entrepreneurship. The emerging dynasties fail to meet this requirement, but do satisfy the other two criteria. Sometimes, as in this chapter, the term "ownership sphere" is used to designate a conglomerate of firms controlled by a single family.

---

[1] There are several examples of family firms that have survived for many generations without being dynasties. In sixteen generations, starting in the thirteenth century, the family firm Kikkoman Soy Sauce has produced and sold soy sauce. The French Wendel family has pursued various industrial activities for thirteen generations, a timeframe similar to that of the Swedish family firm Berte Qvarn, which is mostly associated with SIA Glass today.

The objective is to analyze the evolution of large firms in Sweden from the late nineteenth century onward. The focus is on entrepreneurship, innovations, organizational structures, and value creation, in general, using particular case studies as examples. The evolution of Swedish dynasties illustrates the diverse pathways through which large family firms have faced the challenge of technological change since the Industrial Revolution, with success or with failure. Business life is institutionally determined, even when markets are global. Thus, the strategies of the Swedish dynasties reflect certain cultural identities, in the same way that the evolution of the actual dynasties, to some extent, mirrors the transformation of the Swedish model (Sjögren 2008). First, the Swedish case clearly shows that family business groups are not just products of emerging market imperfections: they are also able to start and survive in well-governed and highly industrialized countries such as Sweden. Second, it is time to revise the view of the family as just a source of trust: the controlling family is also a hub of industrial and business competence backed by long-term active leadership. Finally, the chapter demonstrates the pros and cons of "persevering capitalism" as opposed to what characterizes "quarterly report capitalism" (short-termism).

The chapter starts with an overall description of the role of these dynasties in economic history, which emphasizes their origin, type of business, and company-control systems. After a notion of key characteristics in the corporate governance system, there is an analysis of structural and strategic continuation vis-à-vis the discontinuation of dynasties. In the final sections, the pathways, in terms of innovation and entrepreneurial leadership, are discussed.

FAMILY DYNASTIES IN THE AGE OF CAPITALISM

Family dynasties have often gone through the following development pattern: the founder of a family firm possesses entrepreneurial skills that have made it possible for him or her to develop a technological, organizational, or marketing innovation. Succeeding generations have then expanded the enterprise and a number of principles, based on successes as well as failures, for operating the family-owned business have been developed. Financial crises may have forced the owning family to rely on outside assistance from banks, national and local government funds, relatives, friends, and other outside financiers to guarantee continued control of the enterprise. At these critical points, the confidence of the market in the owning family is tested, as well as its social usefulness in the case of cabinet ministers with government funds to allocate. During prosperous economic times, a financial base that enables further growth of the enterprise is built up. Knowledge capital is renewed through recruitment, preferably within the family. Thus, a number of family members are placed in élite schools and/or are guided through a practical training program. As a second best solution, should the necessary capability not be found within the family, highly promising individuals with a suitable education from outside the family are recruited. They will then be schooled in the business, tested in various positions, imbued with the family's traditional values, and, through their work, contribute to maintaining family control.

If success continues, which depends not just on the profitability of the firms in question, but also on the political climate, an ownership group might develop into a dynasty after a few generations. The controlling companies will have grown and some will have become well-known trademarks. Within the family, strong identity with the enterprise, together with pride over what the past and present generations have accomplished for the benefit of the family, the nation, and/or the entire society, will develop. Controlling holdings will often be protected through various arrangements, for example, shares with differing votes, cross ownership, and/or overlapping boards of directors.

Within the family, the practical ownership experience will have created a deeper understanding of the dynamic mechanisms in the economy. It will have created a silent knowledge of what constitutes a winning ownership philosophy. This, in turn, will have been convincingly transferred to the leading officers in the firms controlled by the family. The network of principal executives will establish the boundary between the firms that "are ours" and those that belong to "others." These selected individuals will have entered into an informal contract with the owners, one that requires absolute loyalty to their own sphere. Should the owners detect signs of insufficient loyalty on the part of their associates, various methods are available to restore order: the network can operate both to include *and* to exclude. The methods are perhaps not as drastic as in *The Godfather* – "never go against the family" – but effective nonetheless. At the same time, the ownership control of large family-owned firms was characterized by caution and careful consideration, which always bore in mind the fact that the high regard in which the family was held was always at risk. The family was now motivated not only by entrepreneurial consideration, but also by regard for dynastic aspects. Thus, even the recounting of the family's history was an important aspect of the efforts to maintain the family's prominent position within the business world. Another aspect of a fully mature dynasty is the funneling of part of its profits into foundations. Here, several different motives can play a role: to create a culture of donations, to avoid taxes, as a buffer during economic downturns, or to exclude unreliable relatives and family members from ownership influence.

This schematic presentation implies that the road to becoming a family dynasty is a long one, and that it is possible to decide whether or not the firm has become a dynasty only after the fact. Furthermore, it is uncommon for a firm to be founded with the goal of developing into a dynasty. However, within some of the family firms that today bear the label of "dynasty," it is possible to trace signs of a *dynastic drive* all the way back to their infancy. A classic example of this can be found in the Wallenberg dynasty, through the financial and industrial operations in the late nineteenth and early twentieth century by André Oscar Wallenberg and his two sons. (Among others, see Nilsson 2001 and Lindgren 2011.) But the fact that the family had the intention of building a corporate empire is not sufficient – a number of fortunate circumstances are also required for their vision to be realized. And it is here that the political climate and the entrepreneurial possibilities play a role. In the case of the Wallenbergs, the road to success might have come to an abrupt end as early as 1878–9 with a financial crisis. The Swedish state, however, decided to save the family bank from sinking beneath the waves. The opposite occurred in the case of the financier Ivar Kreuger. If it had not been for the Wall Street Crash, his empire might well have evolved into a dynasty. In this case, too, the Swedish state had a finger in the pie. During the 1980s, even some speculators – Erik Penser, Robert Weill, and Anders Wall – might, under more favorable circumstances, have joined the exclusive ranks of the dynasty founders.

The academic literature concerning long-lived family firms, in which studies of family dynasties play only a modest role, emphasizes the importance of carefully considered decisions and low levels of debt in achieving success. The explanation for a degree of care is that the social cost of an error can be enormous, as bankruptcy is likely not only to wipe out the family's fortune, but also to destroy its reputation for business competence. Family firms have been said to resemble ants that opt to continue accumulating assets and growing organically, in contrast to non-family-controlled joint stock companies – grasshoppers – that use purchases and mergers to grow more quickly, but at the cost of greater debt and widely dispersed ownership. Moreover, the grasshoppers occasionally crash land while the ants often stick to previously traveled paths that lead straight to their goal (Miller and Le Breton-Miller 2005).

Tending to offset this positive picture is the fact that family dynasties have had a tendency to accumulate substantial amounts of market power, which has resulted not only in more or less permanent monopolies, but has also stifled other new entrepreneurs. Thus, family dynasties can be harmful to the economy by forming both economic and political alliances that result in higher consumer prices and by hindering new innovations and preventing the growth of profitable small businesses. The political ties were intended to create various advantages, including tax rules, which, if successful, gave them a competitive edge vis-à-vis other firms. It is also argued that family firms were bastions of male exclusivity in which closed brotherly networks, with in-law aspects and other types of corruption, ruled. In a world striving for openness, family firms thus constitute a threat to democratic values because their structure lacks transparency and their organizations have good motives for obscuring some of their behavior (Morck 2005). The structure of family dynasties tends to reflect the institutions and the culture that exist in the countries in which they operate. In countries with high tax rates, there might be incentives to safeguard the family fortune by shifting ownership and profits to countries with less onerous tax systems, which, in turn, results in complex legal structures. In developing countries with governments that are corrupt and difficult to navigate, there may well be other reasons for making dynastic arrangements more opaque.

In the industrial countries, family dynasties developed in parallel with a tendency for the ownership and the administration of firms to become increasingly separate, a trend that began with the emergence of large American firms in the post–World War II period. The challenge now faced by the family-controlled firms was to create the conditions necessary for continued investments and innovations while still retaining ownership control within the family. Many families failed in this endeavor and were forced to abandon control to an independent management and/or to accept a widely dispersed ownership, including both private and public owners. Other families, however, succeeded in maintaining control even when their firms needed additional risk capital to keep up with domestic competition and internationalization. In this regard, the importance of tenacious private capitalists proved to be decisive. Research on the topic has demonstrated that family dynasties were created on the overlapping border between breakthrough innovations and entrepreneurial leadership. The fact that innovations often take substantial amounts of time and require support from actors well versed in the business presents an advantage to long-term owners, such as a family. As a result, many surviving foreign and Swedish family dynasties display a high level of industrial competence that has rendered them capable of both leading and developing their control spheres over a long period of time (Sjögren 2005).

The history of the fully mature Swedish family dynasties goes back to the industrial breakthrough in Sweden during the second half of the nineteenth century. The emerging dynasties, on the other hand, can be traced back only to the post–World War II period. All of these dynasties are considered to be Swedish because they were founded by Swedish citizens, and their first incorporation was registered in Sweden. We should, however, be aware that control of the family fortune might, over time, have shifted abroad. This, for example, is the case with the Kamprad and Rausing families and their controlling companies. In some dynasties, the key holdings, or even the family company itself, might not be listed on any stock market. This situation applies, among others, to the Bonnier Group (media), IKEA, the Johnson Group (trade), and Tetra Laval. In several cases, the ownership is associated with large fortunes. Ingvar Kamprad (IKEA) and Stefan Persson (H&M) have appeared on lists of the twenty richest individuals in the world, while the Rausing family (Tetra) has long been among the richest families in the United Kingdom.

In terms of the market value of their controlling interests, H&M is in first place among Swedish stock market listed holdings, while the fully mature Wallenberg sphere is in second place. The latter's largest holdings are Investor, Saab, Electrolux, SKF, StoraEnso (STORA), Atlas Copco, Ericsson, SEB, OMX, ABB, SAS, and Astra Zeneca. Next among the ownership spheres list on the Stockholm Exchange is the Handelsbanken Group, which has traditionally lacked family ownership, but in which the Lundberg family slowly but surely is accumulating ownership influence through direct ownership of the companies controlled by Handelsbanken's foundations and its holding company, Industrivärden. Furthermore, Fredrik Lundberg is represented on the boards of Industrivärden and Svenska Handelsbanken. A combination of the Lundberg and Handelsbanken spheres might form the basis of an additional Swedish family dynasty. In fourth place among the listed ownership groups is the Stenbeck sphere, with its controlling holdings in Kinnevik, Metro, MTG, Tele2, Millicom, and Korsnäs (Carlsson 2007: 1042).

THE KEY PRINCIPLES OF CORPORATE GOVERNANCE

When family dynasties are examined, an interweaving of entrepreneurship, blood ties, ownership power, leadership, as well as political and

economic history, is revealed. Every such study thus stretches over a
number of academic disciplines such as business economics, economic
history, ethnology, and sociology. This, in turn, creates a challenge to
find concepts that are sufficiently wide to encompass broad questions,
while, at the same time, developing analytical tools that are sufficiently
precise to guide us through the empirical material to appropriate general
conclusions.

A general assumption concerning a prosperous society with a rapid rate
of innovation and a high level of employment is that private owners –
control owners – who actively reformulate economic activity and thus
guarantee a constant (industrial) renewal, are required. History has
demonstrated that the most common type of such control owners is that of
individuals or families that exercise *long-term active ownership* in firms.[2]
To be an *active* owner requires at least an ownership interest amounting
to at least 5 percent of the share votes or a role as the firm's principal
provider of credit, as well as a seat on the board of directors and the ability to follow and help to direct the functions of the firm closely. The latter
refers to participation in decisions that concern the company's long-term
direction, changes in high-level personnel, and sometimes even direct leadership. It should be noted that establishing exact borders for these activities involves considerable difficulty and, thus, that the percentages and
absolute numbers presented here should be viewed as approximations.

For a holding to be labeled *long-term*, it must have passed through at
least two downturns, that is, have remained stable during two periods
of weak demand and low profitability. In view of the varying length
of downturns, both generally and in particular businesses, ownership
measured in years should not be less than a decade to be considered
long-term. At the level of the board of directors, this implies that one or
more individuals representing the ownership interest served on the board
during the period in question.

Both of the requirements concerning the length and the extent of long-
term ownership seem modest in the case of family dynasties, as these often
involve 100 percent owned companies and core holdings that stretch
over several generations. If stricter requirements are prescribed, however,
families that have minority positions in large multinational firms and/or

[2] For a more detailed discussion of these concepts, see Sjögren (2005), pp. 14–16, and
Sjögren (2007), pp. 7–22. For additional studies of long-term active ownership, social
capital, and networks, see, among others, Glete (1994); Håkansson and Johanson (2001);
Arregle et al. (2007); Brundin et al. (2008); Peason, Carr, and Shaw (2008); Lumpkin,
Brigham, and Moss (2010); and Lindgren (2012).

follow strategies that involve the buying and selling of firms would be excluded. Thus, for example, the Wallenberg dynasty would fall outside our area of study. Moreover, the qualitative aspects may well be more important. In other words, what is the true goal of the active long-term ownership control that is often concentrated in a majority-owned investment or holding company or a family foundation? It therefore makes sense to take the view that *long-term active ownership* in the case of family dynasties implies that the family assumes responsibility for business renewal and restructuring while, at the same time, stable ownership provides job security and the financial backing necessary to undertake investments that can be expected to be profitable only in the long run. This definition fits well as an overarching concept of long-term ownership as practiced by the successful family dynasties.

One characteristic common to the Swedish family dynasties is that they possess *networking capacity*. This means the ability to create, as well as to renew and widen, the relationship of trust with other individuals or groups of individuals. The level of network capacity guides the controlling owner in his or her choices with regard to human capital, personal competence, and information. Access to a relationships-based network of high quality makes it easier for the owner to achieve his or her predetermined economic goals. Moreover, the social network facilitates the ability to take quick advantage of opportunities as they arise. The effective utilization of the networking capacity reduces the transaction costs associated with creating trust in business transactions as well as the ability to keep, renew, and expand the available stock of competence within the controlled company. It also increases the ability to encourage individuals, political parties, interest organizations and enterprises outside the family's business sphere to take an interest in the future of the companies. A high networking capacity is thus a prerequisite for a living dynasty.

COMPARISONS OF SWEDISH FAMILY DYNASTIES

It is clear that today's family dynasties began on a small scale, for example, a new type of container for liquids (tetrahedrons, Tetra Pak) or Windsor (spindle) chairs that could be placed in a package and left on a farmer's milk pickup platform (IKEA). The common characteristic is that the individual or individuals involved challenged previously existing products or procedures with creative thinking and entrepreneurship. An idea had been transformed into a prototype and had become an innovation with large-scale production. In its earliest phases, the entrepreneurial activity had often required access to outside capital, such as a bank loan, risk capital, or some other source of seed capital. Once profits started to accumulate, the family firm's need for financiers declined substantially, and it is worth noting that many companies belonging to family dynasties are unlisted: they simply had no need for the stock market to expand. Being stock market listed, moreover, is associated with substantial costs. In addition, living constantly in the spotlight from the market and media increases transactions costs. It is even likely that avoiding the public scrutiny associated with the so-called quarterly report capitalism permits company operational flexibility and practices that otherwise would not be possible. Two arguments commonly offered by control owners who have avoided having their firms listed are that the market is inefficient in valuing strategic choices and that it is beneficial not to be dependent on (short-sighted) owners and financiers who do not share the family's goals. This ideal world, however, is attainable only if the need for investment and liquid capital can be met in some other way. Yet another motive for staying away from the stock exchange is that it might make it possible for the family, as controlling owners, to act in their own financial interest, even at the expense of the firm.

Stick to What You Know, or Not

The founding of a family firm on the basis of a given innovation will connect the firm to a particular type of business. Most dynasties have retained their principal enterprise within the same business over all the generations. The third generation of H&M is still in the clothing business, just as the founder, Erling Persson, was during the 1950s and 1960s. Similarly, Dan Olsson (Stena Line), exactly like his father and grandfather, is still a shipowner on the West Coast of Sweden. The Bonnier family has sold books and newspapers for six generations. The two daughters (born in 1979 and 1981) of Fredrik Lundberg (Lundberg sphere) are being prepared for leadership in the real estate empire that their grand-father built up, by seats on the board of Lundberg's firm. The list need not be made any longer. The pattern is apparent – most dynasties stick to the industry in which their story or business originated. But the orig-inal innovation has, of course, been developed and improved, as in the case of the IKEA distribution system, the packaging at Tetra Pak, and the marketing and design departments within H&M. The most vigorous large family firms are thus characterized by a continuously ongoing devel-opment and expansion into new areas of the innovation around which the enterprise originated. However, there are a number of exceptions to the maxim of "sticking to what you know." The enterprises within the Stenbeck sphere have moved further and further away from their original core activity, while, in the case of the Lundberg sphere, a recent broadening has occurred with forestry, mechanical engineering, and finance now complementing the original real estate holdings.

Several of the family dynasties followed the common structural evolution that occurred during the second half of the twentieth century. First diversification through the forming of conglomerates that was then reversed through corporate pruning and outsourcing resulted in a return to the emphasis on core competence and activities. Viewing the changes in enterprise structure from World War II until the beginning of the twenty-first century reveals a chain of events in the form of cause and effect. The strict legislation against increased concentration in the economy during the 1950s resulted in a diversified and decentralized concern structure. Conglomerates were the extreme examples of this tendency. As such, they were glorified by both business theoreticians and practical businessmen. They were considered the ultimate form of enterprise organization. These developments were inspired by the unparalleled success of American firms and the new management ideas coming from the United States. After only a few years could researchers report that European firms were catching up with their American counterparts in the race to establish divisional corporate structures. While the share of multidivisional large firms in America had risen from 20 percent to 77 percent during the twenty years preceding 1969, by then the shares in Germany, France, Italy, and Great Britain had reached 40, 43, 26, and 70 percent respectively. These developments were taken as evidence that the multidivisional firms were in the process of marginalizing all other forms of corporate organization (Sjögren 2005: 28).

Conglomerates had their own theoretical rationale and had a major impact on corporate organization in the Western world. However, by the beginning of the 1970s, the practice had come to be viewed as burdensome. The endless mixtures of activities led by a financially dedicated leadership eventually led to fewer opportunities to innovate, improve products, and broadening of the markets. The pendulum thus swung back in the direction of increased focus on core activities, with the hope of improving the utilization of resources and of increasing profits. The new mottos were *outsourcing*, *back to basics*, and downsizing. Profits largely depended not on productivity increases, but on the purchase and sale of firms, first by creating diversified companies and then by dismantling them. In terms of corporate control, the center of gravity shifted from independent managements to institutional investors who demanded short-term results. Most of the new investors had no interest in active industrial ownership. The turnover of ownership capital became increasingly rapid and was decreasingly used as a tool for long-term value creation (Sjögren 2005: 21–31).

Many large Swedish firms followed the American pattern and became increasingly diversified. Among these were Wallenberg-owned companies such as Swedish Match and Astra, but also included firms without strong leadership owners such as Volvo (Procordia). The American norm, however, was historically far from new. A large family firm that had started to diversify at an early stage was the Johnson group. During Consul General Axel Axelsson Johnson's time, the second generation after the founder and entrepreneur Axel Johnson, the enterprise was expanded into a very diverse group of firms. The traditional trading activity was complemented with industrial, transportation, and building firms. This pattern was not unusual among merchant houses during the breakthrough of industrialization. During the next generation under mining engineer Axel Axelsson Johnson, the concern was effectively a conglomerate, while foreign expansion was eagerly pursued by the family. The conglomerate experienced severe difficulties in the 1980s when world market competition for raw materials, petroleum, and steel tightened. As a privately owned, widespread group, the Johnson Group lacked the resources required to match their competitors' investments and production capacity. The conglomerate was broken up when its industrial commitments were pruned, thus freeing resources that had been tied up in long-term fixed assets.

Within Nordstjernan, the activity was concentrated on construction with the creation of NCC, while, in Axel Johnson, there was a reorganization that emphasized wholesale and retail trade. The changeover to a core activity without industrial connections was a thorough and dramatic process in the long history of the Johnson family, and, in time, proved to be successful. In contrast to several other shipowning Swedish companies, the Johnson group never became insolvent and was able to retain its independence. It was, however, a close thing: the leadership repeatedly had to scramble to meet their payroll while the SE Bank had plans to force the company into bankruptcy. The restructuring was successful and the Johnson Group's renewal of its original enterprises benefited from the changeover to a postindustrial society (De Geer 1998: 552–4; Ericson 2007).

The story of Bonnier Group exemplifies the difficulties that arise from long-term diversification when involvement and network capacity has to be transferred to a new generation of family members. The network of Lukas and Albert Bonnier Jr. contained a clear hierarchy, which meant that it performed various functions. In the media arena, contacts with editors and journalists were cultivated. It sought out persons who could "wield the power of the pen," that is to say, they could assemble interesting news stories and present information and facts in a way that appealed to the public. But it was not in this network that decisions regarding strategy and organization were taken. For that, an élite network existed, including the leadership for Åhlen and Holm and the directors of the Bonnier enterprises. Both of these networks contained long-term relationships with individuals with varying types of competence.

The transfer of the media network did not present great problems when succession within the dynasty required the replacement of Lukas and Albert Jr. Both family members and other executives had been trained and become experienced in the family's core activities over a long period. The extended family also contained a distinct general interest in the media activities, an interest that rested on the position and the recognition in book publishing and newspaper production that the family had achieved in Sweden. The entry into the industrial sector that had occurred during the 1950s to 1970s, with the purchase of firms in, among other businesses, mechanical engineering, furniture production, and the paper industry, however, became problematical. Here, the network was more compact and no family member in the generation after Albert Bonnier Jr. wanted, or was capable of taking over, the responsibility for the administration of these firms. The fact that several of these firms were struggling with major financial problems did not make them more attractive. The main reason that these activities were disposed of after the death of Albert Bonnier was that the family's long-term interest, competence, and work motivation was concentrated in the media arena. Thus, the Bonnier dynasty returned to a total focus on its core activities, following the principle of doing what you know and understand best (Larsson 2006: 348–9; Larsson 2001: 147–51).

Too Much Tradition Kills

The business history of Sweden also shows that lack of entrepreneurship and excessive regard for tradition is a bad combination. This conservative characteristic, which can take the form of uncritical acceptance of the strategies of earlier generations or rejecting new initiatives, can be a substantial obstacle to new ideas and renewal. In the long run, this might result in less-sentimental (non-family owned) companies developing more rapidly. Indeed, history is packed full with mature and emerging dynasties that have lost economic and political importance and more or less expired. In his chapter in this anthology, Andrea Colli, in particular, highlights the fact that family firms sometimes tend to lose market positions by being too conservative strategically.

In the case of Sweden, such losing families include Broström (shipping), Kemple/Carlgren (forestry), Kockum (shipbuilding), Mark and Carlander (textiles and ball and roller bearings), Wehtje (construction and cement), and Åhlen (department stores). In addition, the case of the Salén family is discussed in the following paragraphs. Several of these expired large family firms share the misfortune of belonging to industries that have lost competitiveness due to increased internationalization (shipbuilding, shipping, and textiles). In other cases, the family has lacked competence and/or the financial strength required to maintain ownership control. Two critical factors have been the family's inability to maintain their financial hold (high liquidity) and to recruit qualified and motivated co-workers. Weakness in terms of these important functions has also caused the boards of directors to lose their ability and courage to make important long-term investment decisions, which has been especially damaging when faced with weak markets.

The case of Saléninvest, a highly diversified family concern with large investments in shipowning in the 1970s, is a good example of the fact that too much tradition could be devastating. The concern was listed on the stock exchange but with controlling blocks of shares held by family members and the leaders of the concern. In this case, however, the de-diversification came too late, resulting in the firm's inevitable bankruptcy in 1984. The fact that the company had even survived so long was partly the result of new sources of credit and partly the result of assets that could be sold. Most of the board members and top managers of Saléninvest had a strong aversion to abandoning the firm's core function, preferring, instead, to sell off profitable side activities. During the second half of the 1970s, a share portfolio whose return stabilized the liquidity variability that characterized the shipowning branch had been accumulated. There were also other profitable activities in the areas of real estate, oil production, trading, and the importation of passenger cars (Toyota). Without the revenues from these operations, Saléninvest would have already been insolvent in the 1970s.

When the lack of liquidity became acute, however, none of these profitable activities was retained. The family saw itself as shipowners with their key competence in the area of shipping, and the problems in this industry were judged to be temporary. An exaggerated regard for the strategies followed by earlier generations existed, which resulted in the leadership refusing to abandon the unprofitable shipping business. This conservative tendency, which is often present in family firms, unquestionably impeded Saléninvest's renewal ability. Furthermore, the strategic inertia was also the result of a commission agreement that made the capital in the mother company subject to centrally planned investment decisions. A sale of the tankers would automatically reduce the security situation for the banks that provided credit. Because they had not lent money to the tanker fleet specifically, but to the concern as a whole, they opposed sales that would result in losses.

But the bankruptcy did not dissipate the vitality of the Salén family: there was sufficient financial capital and networking capacity to utilize the bankruptcy procedures to reorganize the ownership. The largest subsidiary – at the time of the bankruptcy, the world's highest tonnage cold shipping fleet – went through an unofficial reconstruction before the bankruptcy date with the members of the Salén family obtaining influence on the board of directors of several of the newly created companies. Together with other leading managers, the family was able to create competence clusters in a number of the new organizations. To a large extent, this was made possible by sums that had been placed in the family foundation, Salénia. The reincarnation of the concern was applauded by most of the creditors, and the house bank (the SE Bank) continued to support the family's transactions. Together with new risk capital, the future of the new cold shipping company, baptized Cool Carriers, was secured. From a long-term perspective, the bankruptcy of Saléninvest and its postlude was an example of creative destruction, with the family escaping the burden of unprofitable tankers in their ownership portfolio and being able to shift their resources to more profitable businesses, including air transport (Skyways). The family firm succeeded in rising like a phoenix with sooty wings from its own ashes (Sjögren 1999).

The case of Salén indicates similarities with the Haniels and Wendels, two large family firms discussed by Harold James in Chapter 3 of this volume. These families (and family foundations) showed coherence through considerable turbulence and were as a result able to reinvent themselves. But the Salén-case also echoes the development of the Italian family business group Falck, whose strategy was to stick to the tradition (once a steel company, always a steel-company), and which diversified too late and consequently lost weight in the Italian economy (James 2006).

New Business Logic

Dynasties have renewed industry by changing the logic of a certain business. Among the mature industries, the innovations were often made within the engineering industry, following the direction of the Swedish industrial revolution. The emerging dynasties from the postwar period are, to a great extent, based on non-technology innovations. This is true for IKEA, whose key invention is a new distribution system, and H&M, which based entrepreneurial thinking within marketing and consumer preferences. Ingvar Kamprad's insights as an entrepreneur and furniture dealer are profound and extend over more than half a century. In his detailed handbook, *A Furniture Dealer's Testament*, he emphasizes the importance of the range of goods and services provided, which were the basis of IKEA's identity and trademark. A basic rule is to offer a wide range of household furnishings of appropriate design and function at prices so low that as many people in the world as possible would consider them affordable. His national competitors were threatened, and, when they tried to marginalize him, he set up a production line in Poland to be able to pursue his vision of inexpensive furniture.

The innovation of IKEA also concerns the establishment of a trademark that emphasizes the importance of creating a team spirit and creating an atmosphere in which customers, suppliers, and co-workers feel that they all play a part. Comparisons with a soccer team are relevant. The leader may have a duty to develop and push his players, but each of them also has an obligation to help improve the team as a whole. Ingvar Kamprad highlights the importance of the people who are the pillars of society:

Take care of our social pillars! These are the simple, quiet and straightforward people who are always willing to lend a hand. They perform their duty and accept their responsibilities without being seen. For them, areas of responsibility are a necessary, but unfortunate, concept. For them, supporting the entire organization is as obvious as helping out and always sharing. (Torekull 2006: 336–9)

The founder of H&M, Erling Persson, also shows a distinctive way of breaking the business logic, referred to as an underwear dealer's testament. His entrepreneurial ideas were concrete, down to earth, and strongly characterized by the business logic associated with the apparel industry. One of his ideas was that inventories of unsold goods are both risky and expensive and thus should be avoided as far as possible. Furthermore, he emphasized the importance of a strong financial position to survive future challenges. Many of these value creating rules, bordering on business strategies, concern how marketing and selling should be organized to reach optimal results. Here, he deals with the importance of being able to read other people's minds and how to carry out negotiations. The entrepreneurial aspect was contained in Erling Persson's concept of *controlled imagination*, which was presented together with an admonition to find co-workers who were *constructively creative* and had the ability to implement their ideas. For the family, it is a matter of utilizing its network capacity and of providing space for visionary – not utopian – co-workers (Pettersson 2001: 299–316).

Through their behavior, Erling and his son Stefan Persson have shown the importance of having close contact with the customer. However, instead of the usual relationship of listening to the customer, they had the courage to test the ideas in which they themselves believed. The desire to create something new has also been manifested in an increased reliance on their own design, for example, by hiring a fashion star such as Stella McCartney. Like all successful entrepreneurs, the Perssons have been motivated by curiosity and considerable self-confidence. Like Kamprad in IKEA, the Persson family has violated accepted ideas and brought a new approach to the business. Through the activities of their firms, both Kamprad and Persson have created new markets. Their organizations and products have repeatedly been reorganized to aim at new goals. In the case of H&M, the company deals with what have come to be called "value chains." Control of the underlying delivery systems is used to lower costs and maintain low consumer prices. By eliminating middle men and integrating backward, they have become their own wholesalers, and the resource supplements that have resulted have systematically been devoted to investments and geographic expansion. To reduce costs further, the production of clothing has been located in low-wage countries in southern Europe and Asia (Pettersson 2001: 315–16).

The entrepreneurial leadership in the Persson family is based on simplicity, anti-bureaucratic principles, and a rejection of academic cleverness. In this regard, they are very similar to Kamprad's pragmatic business ideas of how a firm should be built up and expanded worldwide. But there are also similarities to how Ruben Rausing steered the expansion of Tetra Pak, also an emerging dynasty founded in the postwar period. One explanation for why some of the ideas of these three family dynasties overlap was that they were founded at about the same time as a response to the common need to rationalize the distribution of goods for mass consumption during the 1950s and 1960s. When welfare and wages in Sweden rose, it increased the demand for consumption goods while, at the same time, creating pressure for lower personnel costs in production. The Hennes Company (embryo to H&M) responded by offering reasonably priced, fashionable clothes as an alternative to expensive trademarked items. Hennes' marketing was based on aggressive displays and advertising, as well as on stores with large display windows sited in the best store locations in Swedish cities. Kamprad put his products into flat packages and thereby saved delivery costs while shifting other costs on to the customers. Rausing's innovation – the tightly closed milk carton – also resulted in a distinct simplification of distribution. However, in other regards his vision deviated from those of the others, in that Tetra Pak activities, to a large degree, followed the engineering tradition within the classical Swedish mechanical manufacturing industry (Pettersson 2001: 314).

Entrepreneurship Is Everything

The stress on pragmatic entrepreneurship is something that binds both mature and emerging Swedish dynasties together. In the case of Wallenberg, a key expression has been *First the captain, then the ship*, coined by District Judge Marcus Wallenberg, in the first half of the twentieth century. The meaning is that the firm's culture should encourage and develop a leadership based on drive, creativity, determination, and constructive expansion, that is, a strong entrepreneurship. Thus, organizational effort has priority over individual effort. The belief is that no firm is so bad that a good chief executive cannot restore it to its feet, and that no firm is so good that bad leadership cannot sink it. A related idea in the Wallenberg dynasty is that technologically knowledgeable firm leaders are the alpha to omega in several of the sphere's control holdings. The starting point here is that the family chose to become involved in manufacturing industries through companies such as ASEA, Atlas Copco, and Ericsson, where a civil engineer with economic competence is required as chief. Thanks to the numerous control holdings, a pool of highly qualified colleagues that could be shifted between positions and assignments has been available. Promising young individuals were tested, and, if they proved capable, have been given increasing amounts of responsibility as the heads of larger and larger companies within the sphere.

Kamprad's philosophy is that the path toward the goal yields greater satisfaction than the final achievement of the goal. This insight accords well with a motto employed during five generations of Wallenbergs: *The only tradition worth holding on to is the need for constant renewal.* To achieve these goals, continuous entrepreneurship is *the* method. This applies to all living dynasties in this study. Entrepreneurial ability should be the strongest driving force in their own firms, as well as in other firms, and, indeed, in the economy as a whole. This ambition means that the firms have new technology and soft innovations at the forefront. This vision is, in fact, part of a Swedish identity, supported by the school system, universities, and a public innovation system.

The reason for stressing entrepreneurship and exporting firms is Sweden's dependence on export markets. Considering the small domestic market, to make a profit and survive, firms with investments in R&D have to be strongly competitive internationally from the very beginning. Thus, the products that were developed during the industrial breakthrough period were at the forefront of worldwide technology and paved the way for large profits and the high level of welfare in the Swedish peasant society. The innovation belonged to the so-called genius industries, where Swedish entrepreneurs, inspired by trips abroad, received government and private capital to commit to domestic industrial activity. During the mature industrial society, the tradition of product development directed at export markets continued, and traditional products and services were complemented with product innovations within newly developing businesses such as pharmaceuticals, aviation, and automobile production. This trajectory in Swedish economic history is also triggering the entrepreneurship and family firms in the early twenty-first century.

CONCLUSION

The early successes of Swedish dynasties were based on temporary monopolies created by innovations. In most cases, a single path-breaking innovation was insufficient for survival. Instead, continuous entrepreneurship and a constant flow of innovations were required for survival in the market place. Another key feature was that the first generation of the dynasty broke with the accepted institutional rules and business logic of the time. In opposition to, or in cooperation with, the controlling authorities, they changed market conditions, thereby creating opportunity space that allowed them to become established and to grow. To achieve these changes in market conditions, they had to function as lobbyists or create strong relationships with those possessing political power. Through their enterprises, *they created new markets* and benefited the economy by creating more employment opportunities.

Once the firms became large employers, and thus important for the country's labor market, they also attracted the attention of politicians. As long as they remained good (donating) capitalists and contributed to the welfare state, they were favored by the authorities, for example, through special, favorable tax rules. The owners had become part of the establishment and had developed relationship capital with politicians, the public and, sometimes, with members of the royal family. The ultimate goal was to strengthen the trademark, both of the enterprise and of the family dynasty.

These observations should be weighed against the fact that the power spheres threaten to create monopoly-like economies and slowly to adjust structures that inhibit both entrepreneurship and the creation of new enterprises outside the dominant ownership spheres. In a small country such as Sweden, the combination of alliances among private capitalists and representatives of the authorities can be harmful to consumers in the long run. At the corporate level, a family's efforts to maintain control over firms at any price can result in a loss of competency from the firm when co-workers from outside the family are forced to make way for (less competent) family members.

The latest development within the family dynasties, with more women holding important positions, demonstrates a growing breadth and a larger meritocracy component in the leadership culture. Blood relationships will no doubt continue to play a major role, but competence, as measured by educational achievements and entrepreneurial skills, will probably be elevated even more.

References

Andersson, Per (2000). *Stenbeck: Ett reportage om det virtuella bruket*. Stockholm: Norstedt.

Andersson, Peter, and Tommy Larsson (1998). *Tetra: Historien om dynastin Rausing*. Stockholm: Norstedt.

Arregle, Jean-Luc, Michael. A. Hitt, David G. Sirmon, and Philippe Very (2007). "The Development of Organizational Social Capital: Attributes of Family firms." *Journal of Management Studies*, 44(1): 73–95.

Braunerhjelm, Pontus, and Göran Skogh, eds. (2004). *Sista fracken inga fickor har. Filantropi och ekonomisk tillväxt*. Stockholm: SNS Förlag.

Brundin, Ethel, Emilia Florin Samuelsson, and Leif Melin (2008). "The Family Ownership Logic: Core Characteristics of Family Businesses." *Jönköping*

International Business School, Centre for Family Enterprise and Ownership, Working Paper 2008: 1.

Carlsson, Rolf H. (2001). *Ownership and Value Creation. Strategic Corporate Governance in the New Economy*. Chichester, UK: John Wiley & Sons.

Carlsson, Rolf H. (2007). "Swedish Corporate Governance and Value Creation: Owners Still in the Driver's Seat." *Corporate Governance*, 15(6): 1038–55.

Colli, Andrea (2003). *The History of Family Business*. Cambridge: Cambridge University Press.

De Geer, Hans (1998). *Firman: familj och företagande under 125 år: Från A Johnson & Co till Axel Johnson gruppen*. Stockholm: Atlantis.

Ericson, Bengt (2007). *Antonias revansch*. Stockholm: Fischer & Co.

Glete, Jan (1994). *Nätverk i näringslivet*. Stockholm: SNS.

Håkansson, Håkan, and Jan Johanson, eds. (2001). *Business Network Learning*. Oxford: Pergamon.

Henrekson, Magnus (1996). *Företagandets villkor. Spelregler för sysselsättning och tillväxt*. Stockholm: SNS Förlag.

James, Harold (2006). *Family Capitalism*. Cambridge, MA: Harvard University Press.

Karlsson Stider, Annelie (2000). *Familjen & Firman*. Stockholm: EFI, Handelshögskolan. Diss.

Landes, David (2007). *Dynastier: De stora familjeföretagen och deras mer eller mindre lyckade affärer*. Stockholm: SNS Förlag.

Larsson, Mats (2001). *Bonniers – en mediefamilj. Förlag, konglomerat och mediekoncern 1953–1990*. Stockholm: Bonnier.

Larsson, Mats (2006). "Succession och nätverk. Bonnierföretagen i media och industri 1942–1990." In Ylva Hasselberg and Tom Petersson (eds.), *"Bäste broder!" Nätverk, entreprenörskap och innovation i svenskt näringsliv*. Hedemora: Gidlunds.

Lindgren, Håkan (2007). *Jacob Wallenberg 1892–1980*. Stockholm: Atlantis.

Lindgren, Håkan (2012). "The Long Term Viability of the Wallenberg Family Business Group. The Role of 'a Dynastic Drive'." In Anders Perlinge and Hans Sjögren (eds.), *Biographies in the Financial World*. Hedemora: Gidlunds.

Lumpkin, G.T., Keith H. Brigham, and Todd W. Moss (2010). "Long-term Orientation: Implications for the Entrepreneurial Orientation and Performance of Family Business." *Entrepreneurship & Regional Development*, 22(3–4): 241–64.

Miller, Danny, and Isabelle Le Breton-Miller (2005). *Managing for the Long Run. Lessons in Competitive Advantage from Great Family Businesses*. Boston, MA: Harvard Business School Press.

Morck, Randall, ed. (2005). *A History of Corporate Governance around the World: Family Business Groups to Professional Managers*. Chicago: University of Chicago Press.

Nilsson, Göran B. (2001). *Grundaren*. Stockholm: Atlantis.

Olsson, Ulf (2000). *Att förvalta sitt pund. Marcus Wallenberg 1899–1982*. Stockholm: Ekerlids Förlag.

Pearson, Allison. W., Jon S. Carr, and John C. Shaw (2008). "Towards a Theory of Familiness: A Social Capital Perspective." *Entrepreneurship Theory and Practice*, 32(6): 949–69.

Pettersson, Bo (2001). *HandelsMännen. Så skapade Erling och Stefan Persson sitt modeimperium.* Stockholm: Ekerlids.

Sjögren, Hans (1999). *Spelet i Saléninvest.* Stockholm: Ekerlids Förlag.

Sjögren, Hans (2005). *Den uthålliga kapitalismen. Bolagsstyrningen i Astra, Stora Kopparbergs Berg och Svenska Tändsticksaktiebolaget.* Stockholm: SNS Förlag.

Sjögren, Hans (2007). *Kapitalismens värdekontrakt och relationskapital.* Stockholm: Norstedts.

Sjögren, Hans (2008). "Welfare Capitalism: The Swedish Economy 1850–2005." In Susanna Fellman, Martin Iversen, Hans Sjögren, and Lars Thue (eds.), *Creating Nordic Capitalism. The History of a Competitive Periphery.* London: Palgrave Macmillan.

Stenebo, Johan (2009). *Sanningen om IKEA.* Västerås: ICA.

Torekull, Bertil (2006). *Historien om IKEA: Ingvar Kamprad berättar för Bertil Torekull.* Stockholm: Wahlström and Widstrand.

6

Cultural Forces in Large Family Firm Persistence

A Model Based on the CASE Project

Vipin Gupta

INTRODUCTION

Across cultures, family businesses are subject to high hazard rates. Fewer than 3 percent of all family businesses are estimated to survive beyond the fourth generation (Vallejo 2008). Assuming that each generation of ownership lasts an average of twenty years, a survival rate of 3 percent of the organizations over a century is perhaps not worse than that of non-family businesses. However, a priori, one might expect family businesses to have a significantly lower hazard rate than non-family businesses. This longevity may be expected because of the distinctive advantages of family business, including stewardship values toward the stakeholders, emphasis on continuity through the family dimension/line and change through intergenerational succession and business and non-family dimensions, and a committed and enduring vision of the founders and the families to leave a legacy for their successors (Gallo 1991; Vallejo 2008).

Ward's pioneering study underlined three factors as highly correlated with family firm longevity: frequent family meetings, reflecting open communication; strategic planning, and an active board of directors, reflecting participatory decision making (Ward 1987). Ward concluded that a well-functioning family with strong values is the greatest resource for a family business. Factors such as family meetings that facilitate open communication help the ownership tap the potential power of the family to drive its business. Thus, business can be used as an opportunity for the family to grow, develop its potential, and manifest its values and dreams in society. The future of the business as well as the family involvement and succession can be planned in an orderly and constructive way. Successive studies confirmed these factors (e.g., Fahed-Sreih and Djoundourian 2006). Some identified additional important factors, such as a written succession plan and the preparation of successors (Lank 2001), as well as upkeep of knowledge and its transmission across generations (Chirico 2007).

Though previously not recognized, many of these factors, such as well-functioning families who meet frequently and an independent board of directors who strategically plan both succession and new value streams, are culturally sensitive. For instance, strategic management research suggests that many Japanese firms enjoyed longevity during the twentieth century because they let strategy evolve and form, rather than planning for it. The American firms that planned their strategies found it difficult to adjust and to adapt to the changed global environment, and many failed to survive as a result (Aoki and Choi 1999).

Theoretically as well as empirically, enduring competitive advantage correlates with organizational size, which in evolutionary economics is often associated with inherent core capabilities and investment efficiencies (Nelson & Winter, 1982). Conversely, the size of organizational scale and scope is associated with the accumulation of greater, and often more diverse, resources, which allow a firm to be more resilient in response to environmental contingencies and to be able to allocate resources for both continuity and change (Chandler 1990). But large firms – because of their inertial tendencies – are also highly vulnerable to ecological selection and risk demise if efficiency, innovativeness, and ethics are not maintained (Söderbom, Teal, and Harding 2006).

The existing organizational theories, as summarized in Table 6.1 and related empirical research, implicitly assume the factors both contributing to and hindering organizational endurance as near-absolutes. Most cross-national studies of organizational endurance often also adopt a similar view. Chandler, for instance, discusses the significance of large firms in different nations making three-pronged investments in organization, production, and marketing to survive and endure (Chandler 1990). Similarly, Porter discusses the importance of the quality and co-specialization of four linkages – factor endowments; demand conditions; related and supported industries; and strategy, structure, and rivalry – as well as the role of government in supporting these – as key factors in the endurance of large firms in different nations (Porter 1990).

One of the challenges in studying the longevity of large family businesses is to recognize the wide diversity across cultures and over time (Gupta et al. 2008b). Given the variation in the nature and form of family businesses across cultures, one would expect the dynamics of

TABLE 6.1. *Selected Theories and Schools of Thought on Enduring Organizations*

Theory and School of Thought on Enduring Organizations	Sample Citation
Change, Learning and Complexity theories	
– Organizations are inertial and adapt through large, infrequent change	Gersick 1991
– Organizational learning helps acquire knowledge to adapt via continuous change	Senge 1990
– Organizations accelerate change under complexity to gain competitive advantage	Matthews, White and Long 1999
Contingency and Power theories	
– Organizations constantly align their internal characteristics to the changing external environment characteristics	Lawrence and Lorsh 1967
– Organizations constantly lead change in external environment to match their internal characteristics	
Continuity and Balance theories	
– Organizations maintain continuity between elements of past, present, and future	Srivastava and Fry 1992
– Organizations maintain balance between opposing forces, such as cost reduction and revenue enhancement, transactional leadership and transformational leadership, traditions and change.	Gupta, Gollakota, and Srinivasan 2008
Institutional and Period theories	
– Organizations gain legitimacy in their societies by following the institutional norms at their founding and later periods	Lawrence 1999
– Organizations mobilize network of support to gain legitimacy for their characteristics through institutional change	Seo and Creed 2002
Identity, Image and Culture theories	
– Organizational members develop self-identities around what is core, unique, and enduring about their organizations	Gioia, Shultz and Corley 2000
– Organizations construct formal as well as social images that help them endure	Goffman 1959; House et al. 2004
– Organizational cultures include shared meanings, languages, and history, and offer solutions to major challenges	

(*continued*)

TABLE 6.1 (*continued*)

Theory and School of Thought on Enduring Organizations	Sample Citation
Diversity, creativity and innovation theories	
– Diversity of perspectives helps anticipate and resolve threats and exploit opportunities	Lockwood 2005
– Nurturing creativity attracts human capital talent and renews the organization	Styhre and Sundgren 2005
– Innovation allows distinctive advantage	Van de Ven 1986
Competency, advantage and dependency theories	
– Core competencies are the foundations for evolving new value-adding solutions	Prahalad and Hamel 1990
– Organizations are founded with, bundle, and re-bundle their unique resources	Barney 2001
– Organizations manage, preempt, and coopt the power of other firms on whom they depend for key resources	Thompson 1967
Strategic leadership and network theories	
– Leaders influence organizational endurance through their vision and values, and their influence on and inclusion of groups	Bryman 1996
– Leaders and organizations also build and mobilize networks to gain advantage	Powell 1990

Source: Adapted from Kotecki (2000).

organizational endurance also to vary cross-culturally. In this chapter, we deconstruct the endurance of large family firms, using a cross-cultural approach. Our starting point is a set of culturally varying unique characteristics of family businesses. We propose that different geographical systems and group orientations will enhance or negate the effects of these unique characteristics on the endurance of large family businesses. We construct a conceptual model and develop hypotheses based on two major cross-cultural studies: the GLOBE Program (House et al. 2004) and the CASE Project (Gupta et al. 2008c). In conclusion, the implications and the limitations of the studies are highlighted.

THE RESEARCH MODEL

Culture may have two types of effects on the factors associated with organizational endurance: (1) independent and (2) moderating (see, e.g., Tsui, Nifadkar, and Ou 2009). A useful way of measuring the independent effects is in terms of fixed geography effects, which capture the holistic systemwide influences of geographical cultures. However, there are two philosophical challenges. First, the fixed geography effects capture a range of influences, including economic development, physical climate, and institutional factors. The second is the question of how to account for the subgeography effects that reflect the heterogeneity of the sample studied, including organizational and participant demographics and psychographics and industrial and technological factors.

Two landmark studies on culture – Hofstede and GLOBE – offer contrasting ontological views on the effects of these challenges (Hofstede 2001; House et al. 2004; see also Wyer, Chiu, and Hong 2009 on how leading contemporary scholars either follow or adapt these opposing views). For Hofstede, the impact of the noncultural as well as the subgeography effects must be controlled if one is to assess the true culture effects. GLOBE (Global Leadership and Organizational Behavior Effectiveness Program) challenges the view that the noncultural and subgeography effects are independent of the cultural factor. Hofstede's approach reduces culture to just one other variable, in the multiple levels and types of variables that influence the factors of interest. GLOBE's approach, in contrast, considers culture as ontologically prior to all other factors, in other words, as having a systemwide effect. In other words, in Hofstede's approach, culture operates as a variable, whereas in GLOBE's approach it operates as a system.

If one takes a broader view of culture, as in GLOBE, then the various other influences at the cultural level of analysis – such as economic development – are interpreted as the forces that account for the cross-cultural variations. Similarly, the subgeography effects, which represent the heterogeneity of the sample studied within a given geography – because of subregions, generation, industry, ethnicity, and other demographic and psychographic variables – are a product of the cultural system.

The moderating effects of culture on the factors associated with organizational endurance can be measured using measures of cultural dimensions. Scholars often find that the relationships between the hypothesized factors and the consequential outcomes vary in different cultural geographies. For instance, Robert, Probst, Martocchio, Drasgow, and Lawler (2000) found empowerment to be negatively related with job satisfaction in India but positively related in the U.S., Mexican, and Polish samples. In these cases, specific measures of cultural dimensions, such as power distance, can help explain the variations. For the culture to have a moderating effect, it is critical that the factors researched are culturally sensitive.

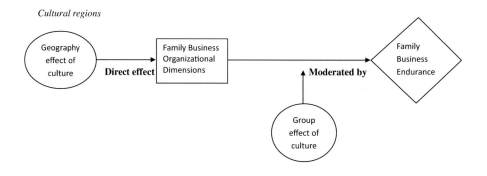

Cultural regions

FIGURE 6.1. Culturally sensitive model of family business endurance.

In other words, the factors should have varying effects, in some cases positive and in others negative, in different geographies, contingent on their orientations on cultural dimensions.

A research model for the cross-cultural variations in the endurance of large family firms is summarized in Figure 6.1. In this model, culturally sensitive family business organizational dimensions are hypothesized to be related to organizational endurance. The culture is hypothesized to have an independent influence, captured as fixed geography effects, on these organizational dimensions, as well as a moderating influence on their relationship with large family business endurance.

Several typologies of cultural dimensions are available in the literature, including the four measures of Hofstede (2001), the nine of GLOBE (House et al. 2004), the seven of Trompenaars (1994), and the three of Schwartz (2009). This chapter uses the GLOBE typology because of its robust cross-cultural collaborative research methodology.

Table 6.2 summarizes the definitions of the nine GLOBE cultural dimensions. All five dimensions of Hofstede have been refined by GLOBE. Furthermore, all three dimensions of Schwarz are captured by the broader GLOBE typology, with significant conceptual and empirical correlation (Mastery/Harmony with Performance orientation, Hierarchical/Egalitarian with Power distance, and Embedded/Autonomy with In-group collectivism). Similarly, many of Trompenaars' dimensions are also conceptually and empirically correlated with GLOBE dimensions.

We rely on the CASE project for the typology of culturally sensitive family business organizational dimensions (Gupta et al. 2008c). The

TABLE 6.2. *Description of GLOBE Dimensions of Societal Culture*

Dimension	Description
In-group collectivism	the degree to which individuals express pride, loyalty, and cohesiveness in their families
Power distance	the extent to which a community accepts and endorses authority, power differences, and status privileges
Uncertainty avoidance	the extent to which a society relies on social norms, rules, and procedures to alleviate the unpredictability of future events
Performance orientation	the extent to which a community encourages and rewards innovation, high standards, excellence, and performance improvement
Gender egalitarianism	the degree to which a collective minimizes gender inequality through gender role and position overlap
Future orientation	the degree to which a collectivity encourages and rewards future-oriented behaviors such as planning and delaying gratification
Assertiveness	the degree to which a collectivity encourages and rewards active self-assertion in order to master, change, and exploit the natural and social environment to attain personal or group goals.
Humane orientation	the degree to which a community cares about particular needs and claims of members, over general rules, codes, values, and standards
Institutional collectivism	the degree to which a collectivity emphasizes holistic and often synergistic consideration of the system, with overlapping lives where business and social relationships are managed together

CASE (Culturally sensitive Assessment Systems and Education) project is an important source of assistance to global managers. Over 2005–9, building on the GLOBE Program, a five-member research team applied the GLOBE regional clusters framework to the study of family business in ten cultural regions of the world. A special side study of gender issues in family business was also added. Although a growing body of knowledge about family business in different cultures exists, it tends to be centered on a few cultures, for instance, the Anglo-Saxon, and is dispersed. The CASE project was a pioneering effort that aimed (1) to examine the varying conceptions of family business around the world; (2) to formulate the culturally sensitive typology of family business dimensions; (3) to construct culturally varying models of family business, including the gender aspect, in different cultural regions; (4) to compare and contrast

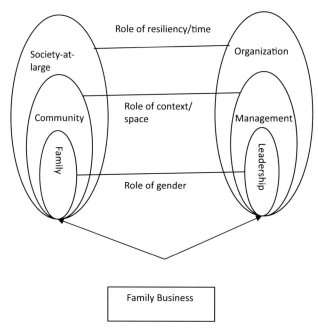

FIGURE 6.2. CASE framework for identifying cross-cultural family business dimensions.

family businesses in different cultural regions; and (5) to examine the factors that account for the cross-cultural variations in the family business dimensions.

The CASE project used a typology of nine dimensions of family business characteristics. The first three examine the correlation of the family business with the family, the community, and society-at-large. The next three examine the correlation of the family business with organization, management, and leadership. The final three examine the correlation of family business with gender, linking family and leadership; time, linking society-at-large and organization; and space, linking community and management. These dimensions are summarized in Figure 6.2 and Table 6.2.

In Table 6.3, we advance specific hypotheses on how cultural dimensions will moderate the relationship between the family business characteristics and the endurance of large family businesses. For each family business characteristic, two cultural dimensions are identified as moderators. The first dimension is embeddedness/in-group collectivism

TABLE 6.3. *Description of CASE Dimensions of Family-Business Characteristics*

Dimension	Description of CASE Dimensions of Family Business Characteristics
Regulated boundary	The criteria for the family business' access to family resources are clearly regulated; the access to these resources is not unregulated.
Business reputation	Family resources are involved only if it makes business sense; the involvement of these resources is not guided by primarily family interests.
Bridging relationships	Family business breaks out to access resources outside the family networks; it is not tied to only the family networks for core resources.
Organizational professionalism	Family business employs professional manpower and methods at all levels; these are not limited to only the lower levels or to only select parts of the organization.
Regulated family power	Family business has a structure to be protected from the dynamics of family; family – as a collective or a divisive entity – does not create uncertainty for it.
Competitive succession	The successors must demonstrate competence to earn employment and leadership in the family business; kinship alone does not create the privilege to be employed and to lead the family business.
Gender-centered leadership	Women family members play important strategic roles in the family business; they are not merely silent and invisible members of family in business.
Operational resiliency	Family business has access to the reservoir of family or market resources to wither temporary crisis or to overcome more enduring challenges; it is not without any patient and /or accessible capital.
Contextual embeddedness	Family business evolution is founded on the co-specialized and dedicated resources, such as deep experiences and localized endowments.

(House et al. 2004; Schwarz 2009), which focuses on the pride and cohesion among the members of the family and in group. We expect this to be a critical dimension that moderates all aspects of family business characteristics. The second moderating dimension differs for the different family business characteristics. Using the insights from GLOBE and related research (House et al. 2004), each of the other GLOBE societal culture dimensions is identified to be the dominant moderator of one CASE family business characteristic.

Vipin Gupta

TABLE 6.4. *Summary of Culturally Moderated Hypotheses on Family Business Endurance*

CASE Family Business Dimension	GLOBE Societal Culture Moderator	Level	Effect on Family Business Endurance
Regulated boundary	Assertiveness	Hi	+ (assert control over sub-system)
		Lo	− (holistic harmony emphasized)
Business reputation	Humane orientation	Hi	− (relationships precede contracts)
		Lo	+ (neutral universal codes)
Bridging relationships	Power distance	Hi	− (core periphery bonding)
		Lo	+ (emphasis on shared interests)
Organizational professionalism	Uncertainty avoidance	Hi	+ (specialized knowledge/institutions)
		Lo	− (low commitment investments)
Regulated family power	Institutional collectivism	Hi	− (collective family/business interests)
		Lo	+ (protect separate business interests)
Competitive succession	Performance orientation	Hi	+ (merit criteria)
		Lo	− (support from constituencies key)
Gender-centered leadership	Gender egalitarianism	Hi	+ (women able to exercise leadership)
		Lo	− (women as leaders not supported)
Operational resiliency	Future orientation	Hi	+ (knowledge intensive investments)
		Lo	− (structurally unattractive sectors)
Contextual embeddedness	In-group collectivism	Hi	+ (roots in home base and relations)
		Lo	+ (roots in home base and relations)

Note: The hypothesized effect will reverse at extreme levels of societal culture characteristics and may also deviate with transformative strategic leadership; will be stronger for the larger firms; and not supported unless using GLOBE methodology and accounting for the varying forms of family business.

HYPOTHESES

The Relationship with the Family: Regulated Boundary and Family Business Endurance

Regulated boundary refers to the extent to which the criteria for the family business' access to family resources, and the access itself, are clearly regulated. Regulated boundary pertains to the criteria or rules that families use to achieve and grant the desired level of access to information, space, and the resources of the family business (Altman 1975). In some geographies, the boundaries between the family and the business are strongly regulated, whereas in others they are permeable.

Families from assertive/mastery cultures believe that, with sufficient resources and investments, any goal can be achieved. They identify specific achievements for each subsystem as goals and see goals as intentions of asserting control over each subsystem (Schwartz 2009). *Thus, boundary regulation is likely to promote family business endurance in assertive/mastery cultures.* In contrast, families from nonassertive/ harmony cultures seek to operate in concert with the world around them, to see the environment and the family as part of a systematic whole, and to keep the system in balance. They support each subsystem exploiting the resources of other subsystems but have strong norms of reciprocity to ensure that no subsystem is exploited more than it can bear, and of frugality to ensure that each resource is best utilized across the subsystems. They identify systemwide goals and seek to improve linkages among various subsystems to achieve these goals (Schwartz 2009). *Thus, boundary regulation is likely to hinder family business endurance in nonassertive/harmony cultures.*

The Relationship with the Community: Business Reputation and Family Business Endurance

What governs the relationship of a family business with its broader community? In some geographies, the relationship of a family business is guided by its reputation in the business community – that is, how far it meets the codes and standards set by the business community and the legal system (Richman 2006). In others, the concept of family identity and reputation plays a more important role (Ben-Porath 1980). The family reputation accrues through the intergenerational involvement of the members of the family in the community and in industrial activities

(Iyer 1999). Business reputation influences the logic of the involvement of family resources – it reflects the extent to which family resources are involved only if it makes business sense, and the involvement of these resources is not guided primarily by family interests.

Families from humane-oriented/particularism cultures show a sense of deep concern for the emotions and well-being of the members of their communities and look at relationships and particular situations to decide what is right (Trompenaars 1994; House et al. 2004). The contractual business agreements are less important than the relationship that is built up by the family with the community – contracts may be revised or ignored if the relationships and the situations so demand. Strict application of contracts may be good from the business logic of reputation, but is perceived as a breach of trust from the family relationship logic. Therefore, *an emphasis on business reputation will hinder family business endurance in particularism cultures*. In contrast, families from non–humane-oriented/universalism cultures seek to develop rules and codes that are neutral to the emotions of the members and are applicable in all situations. The relationships with the community are defined as contractual agreements, with standardized codes enforceable by the parties and through legal institutions. Thus, *an emphasis on business reputation will promote family business endurance in non–humane/universalism cultures*.

The Relationship with Society-at-Large: Bridging Relationships and Family Business Endurance

In Chapter 7, Guillén and Garcia-Canal observe that family multinationals derive their advantage based on their trust-based organizational connections. Trust-based connections may be grounded in bridging or bonding relationships. Bridging relationships refer to the extent to which the family business does not rely exclusively on resources within the family and the home community; instead, it breaks out to form new relationships. Bridging relationships extend to society-at-large versus bonding relationships that occur within kinship and friendship enclaves (Putnam 1995). Salient ethnic identities produce exclusive, homogeneous "bonding" relationships between business families and their kin and community. The concept of bridging relationships focuses primarily on the direct and indirect external links of a family with other actors beyond the immediate collective. As Sharma (2003) notes, similar to other organizational forms, family firms are dependent on external constituencies to meet their resource needs.

Families from hierarchical or high-power distance cultures rely on hierarchical boundaries for the use of power based on ascribed roles to ensure responsible behavior (Schwartz 2009). The stratification and differentiation of power, roles, and resources are practiced (House et al. 2004). A system of vertical cooperation and linkages often evolves with support from more powerful families and institutional actors, which protects the business interests of the less powerful families, particularly during times of crisis, in exchange for the latter sacrificing a greater share of their profits during good times. Bonding relationships are a priority through a system of flexible specialization, characterized by a network of peripheral relationships with society-at-large, which bears the brunt of all the crises and has more limited trust capital (Piore and Sabel 1984). Therefore, *an emphasis on bridging relationships will hinder family business endurance in hierarchical/high-power distance cultures.* In contrast, families from egalitarian/low-power distance cultures rely on the transcendence of selfish interests in favor of stewardship behavior that emphasizes shared interests and welfare beyond in-group bonds. Therefore, *an emphasis on bridging relationships will promote family business endurance in egalitarian/low-power distance cultures.*

The Relationship with the Organization: Organizational Professionalism and Family Business Endurance

Organizational professionalism refers to the extent to which a family business employs professional manpower and methods at all levels; they are not limited only to the lower levels or to selected parts of the organization. The dimension of organizational professionalism blends the organizational systems with the professional systems (Kadushin and Harkness 2002). In other words, organizational strategies and structures are designed in a way that upholds professional principles and objectives. This offers the strengths of organizational change to involve non-family resources, with their distinctive capabilities and competencies, in key decisions and in their implementation (Yeung 2004).

Families from uncertainty-avoidance cultures rely on contemporary, expert, codified, abstract, diffused, and specialized knowledge to manage and resolve uncertainties (House et al. 2004). Rules and procedures are emphasized to ensure clarity and certainty, which are likely to facilitate the ability to form intergroup connections and to bring in external professional resources. Uncertainty-avoidance cultures tend to develop institutions that support a generalized form of trust in society, and that makes this trust enforceable through broader norms of reciprocity and solidarity (Fukuyama 1996). Therefore, *an emphasis on organizational professionalism will promote family business endurance in uncertainty-avoidance cultures.* Families from uncertainty-tolerant cultures rely on spontaneity; rules of thumb; and concrete, hoarded, and generalized knowledge to tolerate and survive uncertainties. Uncertainty-tolerant cultures tend not to have well-developed institutions and instead rely on low-commitment exchanges and investments (House et al. 2004). The cost of ensuring generalized trust and attracting professionals in these cultures can be prohibitive. Therefore, *an emphasis on organizational professionalism will hinder family business endurance in uncertainty-tolerant cultures.*

Consider the case of Germany, which is high in uncertainty avoidance but low in in-group collectivism society. German-Luxembourg family firm Villeroy & Boch, also discussed in Chapter 3, has endured for more than 250 years and nine generations. The firm started as an iron foundry and maker of simple earthenware tableware, but has since diversified into bathroom and kitchen fixtures and tiles. Its chief strategic officer (who is a non-family member), Volker Pruschke, says that the family backing has given an authenticity to the brand and contributed a spectrum of experience that has kept the firm strong and flexible over the centuries. At the same time, the family relies on professional managers and board members, and, in 2007, it hired a non-family member to succeed as CEO. Pruschke says, "At the end of the day, they want the kind of management capability and they have a willingness and determination to find the best person for the job" (Perman 2008: http://www.businessweek.com/stories/2008–05–14).

The Relationship with the Management: Regulated Family Power and Family Business Endurance

Regulated family power refers to the degree to which the family business has a structure that is seen as needing protection from the dynamics of family; family – as a collective or a divisive entity – does not create uncertainty for it. Family businesses establish legitimacy with customers, employees, and investors by regulating the family's exercise of power (Muntean 2008). Some cultures frown upon a family's paternalist control of the management and have mechanisms that protect the family business from the vagaries of family conflicts and splits. In other cultures, the paternalist power of the family may provide reassurance and certainty for stakeholders, who are aware of the family's beliefs and priorities;

and the dynamics of family conflicts and splits are also played out in the family business.

Families from institutionally collective/diffused cultures consider family and the family business to be interrelated, and together they are seen as more than the sum of the parts, whose collective interests a family business seeks to emphasize (House et al. 2004). Family is accepted as having an influence at all levels of the business, and business members are also accepted as family members and are invited to family functions. Business and social matters are discussed, critical information is shared, and key decisions are taken with equal ease at family dinners, as well as at business meetings. Therefore, *regulated family power will hinder family business endurance in institutionally collective/diffused cultures.* In contrast, families from less institutionally collective/specific cultures maintain highly purposeful and well-defined interactions with the family business, which emphasize the individual interests of the family and of the business (House et al. 2004). The business domain is separated from the family domain, and the family is not expected to exercise informal and situation-based influence in the business domain – except in the capacity of the specific and formal management, leadership, and governance roles. Therefore, *regulated family power will promote family business endurance in less institutionally collective/specific cultures.*

The Relationship with the Leadership – Competitive Succession and Family Business Endurance

Competitive succession refers to the degree to which the successors must demonstrate their competence to earn employment and leadership in the family business; kinship alone does not guarantee the right to be employed or the privilege of leading the family business. Cultures vary in terms of how competitive the process is for selecting, nurturing, and advancing the leaders (Handler 1994). In some cultures, the leadership is decided based on nepotist norms, such as kinship and kinship-like relationships; in others, merit and competency are the criteria that guide the competitive process.

Families from high-performance–oriented cultures find it important to use merit criteria for succession. The successors are appointed to existing positions, with their competencies matching the defined strategic needs (Breton-Miller, Miller, and Steier 2004). The external market for corporate control also evaluates the family business based on its commitment to performance-oriented goals and compensation. Otherwise, it is difficult to attract and retain relevant human, financial, and other types of resources. Therefore, *competitive succession will promote family business endurance in high-performance–oriented cultures.* In contrast, families from low-performance–oriented cultures emphasize ascribed value characteristics such as age, education, family, and profession, along with performance and performance-related competencies (House et al. 2004). Success depends not only on developing competencies to achieve business goals but also on the more arduous task of gaining support from key constituencies on the basis of one's background. Goal-related merit is tempered with kinship and patriliality in preparing and deciding successors. Therefore, *competitive succession will hinder family business endurance in low-performance–oriented cultures.*

The Link between Family and Leadership: Gender-centered Leadership and Family Business Endurance

Gender-centered leadership refers to the degree to which female family members play important strategic roles in the family business; they are not merely silent and invisible members of family in the business, as indicated in Chapter 9 by Blondel and Niforos in this book. In some cultures, a largely "invisible" – excluded, behind-the-scenes, or subordinated – role of women in the family business leadership is accepted and endorsed, and few women have the opportunity to lead family businesses from the front in visible and significant roles (Cole 1997). In others, the impediments to women assuming "visible" – inclusive, front-end, independent, and senior – leadership roles are challenged, and many women are able to secure opportunities for such leadership roles.

Families from gender-egalitarian cultures tend to have limited gender-based role differentiation and support and accept role overlap and women in the decision-making roles (House et al. 2004). Here, women are able to use their vantage positions to be the champions of gender-centering the organizational structures, which strengthen the ability of family businesses to attract and retain more diverse pools of talent. They are likely to introduce several changes not only for their own selves, but also for all the employees – women as well as men – including flexible work hours and work sites, access to traditionally male positions, and opportunities and challenges for personal and professional growth (Frishkoff and Brown 1993). Therefore, *gender-centered leadership will promote family business endurance in gender-egalitarian cultures.* In contrast, families from gender-stratified cultures are reluctant to support and accept women in the decision-making roles, and even if they do, find employees and other stakeholders resisting and not taking women in leadership roles seriously (Rosenblatt et al. 1985). Prospective employees may not want to report to female leaders, and prospective business partners may not be comfortable in negotiating and working with female leaders. Therefore, *gender-centered leadership will hinder family business endurance in low–gender-egalitarian cultures.*

The Link between Society-at-Large and Organization: Operational Resiliency and Family Business Endurance

Operational resiliency refers to the degree to which the family business has access to the reservoir of family and community resources to weather temporary crises or to overcome more enduring challenges; such a reservoir is referred to as patient and loyal capital. This dimension is reflective of the flexibility, agility, stability, sustainability, and longevity of the family business. Family business enjoys certain organizational capabilities and challenges by virtue of its unique familiness. Its capabilities include strong social networks, shared family values, and financial independence (Kets de Vries, Carlock, and Florent-Treacy 2007). The challenges include entrenched leadership, enmeshed systems, and financial strains. In some contexts, capabilities dominate the challenges, creating resilience for seizing opportunities and resolving threats. In others, the challenges erode the capabilities, thereby compromising such resilience.

Families from high future–oriented cultures build operational resilience in their family businesses through a long-term commitment, and this patient capital helps them ride the periods of crisis as well as the periods of change. This intergenerational commitment also helps family businesses build trust relations with their business partners, customers, as well as their employees, thereby allowing greater confidence in delegation and collaboration and in an involvement-oriented management philosophy (Salvato 2002). Family firms in future-oriented cultures are more likely to be able to grow and to innovate by finding new ways to integrate managerial cohorts and special corporate governance strategies, which reflect the institutional, social, economic, and cultural realities of their market and allow them to maintain family influence (Colli 2003). They are also more likely to be pioneers of new technology and new flexible work practices and to show greater openness to pursuing profitable diversification opportunities. Therefore, *operational resilience will promote family business endurance in high future–oriented cultures.* In contrast, *families from low future–oriented cultures* are likely to develop operational resilience by keeping the business concentrated in light, labor-intensive, and specialized sectors, where other families in their community have had long experience, and where the family members can easily join. These structurally unattractive industries require limited resources and face few entry barriers (Gallo 1991), which make it difficult for the family businesses to capture the value inherent in their operational capability and thus present adverse terms of exchange and survival. Strong mental models, such as tradition, lock a family firm in existing practices and reduce its ability to find adequate external help during a crisis. Therefore, *operational resilience will hinder family business endurance in low future–oriented cultures.*

To illustrate this, consider the case of Lyman Orchards, based in Middlefield, Connecticut, which was founded in 1785. In the GLOBE study, the United States is identified as a society that is moderately high in future orientation and very low in in-group collectivism. Thus, we predict that operational resilience should promote family business endurance for a U.S.-based family business. Indeed, Lyman's family attributes its endurance to "remaining tied to the land as well as continuously diversifying offerings." Its current CEO, John Lymans, says: "We are constantly looking for new opportunities. We've tried to be open to new ideas. We are not heavy risk-takers, but we try not to be afraid of taking risks, too" (Perman 2008).

The Link between Community and Management: Contextual Embeddedness and Family Business Endurance

Contextual embeddedness refers to the extent to which family business evolution is founded on co-specialized and dedicated resources, such as deep experience and localized endowments. This dimension is concerned with the co-management and co-development of the family business and its community context. Hess (2004) identifies three forms of embeddedness: societal (the home base, or the genetic code of where an actor comes from), network (the structure of the relationships of that actor), and territorial (the extent to which an actor is "anchored" in particular territories or places). The concept of contextual embeddedness captures various anchors or roots, including the home base, relations, and territories. Family businesses tend to be embedded within clusters of firms and other participants that offer critical resources, support, and markets (Gulbrandsen 2005). They rely on the traditional strengths of these clusters and work with the cluster participants to generate new networks, capture new global opportunities, and support regional transformations.

In some contexts, the identity and the trajectory of the family business are intricately tied with that of its local or national community. Family businesses – both individually and collectively – act as the critical engines for local or national vibrancy, development, and transformation. In other contexts, the existence, operations, competencies, and the success of the family business are rather independent of its local or national community. Family business has no special role in the history, present identity, and future trajectory of its community – be it local or national.

We hypothesize that the contextual embeddedness will promote family business endurance in high as well as in low in-group collective cultures of the world.

DISCUSSION

Several boundary conditions need to be considered in the application and testing of the family business endurance hypotheses. First, family businesses as well as societal cultures do not have homogeneous or constant characteristics. Some degree of balance is required in all family businesses and societal cultures. For a cross-cultural sample as a whole, at their extremes, the impact of factors on family business endurance is likely to reverse. Extreme cultures imbalance the functioning of a family business and threaten its endurance. Second, family leadership visions and organizational cultures may provide an alternative cultural condition lending support to what is identified as the best practice and "must do" family business characteristics. For instance, families in which the older members believe in empowering women and treating the daughters the same as the sons can help foster an organizational culture in which the roles and contributions of women are acknowledged and in which the structures support flexible participation by women. In such cases, gender-centered leadership can actually be a source of advantage and family business endurance even in the embedded/high in-group collectivism cultures, particularly as the families move toward having only one or two children, who may be solely daughters.

Third, size matters. The size of the family business has important symbolic and substantive meaning. The hypotheses are likely to have stronger validity for large family businesses that have the necessary resources to complement those accessible, based on the compatibility of their organizational characteristics with their societal cultures. Selection forces, based on the compatibility of organizational work culture and societal culture, operate more strongly on larger firms. The larger firms are, the

more visible they are in society, and they are expected to have practices that are compatible with the societal norms – either through con-
formity or through leading a change in the societal culture (Söderbom,
Teal, and Harding 2006). The smaller firms, on the other hand, can
be much more entrepreneurial and nimble and can experiment with
the alternative practices, by investing only limited resources. In addition, smaller family businesses may be founded for motivations other
than being endured transgenerationally (Söderbom, Teal, and Harding
2006). For instance, the motivation may be simply to provide a source
of employment to children or to retired parents in times and contexts of
high unemployment and lack of other opportunities. The family business
may be dissolved when new opportunities emerge, or when the need for
the supplemental income or self-employment of some family members
diminishes.

Fourth, when one talks about an enduring large family firm, it is important to clarify what is being endured. A narrow view assumes a family
firm to have endured if its ownership, leadership, and management remain
in the hands of the founder family, typically along the patriarchal lines.
However, family businesses around the world do not conform to this
assumption (Gupta et al. 2008b). Family businesses may be founded by
a consortium of families, or be succeeded to several family successors,
who may part ways or split the family business later. Family businesses
may also bring in strategic non-family owners, leaders, and/or managers,
to play a minority or dominant role. Families may close the founder
business and then start a new business under the same family business
name; or they may close one business and then start another business
in the same industry using a different name. Often, families may be
engaged in business over successive generations living in the same city
or even in the same ancestral home and may have taken their family
name from the ancestral line of business even though each generation
runs the business under a different name. Some of the family groups may
be the prominent names in their locales or areas, with leadership positions both in industry and in the community; notwithstanding this, they
may operate under intangible common connections of same family values,
visions, mission, language, and social networks, and honor the same family elders, but have distinct tangible business names, ownership, management, and leadership. In some cases, daughters might have married and
taken the family legacy to other geographies and other family groups and
passed that on to start new family businesses with their husbands or their
children.

In imposing a particular definition of endurance, one that conforms to the ideal-typical Anglo-Saxon view of separating the family from the business, the danger is of losing the richness and power of the family business organization, and of devaluing the diversity that various cultures offer to our world (Gupta et al. 2008b). Based on a case study of an established Australian wine family business, Steen and Welch (2006) underline, "how extensive, convoluted, and intertwined family business networks may become, to the point where it is difficult to disentangle business, family, and personal elements." They conclude that, for a family business, "a merger or acquisition might be seen as a legitimate response in a threatening environment rather than an endpoint."

CONCLUSIONS

In this chapter, we have discussed the value and the challenges of the longevity of larger family businesses. Enduring large organizations is a challenge in itself, because size produces inertial tendencies. Globalization, technology, and other forces have increased the intensity and frequency of crisis, which has brought forth new threats to growth and survival. Family businesses have their own added challenges of resource limitations, family conflicts and splits, and succession issues. As a net result, despite their substantial known advantages, the survival rate of the family businesses up to their fifth generation remains less than 3 percent. Scholars have identified a need for the family businesses to put systems in place to manage family communication, plan strategically, and transfer values and knowledge intergenerationally, and to create new streams of value. The emphasis is on resiliency capabilities to manage proactively, and even capitalize on, the adversity, complexity, and crisis in the environment.

This chapter has offered several directions for practitioners as well as scholars. We have furthered the discourse by stressing how differences in the nature of family businesses, and the variations in the cultural contexts of their operation, offer each family business unique pathways based on its unique features and unique context to manage the challenge of longevity.

There is a need in future studies to recognize the appropriate societal and organizational context clearly, before deciding on specific practitioner solutions or scholarly premises about the generalizability and validity of these solutions. In particular, the multilevel, multifocal nature of culture and cultural influences, the differing meanings of the context and contextual characteristics for different members and investigators, and the changing aspirations and values of the leaders and the members should all be appropriately considered.

Finally, it is important to recognize that we are in the midst of epochal change in the cultural attitudes around the world, as a result of globalization, technology, and education. One wonders if the sociocultural changes will bring about fundamental changes in how cultural forces moderate the persistence of large family firms in different regions. This is also where historians can bring a creative tension to address the more ahistorical typologies of GLOBE, which freeze a particular timeframe.

References

Altman, Irwin (1975). *The Environment and Social Behavior*. Monterey, CA: Brooks/Cole.

Aoki, Koichi, and Dae-Ryong Choi (1999). "Japanese Acceptance of Mintzberg's Suggestions." *Strategic Change*, 8(1): 41–50.

Barney, Jay B. (2004). "Is the Resource-based 'View' a Useful Perspective for Strategic Management Research?" *Academy of Management Review*, 26(1): 41–56.

Ben-Porath, Yoram (1980). "The F-Connection: Families, Friends, and Firms and the Organization of Exchange." *Population and Development Review*, 6(1): 1–30.

Breton-Miller, Isabelle Le, Danny Miller, and Lloyd P. Steier (2004). "Toward an Integrative Model of Effective FOB Succession." *Entrepreneurship Theory and Practice*, 28(4): 305–28.

Bryman, Alan (1996). "Leadership in Organizations." In Stewart R. Clegg, Cynthia Hardy, and Walter R. Nord (eds.), *Handbook of Organization Studies* (pp. 276–292). Thousand Oaks, CA: SAGE.

Chandler, Alfred D. (1990). *Scale and Scope: The Dynamics of Industrial Capitalism*, Cambridge, MA: Belknap Press.

Chirico, Francesco (2007). "Improving the Long-run Survival of Family Firms: Knowledge-Management and Resource-Shedding Processes." Ph.D. Diss. in Economics, University of Lugano.

Cole, Patricia M. (1997). "Women in Family Business." *Family Business Review*, 10(4): 353–71.

Colli, Andrea (2003). *The History of Family Business, 1850–2000*. Cambridge: Cambridge University Press.

Fahed-Sreih, Josiane, and Salpie Djoundourian (2006). "Determinants of Longevity and Success in Lebanese Family Businesses: An Exploratory Study." *Family Business Review*, 19(3): 225–34.

Frishkoff, Patricia, and Bonnie Brown (1993). "Women on the Move in Family Business." *Business Horizons*, 36(2): 66–70.

Fukuyama, Francis (1996). *Trust: The Social Virtues and the Creation of Prosperity*. New York: Free Press.

Gallo, Miguel Á. (1991). "The Role of Family Business and Its Distinctive Characteristic Behavior in Industrial Activity." *Family Business Review*, 8(2): 83–97.

Gersick, Connie J.G. (2000). "Revolutionary Change Theories: A Multilevel Exploration of Punctuated Equilibrium Paradigm." *Academy of Management Review*, 16(1): 10–36.

Gioia, Dennis, Majken Schultz, and Kevin Corley (2000). "Organizational Identity, Image, and Adaptive Instability." *Academy of Management Review*, 25(1): 63–81.

Goffman, Erving (1959). *The Presentation of Self in Everyday Life*. New York: Doubleday.

Gulbrandsen, Trygve (2005). "Flexibility in Norwegian Family-Owned Enterprises." *Family Business Review*, 18(1): 57–76.

Gupta, Vipin, Kamala Gollakota, and S. Srinivasan (2008a). *Business Policy and Strategic Management: Text and Cases*, 2nd ed. New Delhi: Prentice Hall of India.

Gupta, Vipin, Nancy Levenburg, Lynda L. Moore, Jaideep Motwani, and Thomas Schwarz (2008b). "Exploring the Construct of Family Business in the Emerging Markets." *International Journal of Business and Emerging Markets*, 1(2): 189–208.

Gupta, Vipin, Nancy Levenburg, Lynda L. Moore, Jaideep Motwani, and Thomas Schwarz, eds. (2008c). *Culturally-sensitive Models of Family Business: A Compendium Using the GLOBE Paradigm*. Hyderabad, India: ICFAI University Press.

Handler, Wendy C. (1994). "Succession in Family Business: A Review of the Research." *Family Business Review*, 7(2): 133–57.

Hess, Martin (2004). "'Spatial' Relationships? Towards a Re-conceptualisation of Embeddedness." *Progress in Human Geography*, 28(2): 165–86.

Hofstede, Geert (2001). *Culture's Consequences: Comparing Values, Behaviors, Institutions, and Organizations across Nations*, 2nd ed. Thousand Oaks, CA: SAGE.

House, Robert, Paul J. Hanges, Mansour Javidan, Peter Dorfman, and Vipin Gupta, eds. (2004). *Culture, Leadership, and Organizations: The GLOBE Study of 62 Societies*. Thousand Oaks, CA: SAGE.

Iyer, Gopalkrishnan R. (1999). "The Impact of Religion and Reputation in the Organization of Indian Merchant Communities." *Journal of Business & Industrial Marketing*, 14(2): 102–21.

Kadushin, Alfred, and Daniel Harkness (2002). *Supervision in Social Work*. New York: Columbia University Press.

Kets de Vries, Manfred F.R., Randel S. Carlock, and Elizabeth Florent-Treacy (2007). *The Family Business on the Couch: A Psychological Perspective*. Hoboken, NJ: John Wiley & Sons.

Kotecki, Mary Lou. (2000). "Building a Future: Creating and Leveraging Organizational Resilience within the Context of History, Change and Continuity." Ph.D. Diss., Benedictine University.

Lank, Alden G. (2001). "Determinants of the Longevity of the Family Business." In G. Corbetta & D. Montemerlo (eds.), *The Role of Family in Family Business:*

Research Forum Proceedings, 12th Annual World Conference of the Family Business Network. Rome (pp. 4–6).

Lawrence, Paul R., and Jay Lorsch (1967). "Differentiation and Integration in Complex Organizations." *Administrative Science Quarterly*, 12: 1–47.

Lawrence, Thomas (1999). "Institutional Strategy." *Journal of Management*, 25(2): 161–87.

Lockwood, Nancy R. (2005). "Workplace Diversity: Leveraging the Power of Difference for Competitive Advantage." *HR Magazine*, 50(6): 1–10.

Matthews, Michael K., Michael White, and Rebbeca Long (1999). "Why Study Complexity Sciences in the Social Sciences?" *Human Relations*, 52(4): 439–62.

Muntean, Susan C. (2008). "Analyzing the Dearth in Family Business Research." In P.H. Phan and J.E. Butler (eds.), *Theoretical Developments and Future Research in Family Business*. Charlotte, NC: Information Age Publishing.

Perman, Stacy. "Centuries-Old Family Businesses Share Their Secrets." *Business Week*, May 14, 2008. Available at: http://www.businessweek.com/stories/2008–05–14 (Accessed June 10, 2008).

Piore, Michael J., and Charles F. Sabel (1984). *The Second Industrial Divide: Possibilities for Prosperity*. New York: Basic Books.

Porter, Michael E. (1990). *The Competitive Advantage of Nations*. New York: Free Press.

Powell, Walter W. (1990). "Neither Market nor Hierarchy: Network Forms of Organization." *Research in Organizational Behavior*, 12: 295–336.

Prahalad, Coimbatore K., and Gary Hamel (1990). "The Core Competence of the Corporation." *Harvard Business Review*, 68(3): 79–91.

Putnam, Robert D. (1995). "Bowling Alone: America's Declining Social Capital." *The Journal of Democracy*, 6(1): 65–78.

Richman, Barak D. (2006). "How Community Institutions Create Economic Advantage: Jewish Diamond Merchants in New York." *Law & Social Inquiry*, 31(2): 383–420.

Robert, Christopher, Tahira Probst, Joseph Martocchio, Fritz Drasgow, and John Lawler (2000). "Empowerment and Continuous Improvement in the United States, Mexico, Poland, and India: Predicting Fit on the Basis of the Dimensions of Power Distance and Individualism." *The Journal of Applied Psychology*, 85(5): 643–58.

Rosenblatt, Paul C., Roxanne M. Anderson, and Patricia A. Johnson (1985). *The Family in Business: Understanding and Dealing with the Challenges Entrepreneurial Families Face*. San Francisco, CA: Jossey-Bass.

Salvato, Carlo (2002). *Antecedents of Entrepreneurship in Three Types of Family Firms*. Jönköping International Business School, Research Report 1, Jönköping, Sweden.

Schwartz, Shalom H. (2009). "Culture Matters – National Value Cultures, Sources and Consequences." In Robert S. Wyer Jr., Chi-Yue Chiu, and Ying-Yi Hong (eds.), *Understanding Culture: Theory, Research and Application*. New York: Psychology Press.

Senge, Peter (1990). *The Fifth Discipline: The Art and Practice of the Learning Organization*. New York: Doubleday/Currency.

Seo, Myeong G., and W.E. Douglas Creed (2002). "Institutional Contradictions, Praxis and Institutional Change: A Dialectical Perspective." *Academy of Management Review*, 27(2): 222–47.

Sharma, Pramodita, James J. Chrisman, and Jess H. Chua (2003). "Succession Planning as Planned Behavior: Some Empirical Results." *Family Business Review*, 16(1): 1–15.

Söderbom, Mans, Francis Teal, and Alan Harding (2006). "The Determinants of Survival among African Manufacturing Firms." *Economic Development and Cultural Change*, 54(3): 533–55.

Srivastva, Suresh, and Ronald Fry, eds. (1992). *Executive and Organizational Continuity: Managing the Paradoxes of Stability and Change*. San Francisco, CA: Jossey-Bass.

Steen, Adam, and Lawrence S. Welch (2006). "Dancing with Giants: Acquisition and Survival of the Family Firm." *Family Business Review*, 19(4): 289–300.

Styhre, Alexander, and Mats Sundgren (2005). *Managing Creativity in Organizations*. Basingstoke, UK: Palgrave Macmillan.

Thompson, James D. (1967). *Organizations in Action: Social Science Bases of Administration Theory*. New York: McGraw-Hill.

Trompenaars, Fons (1994). *Riding the Waves of Culture: Understanding Cultural Diversity in Business*. Chicago: Irwin.

Tsui, Anne S., Sushil S. Nifadkar, and Amy Y. Ou (2009). "Nagging Problems and Modest Solutions in Cross-Cultural Research: Illustrations from Organizational Behavior Literature." In Robert S. Wyer Jr., Chi-Yue Chiu, and Ying-Yi Hong (eds.), *Understanding Culture: Theory, Research and Application* (pp. 163–86). New York: Psychology Press.

Vallejo, Manuel C. (2008). "Is the Culture of Family Firms Really Different? A Value-based Model for Its Survival through Generations." *Journal of Business Ethics*, 81(2): 261–79.

Van de Ven, Andrew H. (1986). "Central Problems in the Management of Innovation." *Management Science*, 32(5): 590–607.

Ward, John L. (1987). *Keeping the Family Business Healthy: How to Plan for Continuing Growth, Profitability, and Family Leadership*. San Francisco, CA: Jossey-Bass.

Wyer, Robert S. Jr., Chi-yue Chiu, and Ying-yi Hong, eds. (2009). *Problems and Solutions in Cross-cultural Theory, Research and Application*. New York: Psychology Press.

Yeung, Henry W.-C. (2004). *Chinese Capitalism in a Global Era: Towards Hybrid Capitalism*. London: Routledge.

7

Family Firms and the New Multinationals

Evidence from Spain

Mauro F. Guillén and Esteban García-Canal*

INTRODUCTION

The last twenty years have witnessed the rise of a new type of multi-national firm, one that, instead of leveraging technology and brands in the traditional sense, has expanded throughout the world on the basis of its ability to organize, manage, execute, and network (Guillén and García-Canal 2009, 2010). The rise of these firms, which predominantly come from upper-middle-income, emerging, and developing countries, marks the coming of age of a tier of countries that have hitherto been passive players in global economic, financial, and political affairs. It is hard to underestimate the importance of this phenomenon, as one industry after another feels the impact of the increasing size, sophistication, and geographical reach of the new multinationals, which challenges our assumptions regarding the division of labor between the developed and the emerging countries. Companies such as Embraer, Tata, Haier, and Cemex are becoming global leaders in their fields as a result of aggressive expansion strategies and the adoption of unconventional organizational structures.

Most of the new multinationals are privately held firms, mainly family-controlled and/or family-owned, though a significant number are state-owned enterprises. For instance, of the one hundred Global Challengers

* We thank Paloma Fernández Pérez, Andrea Colli, and two anonymous referees for their comments and suggestions. Financial support by the Fundación Rafael del Pino, the Spanish Ministerio de Ciencia e Innovación (Project ECO2010-18718), and FEDER is gratefully acknowledged.

listed by the Boston Consulting Group in 2009 (BCG 2009), sixty-three are family firms and thirty-one have the state as a major shareholder. This can hardly come as a surprise, given that family firms are so predominant in developing countries (La Porta, Lopez-de-Silanes, and Shleifer 1999; Claessens, Djankov, and Lang 2000; Iskander and Chamlou 2000). However, the fact that the new multinationals have based their international expansion on resources such as organizational and networking capabilities, which basically rely on the management of the company, lead us to ask whether a family-based ownership structure suits the needs of the new multinationals better than those of the established ones. Much has been written about how second and later generations can squander the legacy of the founders of family firms. However, families can act as a repository for these intangible capabilities, and we have found that the careful preparation of their gradual transfer to the following generation was a crucial factor in explaining the growth of the firms analyzed.

For the purposes of this chapter, we use the definition of family firm of Villalonga and Amit (2006), namely, companies in which the founder or a member of the family is officer, director, or owns more than 5 percent of the firm's equity. According to the data of Villalonga and Amit (2009), about 40 percent of the largest U.S. corporations on the Fortune 500 list are family firms.

In this chapter, we analyze the extent to which being a family firm helps leverage the firm's competitive advantages. Selected cases of new multinationals from Spain are our main source of empirical evidence.[1] This evidence was compiled by the authors for a wider project on the new multinationals (Guillén and García-Canal 2010) and is used here for the purposes of analyzing the impact of family ownership. The Spanish case is especially interesting, as Spain, together with South Korea and Taiwan, has produced the largest number of truly global multinationals among the countries which, back in the 1960s, were still attempting to develop a solid industrial base.[2]

---

[1] Even though some entrepreneurial developments that led to the formation of Spanish multinationals can be traced back to the beginning of the twentieth century (see Sudrià and Fernández-Pérez 2010) – most of them were abruptly ended by the Spanish civil war – the recent rise of Spanish multinational firms is a process that started in the 1980s (Guillén 2005). For a more detailed analysis of the socioeconomic context in which Spanish multinationals came of age, see Guillén (2005).

[2] Spain and South Korea have ten companies listed among the Fortune 500 ranking and Taiwan has eight.

FAMILY FIRMS AND THE NEW MULTINATIONALS

Family firms exhibit several attributes that may confer a sustainable competitive advantage on the (Sirmon and Hitt 2003):

- Firm-specific human capital: Family firms have greater levels of firm-specific knowledge than non-family firms because of lower CEO turnover rates and because the early involvement of the family offspring facilitates the accumulation and transfer of management expertise and know-how.
- Family-specific social capital: Family firms benefit from the network of ties that the members of the family have with external stakeholders. A long-term commitment to the firm allows these relationships to be developed and maintained, and, again, the early involvement of the offspring helps enhance and maintain them as well.
- Patient financial capital and survivability capital: The family-ownership structure offers an advantage when it comes to undertaking risky projects whose returns will be realized in the long term. The family as a shareholder typically does not adopt the short-term orientation of other shareholders and of the financial markets. Hence, the founder has more freedom to develop a business model.
- Lower governance costs as a result of the identification of ownership with managerial control.

Generally speaking, these advantages stem from the long-term commitment that family managers usually have toward both the firm and the other members and generations of the family, a level and depth of commitment that is very difficult to replicate when the management of the company is in the hands of a professional manager (Colli 2010). However, it should be noted that family members do not always act as the stewards of the rest of the family (Schulze et al. 2001; Eddleston and Kellermanns 2007). In fact, empirical evidence on the performance of family firms is quite inconclusive and very dependent on the specific definition of family firm used (see Miller et al. 2007 for a review). According to recent research, a positive impact is observed only in companies managed by the founder (Villalonga and Amit 2006).

Nevertheless, if we compare these advantages of family firms with the distinctive features of the new multinationals, it is plausible to argue that the family character of the firm helps preserve and develop the competitive advantages of the new multinationals. In effect, the main competitive advantages of the new multinationals are based not on technologies or brands but on their organizational capabilities and relational assets (Guillén and García-Canal 2010). Specifically, being a family firm may contribute strongly to the international expansion of the new multinationals in at least three ways: (1) by granting more freedom to the managers of the company to develop their business model; (2) by facilitating the transfer to, and exploitation of, this model in foreign markets; and (3) by making the adoption of governance structures based on trust easier. In the following sections, we analyze these three contributions of the family character of the firm, using specific cases of Spanish multinationals as illustrations.

FREEDOM TO DEVELOP THE FIRM'S BUSINESS MODEL

As noted previously, longer top management tenure at family firms, coupled with the presence of patient financial capital, gives the managers more freedom and more time to develop the business model. This is important because the main advantages of the new multinationals are based on the accrued expertise, skills, and social capital of the top managers. Thus, under these circumstances, the fact that they enjoy more freedom allows the top managers of family firms to develop a coherent business model based on these types of expertise. A prime example of this pattern of growth is Planeta, a company that, thanks to family ownership and control, managed to make the transition from book printing to multimedia, riding successive waves of innovation. In its original business, books, the company still leads the market in Spain, Portugal, and Latin America.

Planeta was founded by José Manuel Lara Hernández in 1949. The name of the company was chosen because, in his own words, "it was the biggest thing that I could think of."[3] In fact, Lara had an ambitious growth plan, first for Spain and, from 1966, for Europe and Latin America. He has been recognized for his ability to expand the market for books and cultural goods in Spanish-speaking countries by acting on both the

---

[3] "Editorial Planeta, el origen de un gran grupo," *Cataluña Económica*, November 15, 2004. This case was based on Lara Bosch (2002, 2006), Peces (2003), Marco and Gracia (2004); published interviews with Lara Bosch (*El Mundo*, September 13, 1999; *El País*, May 21, 1999; *La Razón*, October 19, 2001; *Cinco Días*, October 19, 2002; *Expansión*, December 2, 2002; *El País*, May 4, 2008) and Lara Hernández (*ABC*, June 13, 1967; *La Vanguardia*, August 19, 1994); other newspaper articles and corporate information; and an interview with Luis Elías, Secretary-General, Grupo Planeta.

supply and the demand of these goods.[4] It took more than fifty years and two generations of the family to develop fully a business model oriented to this expansion, something that would have been more difficult in a corporation oriented to short-term results. The business model of the company was based on four pillars: the proactive search for best-selling books written in Spanish; new commercial formulas to sell cultural products; the acquisitions of other publishers to expand its title collection; and alliances with other firms to gain access to content for the Spanish-speaking markets.

To promote books written in Spanish, Planeta organized up to fourteen literary awards to attract the best authors. Thanks to these awards and also to the editorial efforts of Lara, more and more authors were able to earn their living by writing (Peces 2003). The company also pioneered new formulas to sell cultural products. During the early years, it developed a sales force specializing in sales of pricey products, such as encyclopedias, on credit to the final customer. This sales force was the starting point of a division within Planeta devoted to direct sales that today sells not only encyclopedias and luxury editions of books but also a wide variety of items such as multimedia products, dining services, watches, jewelry, and fashion accessories, which are available over the Internet via the company's website. Another innovative formula introduced in the Spanish market was the sale of specialized dictionaries, encyclopedias, and other items in weekly or monthly installments, using newsstands as the distribution channel, and sometimes in collaboration with national newspapers.

The company also expanded through its acquisitions of other publishers. The main goal was to gain control of an expanding catalogue of books in print, but without integrating them into the same publishing firm. Planeta actually kept the acquisitions separate, with their own personality, readership, and brand name, each catering to a specific segment of the market. Over the years, Planeta acquired Ariel (academic books), Seix Barral (innovative novels), Ediciones Deusto (business books), Espasa Calpe (encyclopedias and academic books), Destino (literature in general), and MR Ediciones (novels and practical and esoteric books), among others. The only segment of the book market in which Planeta is still not present is textbooks in Spanish, where the main potential targets are not for sale. Planeta's presence in textbooks is limited to the French market,

---

[4] See, for instance, the biographical article written by Peces (2003). See also Fernández Moya (2010) and Prieto Martín (2006).

where it is the second largest publisher thanks to its acquisition of the Editis Group.

Finally, Planeta entered into alliances with other publishers to gain access to other types of content. A key agreement was the one signed with Larousse in 1963, whereby Planeta published the Spanish edition of the famous French encyclopedia. Another important alliance for Planeta was the 1985 agreement with Italy's De Agostini. This 50/50 joint venture focused on installment publications, interactive products, and comics. The company also entered into alliances with other publishing firms to exploit specific opportunities jointly. Technological change offered Planeta a myriad of opportunities to pursue the multimedia delivery of its content. Armed with several decades of experience and a strong cash flow from operations in Europe and Latin America, Planeta digitized its entire content in order to sell it through the Internet and other channels. The company also entered the distance-learning industry in 2002 by taking over two companies, Centro de Estudios CEAC, a traditional mail-order learning company, and Home English, a distance language teaching company. Planeta and its Italian partner De Agostini also invested jointly in the media and audiovisual industries, by promoting a new company, DeA-Planeta. Since 2003, Planeta has owned a majority stake in the Antena 3 Group, a media group that comprises a leading TV station in Spain and a radio station named Onda Cero, among other companies. Planeta is the main shareholder in *La Razón*, one of Spain's six biggest newspapers, and the sole shareholder of ADN, a free daily newspaper. In January 2010, Planeta sold its participation in Avui, the main newspaper in the Catalan language. The company has also launched an online business school in partnership with the University of Barcelona, for which part of the content is developed by Editorial Deusto (part of Planeta) and by the EAE-Business School, a Barcelona-based business school, which it acquired in 2007. In 2006, Planeta also entered the business of creating content for mobile phones by buying a 25 percent equity stake in Zed Worldwide in 2007. Thus, the corporate growth of Planeta has been a combination of diversification and vertical integration. Through the family office, Planeta has also diversified into unrelated fields such as low-cost airlines (Vueling) and banking (10 percent of Banco de Sabadell). Planeta Group is currently run by José Manuel Lara Bosch, son of the company founder. Initially, the founder of Planeta appointed his two sons, Fernando and José Manuel, as heads of the books and collectables divisions, respectively. However, after the premature death of Fernando in 1995, José Manuel became the first executive of the company.

The international expansion of Planeta started in the 1960s through wholly owned subsidiaries aimed at commercializing cultural products developed in Spain. The firm also started to publish books written by Latin American authors. The company first established operations in Colombia, Mexico, Argentina, and Venezuela (1966), followed by Chile (1968), Ecuador (1981), and Peru (2005). Local sales forces were trained and hired to promote sales on credit.[5] Planeta also made acquisitions in Latin America, including Editorial Joaquín Mortiz in Mexico (1985) and a minority stake in Editorial Sudamericana in Argentina (1984), which is presently owned by Bertelsmann. Its most important Argentine acquisitions were Emecé and Minotauro in 2001 and Paidós in 2003. Emecé is a large general publisher, while Minotauro specializes in fantasy literature and Paidós in social sciences and general interest books. In 2007, Planeta acquired, through a public offer on the Mexican stock exchange, Editorial Diana, which owns the rights to Gabriel García Márquez's books. These acquisitions consolidated the position of Planeta not only in the respective home countries of the targets but also in the entire Spanish book market, given that each purchase brought with it an expanded catalogue of books. In Latin America, Planeta also acquired Casa Editorial El Tiempo in 2007, a large Colombian media group with interests in newspapers, TV stations, book publishing, and Internet content.

Planeta's expansion was not limited to Spanish-speaking markets. The company entered Portugal in 1992 in collaboration with De Agostini. Planeta also bought Editorial Dom Quixote in 1999, although this company was subsequently sold in 2007. Planeta entered Brazil in 2000 by acquiring Barsa International Publishers, a publisher of encyclopedias and luxury editions of books. In Brazil, Planeta also created Planeta do Brazil and acquired Editora Acadamia de Inteligência in 2007, a publisher specializing in self-help books, and signed an alliance with Grupo Globo to launch a series of collectables in Brazil. The entry into non–Spanish-speaking countries taught Planeta that language was not a relevant barrier for the firm. According to Lara Bosch, language per se does not pose a barrier in these countries, whereas the difficulty in finding good local managers and editors do (Lara Bosch 2002). To tap into the Spanish-speaking market in the United States, Planeta signed an agreement with

---

5 In an interview published in 1967, Lara Hernández stated that having their own sales force in Latin America was the only way to reach the final customer for the sale of pricey books and encyclopedias on credit, as other local editors were starting to sell directly to the clients (*ABC*, June 13, 1967, reproduced in Marco and Gracia 2004: 433–4).

Random House in 1993. In 2006, the company entered into an alliance with Harper not just for the Spanish market in the United States, but also for English translations of books in Planeta's catalogue.

In 2008, Planeta acquired EDITIS, the second-largest French publishing group, founded in 1835. With a turnover of 760 million euro in the year before the acquisition, and twenty publishing companies, EDITIS positioned Planeta in the French-speaking countries thanks to both its catalogue of books in print and its distribution and logistics infrastructure. EDITIS' distribution subsidiary, Interforum, with the largest coverage of points of sale in France and branches in Belgium, Switzerland, and Canada, commercializes not only all of the EDITIS catalogue but also the works of eighty other publishing companies in French-speaking countries. Finally, Planeta now sells collectible publications in Poland and Japan.

Planeta has thus evolved from a book publisher to producing and selling a wide range of cultural goods and services through multiple channels, as well as the traditional ones, including the Internet, TV, newsstands, and mobile phones. It has also capitalized on its expertise in Internet sales by launching online travel agencies and online marketing services. In so doing, the company takes advantage of its reputation and expertise in direct marketing. As previously mentioned, it took two generations to develop such a coherent business model fully. Although the founder established the building blocks of the business model, the second generation was pivotal in both the consolidation of this model and its expansion to other businesses. Specifically, the role of Lara Bosch has been crucial in dealing with the challenges of the digital revolution. Although this revolution was undoubtedly a threat to the business model of Planeta, it was also a big opportunity. In his own words:

The digital revolution has generated ... a new customer, very heterogeneous in his or her preferences and in a permanent process of change. ... Firms that do not adapt their business model to the changing preferences and consuming habits of the society, or that are not able to identify them, will be unable to take advantage of the big opportunities of the digital revolution. (Lara Bosch 2006: 179)

Lara Bosch identified an opportunity for expanding the market for cultural goods through the Internet. In a context in which the traditional book loses its market share to new distribution channels and platforms, Planeta has no option but to ride each new wave of technological innovation.

ADVANTAGES IN TRANSFERRING AND EXPLOITING THE BUSINESS MODEL ABROAD

Incoming family members can play a key role in the international expansion of family firms. First, their early and progressive involvement within the firm makes it easier to transfer the accrued expertise to them, a transfer that is easier than in the case of an external manager. Second, this sound understanding of the business model makes it easier for them to transfer the business model to a new country if they are in charge of this transfer. This is especially important, because, in most cases, the business model must be adapted to the local environment, and, in these cases, it is critical to know which elements of the business model can be changed and which cannot.

The international expansion of ALSA into China is a good example of this advantage. Automóviles Luarca SA (ALSA), the market leader in Spain for bus services, was founded in 1923 in Luarca, in the northern region of Asturias.[6] It focuses on the provision of regularly scheduled bus passenger transportation services. The company grew by gradually expanding the number and frequency of destinations. Given that transportation is a regulated industry, growth required either obtaining new licenses or acquiring companies with licenses. After decades of organic growth, ALSA tried to take over Empresa Cosmen, another company located in Asturias and owned by the Cosmen family in 1960. Instead of accepting the offer, the Cosmen family proposed a merger between both companies. This new proposal was accepted and the family received newly issued shares of ALSA in exchange for their transportation business. One year later, José Cosmen assumed the top executive position at ALSA, and the family continued to purchase ALSA shares until they gained full control of the company.

Under the leadership of Cosmen, ALSA grew to become a bus transportation service multinational operating on four continents. This growth was facilitated by an expanding domestic market, with improvements in the highway infrastructure, and quantitative and qualitative changes in the demand for transportation services. Nowadays, ALSA offers four

---

[6] This case was based upon Bueno and Morcillo (1993), Cosmen (1994), Cosmen (2002, 2004, 2005), Bueno and Merino (2006), Fernández and Nieto (2008); published interviews with José Cosmen (*El Mundo*, April 23, 2000), Jorge Cosmen (*Las Provincias*, February 3, 2008; *Expansión*, November 8, 2001), and Andrés Cosmen (*Savia*, June 2005; *Ideas Empresariales*, 95 [2006]); other newspaper articles and corporate information; and an interview with Jacobo Cosmen.

types of service: urban transportation in twenty Spanish municipalities and in Marrakesh, Morocco; regional transportation within thirteen of Spain's nineteen autonomous communities; national transportation connecting virtually all parts of Spain; and, finally, international transportation, operating sixty-five routes that connect Spain with continental Europe, the United Kingdom, and northern Africa. ALSA also operates bus routes in Portugal, France, Belgium, Switzerland, and Germany and is a member of EUROLINES, a network of thirty-two independent European bus companies that provide single-ticket services connecting routes operated by different companies. Outside of Europe, it operates regional services in Chile and in China. ALSA merged in 2005 with National Express (NX), a U.K.-based multinational transportation group with interests in bus and rail transport. As a result of the deal, the Cosmen family became the main shareholder of NX and one of Cosmen's sons, Jorge, was appointed as a non-executive director and deputy chairman. The Cosmen family has retained the ownership of the ALSA businesses in China (where the company has been present since 1984). Similarly to what happened with the absorption of "Empresa Cosmen" by ALSA, the Cosmen family tried to gain full control of NX in 2009 by launching a tender offer. At this time, the company was in a dire financial situation that coincided with the resignation of the CEO. However, the Cosmen family withdrew the offer after exercising due diligence. Notwithstanding this, the Cosmen family remains the biggest shareholder, with a 19 percent stake in NX's equity.

Acquisitions played a key role in ALSA's growth, starting with several small companies (Turytrans, Rutas del Cantábrico S.L., Viajes por Carretera S.A.), and reaching a climax with the 1999 purchase of Enatcar, a state-owned bus transportation company. In 2007, ALSA acquired Continental, the second-largest bus transportation group in Spain, and, in 2008, it bought Transportes Colectivos, a city bus transportation firm.

A second factor in ALSA's expansion was operating efficiency. To standardize service and ensure safety, the firm invested heavily in training and bus maintenance. As Cosmen once pointed out, "our relative success in transportation is based on the establishment of effective, strategically distributed maintenance facilities" (Cosmen 1994: 166). The company trains its drivers at dedicated facilities in Madrid, Oviedo, China, Morocco, and Portugal (Fernández and Nieto 2008). As drivers are normally the only persons of the company who are in touch with clients throughout most of the process, their behavior is critical in ensuring customer satisfaction (in addition to the good use of the buses).

A third factor in ALSA's expansion has been continuous innovation in services, not only to create more customer value (for instance, by selling tickets through the Internet) but also to introduce customized services to specific types of customers. Even though bus routes are concessions in Spain, and bus companies enjoy a monopoly position over them, bus transportation is under threat of substitution by other means of transport such as private cars, railways, or airlines. Over the years, ALSA developed several innovations to persuade customers to switch to bus transportation. An example is the so-called Supra service, a nonstop intercity route that incorporates certain attributes of business class in air travel using luxury coaches with larger seats, more leg room, and complimentary services such as refreshments, newspapers, and, more recently, Wi-Fi.

In terms of international expansion, the company first decided to operate bus routes originating in Spain, and later to extend the business model developed in Spain to other countries.[7]

Despite the success of its international routes originating from Spain, the most important foreign expansion decisions had to do with direct investments. The idea was to exploit the accrued know-how from its Spanish operations to run local or regional bus routes in distant countries. The first important foray was into China, where the company established a series of fourteen joint ventures beginning in 1984. In 1999, ALSA started to invest more aggressively abroad because competition authorities barred it from further domestic growth after the acquisition of Enatcar. In 1999, ALSA won the bid for the concession for urban bus services in Marrakesh, Morocco, and, in 2001, it won approval for regional services in the same part of the country. Also in 2001, ALSA acquired 51 percent of the equity of Autobuses Lit, a leading Chilean transportation company. In 2003, ALSA acquired 49 percent of Tas Choapa, also in Chile, which enabled it to operate some international routes within Latin America. The most interesting project in Chile was the Transantiago, an ambitious undertaking aimed at improving and integrating the public transportation system in Santiago de Chile. However, after the government granted the licenses to other companies in 1995, ALSA limited its presence in this country as a financial investor. ALSA has also invested in several companies in Portugal, Germany, and France.

China was a remarkable experience for ALSA. José Cosmen was always interested in business opportunities, and the existence of an innovative

---

[7] See Fernández and Nieto (2008) for a detailed chronology of Alsa's international expansion.

toothpaste, made in China, that prevented respiratory diseases caught his attention, as many people suffer from these diseases in Asturias (Cosmen 1994). During the process of finding information about this business, he discovered that passenger transportation by bus presented a unique opportunity. China's infrastructure was underdeveloped, and transportation services were backward. However, because of regulatory restrictions, foreign investors could only operate taxis, and only in specially designated areas. Thus, in 1984, the company launched a joint venture with local partners named Nanyio Transportation Services Co. Ltd. operating in Shenzhen, a Special Economic Zone close to Hong Kong, where foreign investors were allowed to operate under certain conditions. ALSA held a 49 percent stake in the equity but considered this investment to be a good platform to learn how to operate in China and adapt to local peculiarities, and do business with a local partner. As José Cosmen observed, "at the beginning, we wanted to transfer all of our business systems and we realized that it wasn't possible. Changes ought to be introduced slowly, justifying each decision" (Cosmen 1994: 164). For a company with a long-term orientation, this early step became a first-mover advantage, as it is not easy to build business relationships with Chinese partners from scratch. Thus, when, in 1990, the government allowed foreign investors to operate bus services, ALSA was fully prepared to take advantage of the opportunity. It created a new joint venture to exploit the route connecting Beijing with the rapidly industrializing coastal city of Tianjing. ALSA offered services that China had never seen, including regular schedules and modern coaches with comfortable seats. New joint ventures were set up to operate routes between Beijing and Shanghai. The company then moved to smaller cities, launching companies in Shijiazhuang and Nanjing. Step by step, ALSA replicated its business model introducing special services such as the Imperial Class, the Chinese version of the Supra service offered in Spain. To overcome the difficulties associated with the subpar infrastructure, ALSA formed joint ventures to build bus stations, assemble buses (in collaboration with the Spanish firm Irizar), and develop and manage maintenance facilities. Over time, ALSA became an expert on the Chinese market, so the company also established an import–export subsidiary to help other companies operate in China. Andrés Cosmen, one of the sons of José Cosmen, has run the company's operations in China since 1987. Summarizing the key factors of ALSA's success in China, Andrés Cosmen noted that:

We have dedicated a lot of time and effort to developing relationships with both our Chinese partners and the Chinese administration [. . .] It is also important to adapt the business concept to China's characteristics [. . .] But it is even more important to know which aspects or processes of our business should not be changed. (Cosmen 2004: 92)

Thus, ALSA's success illustrates the importance of family involvement in the exploitation of home-country expertise in foreign countries that are very different. In fact, in Chile, a less successful experience of international expansion, no member of the family was sent as a full-time expatriate.

With regard to the importance of the family for the accumulation and transfer of managerial knowledge among its members, José Cosmen has acknowledged how being the descendent of a family of entrepreneurs contributed to mold his vision of how a company should be managed. When remembering the importance of family and family values, he stated that:

Family was then, and luckily for us, it is still now, the main center of our life.... It was the starting-point of our business activities, external relationships and new projects.... What happened in the company was always present in everyday family conversations... and, in this way, imperceptibly, my brothers and I grew up in the midst of entrepreneurial activity, because, while we were kids, we helped as we could. (Cosmen 1994: 159)

The early involvement in the company of José Cosmen's sons was also important for the transfer of the accrued management know-how and business model. As Jorge Cosmen stated in an interview, "the best option is for the two generations to overlap during a certain period of time to allow the young generation to acquire an in-depth knowledge of the company and ask for everything they need... Since we were young, we had to learn the ways of the company by working during the summer."[8] In fact, before the four male sons of Cosmen started to hold executive positions in the company, they spent a period of two to three years working in the different functional areas such as procurement, maintenance, sales warehouse, among others, to gain a comprehensive knowledge of the company and its business model. Taking this into account, it is easy to understand why the personal involvement of two generations of the Cosmen family in the Chinese subsidiary was crucial to its success.

EASE IN THE ADOPTION OF NETWORK- AND TRUST-BASED GOVERNANCE STRUCTURES

Having relatives in top management positions can simplify coordination and control tasks within the firm and assist the development of networks.

---

[8] *Expansión*, November 7, 2001.

First, as previously mentioned, family firms benefit from the network of ties that the members of the family have with external stakeholders. In addition, internal organization can be simplified by placing family members in critical positions, or even dividing the corporation into different entities headed by different members of the family.

The international expansion of Corporación Gestamp is a good example of this advantage of being a family firm. Corporación Gestamp is a vertically integrated supplier of steel products for the automotive, electrical appliances, construction, and wind power generation industries.[9] It makes products such as stampings, road barriers, shelves, and tubular steel towers. Downstream, the company also provides logistics services for its clients. Upstream, the firm is also engaged in cooperative relationships with steel manufacturers, especially Arcelor-Mittal. In 2008, Corporación Gestamp had revenues of 4,000 million euro and 15,625 employees.

The origins of Corporación Gestamp go back to the incorporation of Gonvarri in 1958 as a distributor of tin, piano strings, and steel sheets. The company was founded by Francisco Riberas Pampliega, a self-made man, and three friends of his who later left the company. Riberas was keenly aware of the growth potential of the steel sheet market, so the company established commercial links with important clients and secured the supply of steel. However, to exploit this growth potential fully, Riberas realized the importance of setting up a steel cutting line and becoming a steel service center, instead of being a mere steel sheet trader. The business model of steel service centers consists in manipulating and treating steel to provide specialized finishing and processing services to industries that need ready-to-use parts and components. Service centers play a critical role within the steel value chain, as they buy large amounts of structural steel directly from the mills, store it, sell it in small batches with the processing services required by their customers, and deliver it when needed in such a way that the steel is either directly usable by the customer, or the customer's time required to make the steel usable is reduced.

Gonvarri's first processing plant was set up in Burgos in 1966, where Riberas had been born. Riberas anticipated not only the market potential of steel services in Spain but also the importance of establishing strong

---

[9] This case was based on Lillo (2004), Montoro (2005), and Klet and García (2006); published interviews with Francisco Riberas Pampliega (*Diario de Burgos*, January 30, 2006) and Jon Riberas (*El País*, December 6, 2009); other newspaper articles and corporate information; and other data and information provided by Juan Carlos Esteban (manager of Holding Gonvarri).

links along the entire value chain, from steel producers to steel users. For this reason, the expansion of the company started by building service centers close to the main steel mills in Spain, located in Asturias, the Basque Country and Valencia. In 1972, Gonvarri acquired a majority stake in the equity of Hiasa, a small company located close to the plants of Ensidesa (now Arcelor-Mittal) in Asturias. The management of the company remained in the hands of Manuel Álvarez, the founder, until his recent retirement. Gonvarri also set up Ferrodisa in 1978 in Sagunto (Valencia) close to Altos Hornos del Mediterráneo's mill. The company also had an equity stake of 60 percent from 1986 to 1996 in Laminados Velasco, a service center located in the Basque Country, close to Altos Hornos de Vizcaya. Gonvarri ran the risk of downstream vertical integration by the steel manufacturers. To prevent this from happening, in 1992, Gonvarri sold 30 percent of its equity to Sollac Aceros in 1992 (the Spanish subsidiary of France's Usinor) and another 30 percent to Ensidesa in 1993, its two main suppliers. Although the Riberas family ended up holding less than 50 percent of the equity, they retained managerial control. Having both Ensidesa and Usinor as shareholders proved to be far from easy. Even though these two firms are part of Arcelor-Mittal now, they were fierce rivals in the 1990s. After Ensidesa (by then called Aceralia), Usinor, and Arbed merged into Arcelor in 2001, the Riberas family repurchased part of the equity owned by Arcelor, in such a way that they came to control 65 percent, with Arcelor controlling the remaining 35 percent. The only significant change in the ownership structure of Gonvarri since then was the acquisition of a 5 percent stake by Caja Madrid (a large savings bank) in 2007. For several years, as the result of a merger among domestic steel producers, the Gonvarri group kept a 6.67 percent stake in the equity of Aceralia. Gonvarri's most consequential vertical integration, however, took place downstream. The company set up its first service center in Barcelona in 1982, close to key automotive assemblers and component manufacturers. It also founded Gonvauto, a division for steel handling and cutting services for automotive clients.

The most important project launched by Gonvarri involved stamping and the subsequent creation of Gestamp Automoción. In 1986, the year Spain entered the European Union, Gonvarri acquired Estampaciones Arín. The founder of the company thought that Gonvarri could turn the company around by taking advantage of its reputation among automakers. As Francisco Riberas declared in a book describing his business experience: "I believed that I would gain contracts for Estampaciones Arín once acquired, because I had good contacts and I convinced myself that this was our opportunity" (Lillo 2004: 320).

The new stamping division started to supply PSA-Citroën and Renault. As business grew, Gestamp Automoción established two new stamping facilities, co-located with each of the assembly plants. The growth of the stamping business followed similar patterns to the initial expansion of Gonvarri in terms of technology adoption, co-location, and equity links with other firms. For instance, the large steel company Arcelor took a 35 percent equity stake in Gestamp Automoción, and Gestamp Automoción established equity links with the stamping company Sociedad Metalúrgica Hermanos Uceda.

At present, Gestamp's automotive division operates fifty-seven manufacturing plants and thirteen R&D centers in eighteen countries. The company has grown through acquisitions. In 1999, it bought Metalbages, a supplier to Opel (GM), and Matricería Deusto, a stamping firm facing a troubled financial situation. The acquisition of Metalbages was especially consequential as this company operated plants in Argentina, Brazil, and France, and also participated in Aceralia at a time when Gonvarri was also partly owned by Usinor. Through this acquisition, Corporación Gestamp consolidated its position as the main ally of Aceralia in stamping. Gestamp Automoción's main milestones in international expansion include full and partial acquisitions in Argentina (1999), Germany and Portugal (2001), Sweden (2004), and India and Turkey (2007). In 2008, Gestamp set up a greenfield stamping facility in China (in Kunshan), acquired a majority stake in a Korean firm, and entered into a joint venture with Severstal in Russia. Despite being the origin of the group, the international expansion of Gonvarri (the steel service center division) now depends on the decisions made by Gestamp Automoción.[10] As of 2008, Gonvarri had steel service centers in Portugal, Brazil, Mexico, and Slovakia. In the short term, Gonvarri plans to open new steel service centers in countries where Gestamp Automoción has manufacturing facilities, such as India, Russia, and Argentina. The existence of manufacturing plants of Gestamp

---

[10] The first international project of Gonvarri took place in 1992, when acquiring Emilsider, an Italian steel services center, followed by the purchase of Cosider in Portugal one year later. In 1997, Gonvarri established a service center in Morocco, catering to the needs of the household appliances industry, and anticipating the establishment of automobile assembly plants. These early steps, however, were disappointing, and the company sold its facilities in Morocco and Italy in 2006 and 2007, respectively. For this reason, the international expansion of the steel service activities became conditioned by the existence of manufacturing plants of Gestamp Automoción.

Automoción guarantee sufficient critical mass to open a new service center, although, once established in a new country, the company tries to gain new clients in the construction and domestic appliances industries, among others.

A final move downstream along the value chain was in the field of renewable energy. Corporación Gestamp first entered into the solar field as a turnkey contractor of solar power farms, with part of the photovoltaic infrastructure manufactured by the group at one of its facilities. In the field of wind energy, the company is directly involved as a turnkey contractor of wind power farms and as a manufacturer of the towers used to install the wind power turbines.

The company is currently run by the second generation. Two sons of Riberas are in charge of the corporation, Francisco and Jon Riberas Mera (both co-CEOs of Corporación Gestamp), each one running one of the two main arms of the company, Gestamp Automoción and Gonvarri. Both started in the company in junior management positions just after completing their university degrees, Francisco in 1988 and Jon in 1992. According to a biography of Riberas, he prepared his sons for their future involvement in the company from their early childhood and advised them to pursue a dual degree in law and business administration at such a prestigious Spanish institution as ICADE (*Instituto Católico de Administración y Dirección de Empresas*) in Madrid. He argued that:

A dual degree in Law and Business Administration would provide them with a well-rounded education ... Four years after Paco graduated ... Jon started at ICADE ... they were very interested because I inculcated them this idea slowly but surely ... They had lived through the development and expansion processes of my companies since their early childhood ... and thanks to my efforts and their dedication they have an excellent education today, they are capable and also know how to handle people. Having them beside me is the fulfillment of all my dreams, my highest pride, and the guarantee of continuation of my work. (Lillo 2004: 255–8)

Family character thus played a key role in the transformation of this company from being a small trader of steel into a vertically integrated group of companies, not only for the involvement of the second generation, but also by making use of equity links and other associations with other businessmen and other companies, such as Arcelor, and, above all, by capitalizing, in the rest of the world, on the links and reputation developed with car manufacturers in Spain. Riberas has a management style based on trust and reciprocity in his relationships with clients and partners. Manuel Álvarez, partner of Riberas in Hiasa, stated that "we never had problems...Riberas gives me plenty of autonomy...we are good friends, as it is impossible to be good partners without being good friends" (Lillo 2004: 210–11). Ángel Uceda, partner in Sociedad Metalúrgica Hermanos Uceda, stated that "Riberas has been a great partner for us, and we have been great partners for him" (Lillo 2004: 329). He also built a reputation for always honoring his commitments. As one of his clients said, "only a 'yes' on the phone or a handshake was necessary. And, no matter if the market changed or whatever else happened, he always honored his word. With Riberas no legal document was required" (Lillo 2004: 284). All of these relationships and the trust accrued would be impossible to either establish or maintain in the context of a company with a different ownership structure, as the family became a repository of the trust with other agents and as a guarantee of the continuity of the cooperative relationship. As stated by Pedro Velasco, partner of Riberas in Laminados Velasco,

We have several joint companies with the Riberas family...with whom we still have a very good friendship, and the proof of that is the economic relationship that we have. Our sons continue this friendship and are also business partners. (Lillo 2004: 317–18)

CONCLUSION

This chapter links the recent literature on the new multinationals from emerging markets with the literature dealing with the competitive advantages of family firms. We have argued that a family-based ownership structure reinforces the competitive advantages of the new multinationals, which are based on the expertise accrued, the ability to exploit this expertise in other contexts, and in networking.

We have provided case studies that illustrate how the family character of the firm suits the needs of the new multinationals. Even though the institutional environment of emerging countries does not facilitate separation of ownership and control, our cases have shown how, in a country such as Spain, which ranks better in terms of the quality of the institutional environment than the average emerging country, the family character of the firm helps the leveraging of competitive advantages based on the accumulation and development of experience and relationships. The family thus becomes a sort of a repository of both this experience gained and the relationships that continuously support the development of the company. Our research complements previous work by Puig and Fernández (2009) that showed how the internationalization of Spanish family firms was the "outcome of a silent revolution" through which these firms adjusted their resource endowments to the opportunities stemming from their environments. Specifically, our chapter has highlighted the role played by intergenerational knowledge transfer in backing such a silent revolution. Clearly, the knowledge and relational resources transferred from one generation to the next do not need to include other required resources to expand successfully abroad, such as the management of international operations or host country specific knowledge. However, as the ALSA case shows, a sound understanding of the business model is a necessary condition to adapt it to other realities.

Our explanation for the rise of multinational family firms from emerging countries can also be applied to the rise of other multinational family firms from other contexts. We argue that, in any firm whose competitive advantages is based on experience and relations, family character boosts these advantages, for the reasons outlined in this chapter. One example of this can be found in the recent development of medium-sized Italian multinationals, labeled by Colli (2009) as pocket multinationals. These multinationals have emerged from the Italian industrial districts, in which the experience and relations developed inside such clusters or districts were preserved and developed by the family supporting the company.

Last but not least, we should point out that the family character of the firm is not always an advantage. If the family supporting the firm is united, the family becomes an excellent repository for the expertise and relations accrued by the company. However, if there are tensions and conflicts in the family, the firm's family character becomes a liability as the three mechanisms through which family ownerships boosts a firm's competitiveness are deactivated.

References

Boston Consulting Group (2009). *Pamphlet: The 2009 BCG 100 New Global Challengers*, Boston MA: Boston Consulting Group, 2009. Available at: http://www.bcg.com/documents/file20519.pdf.

Bueno, Eduardo, and Carlos Merino (2006). "La Vocación Internacional como Espíritu Emprendedor. La presencia de ALSA en China." *Economía Industrial*, 362: 43–146.

Bueno, Eduardo, and Patricio Morcillo (1993). *La Dirección Eficiente*. 2nd ed. Madrid: Pirámide.

Claessens, Stijn, Simon Djankov, and Larry H.P. Lang (2000). "The Separation of Ownership and Control in East Asian Corporations." *Journal of Financial Economics*, 58(1): 81–112.

Colli, Andrea (2009). "The Revivals of the Family Firm in Italy, 1980–2005." (unpublished paper, Bocconi University).

Colli, Andrea (2010). *The History of Family Business: 1850 to 2000*. Cambridge: Cambridge University Press.

Cosmen, Andrés (2002). "Perspectivas para la empresa española en China: La experiencia de ALSA." *Información Comercial Española*, 797: 71–6.

Cosmen, Andrés (2004). "Los sistemas de gestión de las empresas de transporte en China." *Economía Exterior*, 30: 85–92.

Cosmen, Andrés (2005). "ALSA in China." IRU Shanghai Forum. Available at: http://www.iru.org/en_events_2005_shanghai_speeches_menendez_castanedo.

Cosmen, José (1994). "Experiencia de un empresario español en China." *Política Exterior*, 38: 159–71.

Eddleston, Kimberly A., and Franz W. Kellermanns (2007). "Destructive and Productive Family Relationships: A Stewardship Theory Perspective." *Journal of Business Venturing*, 22: 545–65.

Fernández, Zulima, and María Jesús Nieto (2008). "La internacionalización de ALSA." In J.C. Casillas (ed.), *La internacionalización de la empresa familiar*. Sevilla: Digital @tres.

Fernández Moya, María (2010). "La promesa del gran mercado del libro. Un siglo de editoriales españolas en Argentina 1908–2008." XIII Seminario Complutense de Historia Económica. Available at: http://www.ucm.es/centros/cont/descargas/documento18509.pdf (Accessed in 2010).

García-Canal, Esteban, and Mauro F. Guillén (2008). "Risk and the Strategy of Foreign Location Choice in Regulated Industries." *Strategic Management Journal*, 29(10): 1097–115.

Guillén, Mauro F. (2005). *The Rise of Spanish Multinationals: European Business in the Global Economy*. Cambridge: Cambridge University Press.

Guillén, Mauro F., and Esteban García-Canal (2009). "The American Model of the Multinational Firm and the 'New' Multinationals from Emerging Economies." *Academy of Management Perspectives*, 23(2): 23–35.

Guillén, Mauro F., and Esteban García-Canal (2010). *The New Multinationals. Spanish Firms in a Global Context*. Cambridge: Cambridge University Press.

Iskander, Magdi R., and N. Chamlou (2000). *Corporate Governance: A Framework for Implementation*. Washington, DC: The World Bank Group.

Klett, Pedro, and Antonio García (2006). "El papel de las TIC en el crecimiento e internacionalización de un grupo. La estrategia de Gonvarri." *Economía Industrial*, 361: 133–9.

La Porta, Rafael, Florencio Lopez-de-Silanes, and Andrei Shleifer (1999). "Corporate Ownership around the World." *Journal of Finance*, 54(2): 471–517.

Lara Bosch, José M. (2002). "Sector editorial: El caso de Planeta." *Información Comercial Española*, 799: 219–24.

Lara Bosch, José M. (2006). "La transformación del negocio de la comunicación." In E. Rollano Borús (ed.), *Nuevo paradigma de los medios de comunicación en España*. Madrid: Nueva Economía Fórum.

Lillo, Juan de (2004). *Francisco Riberas contra su destino*. Oviedo: Nobel.

Marco, Joaquín, and Jordi Gracia, eds. (2004). La Llegada de los Bárbaros. La Recepción de la Literatura Hispanoamericana en España 1960–1981. Barcelona: Edhasa.

Miller, Danny, Isabelle Le Breton-Miller, Richard H. Lester, and Albert A. Cannella (2007). "Are Family Firms Really Superior Performers?" *Journal of Corporate Finance*, 13(5): 829–58.

Montoro, María A. (2005). "El modelo Gestamp Automoción en la industria auxiliar del automóvil." *Economía Industrial*, 358: 149–58.

Peces, Teresa (2003). "José Manuel Lara Hernández: Muere el hombre perdura el mito." *Delibros*, 166: 18–21.

Prieto Martín, A. (2006). "José Manuel Lara Hernández." In F. Cabana (ed.), *Cien empresarios catalanes*. Madrid: LID Editorial.

Puig, Nuria, and Paloma Fernández Pérez (2009). "A Silent Revolution: The Internationalisation of Large Spanish Family Firms." *Business History*, 51(3): 462–83.

Schulze, William S., Michael H. Lubatkin, Richard N. Dino, and Ann K. Buchholtz (2001). "Agency Relationship in Family Firms: Theory and Evidence." *Organization Science*, 12(9): 99–116.

Sirmon, David G., and Michael A. Hitt (2003). "Managing Resources: Linking Unique Resources, Management, and Wealth Creation in Family Firms." *Entrepreneurship Theory and Practice*, 27(4): 339–57.

Sudrià, Carles, and Paloma Fernández Pérez (2010). "Introduction: The Evolution of Business History as an Academic Field in Spain." *Business History*, 52 (Special Issue Spanish Business History at the Crossroads): 359–70.

Villalonga, Belén, and Raphael Amit (2006). "How Do Family Ownership, Control, and Management Affect Firm Value?" *Journal of Financial Economics*, 80(2): 385–417.

Villalonga, Belén, and Raphael Amit (2009). "How Are U.S. Family Firms Controlled?" *Review of Financial Studies*, 228: 3047–91.

8

Finance and Family-Ness*

A Historical Overview of Assessing the Economics of Kinship

Christopher Kobrak and Pramuan Bunkanwanicha

It is the human component, the character and intelligence of the people one works and deals with, that calls for art and judgment. . . . Can we count on these people to deliver?

David Landes, *Dynasties*, p. 3

INTRODUCTION

Family business has a long history. Business people have understood its social and economic importance since ancient times, but economists are just beginning to integrate kinship relationships into their theory, sometimes looking at its direct, and sometimes merely its indirect, role. The elaboration of the value of family business has been an interdisciplinary affair, sometimes articulated in more general terms through a discussion of the owner control of firms. Although there is some distinction between family business and tightly held firms, it is hard to deny the overlap between family control and owner control. In many countries and in many periods, concentrated ownership was predominately built on kinship ties. When Adam Smith bemoaned the separation of ownership and control, there were few alternatives to family or sole proprietorship firms. Not until the 1930s, however, did social theorists first take notice of the huge shift away from closely held to widely dispersed ownership, and

---

* Strictly speaking, the word "family-ness" does not exist. We have taken liberties with suffixation, which is usually combined with an adjective to form a noun denoting some state or quality, to draw attention to the characteristics generally associated with family firms.

begin to outline the economic and social ramifications of founding owners, most of whom were families, exiting from day-to-day management,
a process that took hold in earnest in many Western countries around
the turn of the nineteenth century (Berle and Means 1932). Although
Berle and Means focused on the United States, many business historians,
following the lead of Alfred Chandler, have identified the move from
family to management control over a large swath of the world as a necessary part of companies' maturing, developing the capacity to diversify,
and thereby to build on their first-mover advantages (Chandler 1990).
Some recent studies have cast doubt on the Berle and Means story, at
least with regard to its timing and application from country to country
of the loss in relational capitalism. These studies include examinations of
the possible causes for the differences in national ownership structures,
such as legal systems (La Porta et al. 1998, 1999). But few doubt about
the importance of ownership structures for understanding a large part of
the current financial landscape in most developed countries (Rajan and
Zingales 2003; Hannah 2007).

But modern financial economics has tended to ignore, or at least to
diminish, the importance of many institutions to the financial system,
including the role of family business in creating and maintaining economic
value. During the second half of the twentieth century, under pressure
from U.S. and U.K. regulation, huge impersonal equity and debt markets came to dominate finance. Managing investments is largely based on
financial theory, mathematical modeling, diversification, rating agencies,
transparent accounting, and other forms of governance regulation, which
have replaced older forms of trust building, in which families had more of
a competitive advantage. Most financial economists have emphasized the
inefficiencies of family businesses, and their tendency to siphon off private rents or nonpecuniary rewards. Superior voting or other controlling
rights for them led not to better management, but rather to higher premi-
ums demanded by the other investors (Hannah 2011). In short, until very
recently, like many other social scientists, modern financial economists
have had little patience for the internal institutional and corporate governance factors that would draw attention to the positive contributions
of family business.

One obstacle to further study of the relationship between family influence and economics or finance is the problem of definition. Coming up
with a rigorous cutoff to separate family firms that holds up across time
and geography is difficult, to say the least. Many scholars ignore the problem altogether, while others rely on numerical cutoffs of ownership or

voting shares. The importance of definition is an old debate stretching as far back as the ancient Greeks. Like Socrates' critics, many modern social scientists would argue that one can be a cobbler or discuss shoes without articulating the essence of "shoeness." Like the shoemaker and his trade, even without a precise definition of the family firm, most of us recognize that the House of Rothschild in the nineteenth century was a family institution and Citigroup in the late twentieth century was not. Moreover, the numerical cutoffs have the advantage of precision but ignore context. A mere 5 percent of ownership, for example, might hold sway in the hands of a knowledge investor with a close relationship to the firm, as long as other investors are dispersed, while, in other situations, a passive family holding of 30 percent, say, might have no effect on the firms activities. As some researchers have noted, the power of large shareholders is highly influenced by a country's protection of minority rights. We prefer here to think of family firms as ones in which a connection to one or more families has a substantial effect on a business' strategies and competitive advantage, for good or ill. Our notion leaves a large number of gray areas, which we believe is unavoidable. However, what it lacks in precision, it makes up for in its contribution to the conceptual relevance and clarity in relation to the questions in hand.

Despite the definitional issues, during the last ten years, building on the work of social scientists, this picture has changed considerably. But long before finance turned any attention to family firms, business economists and other social scientists rediscovered families as a "fit subject for serious analysis." As early as 1985, Pollack applied Williamson's transactional approach, which had ignored family business, to correct economists' vision of "frictionless firms" and to posit some of the economic benefits of family firms. These included the ability to avoid some contracting hazards, to provide incentives and monitoring, and to add a long-term vision to company management (Pollack 1985).

Mainstream finance first took note of the value-enhancing qualities of family business in the twenty-first century. Although most studies still emphasized the value-destroying qualities of family firms, a few argued that families, by maintaining some involvement in the firms, could serve as engines of economic value. Writing against the trend in financial literature, Anderson and Reeb (2003) actually concluded that S&P 500 firms with strong family presences outperformed non-family firms. Building on the work of some early papers that first articulated the value-enhancing characteristics of families – for example, in balancing the interests of managers – Anderson and Reeb found a surprising number of S&P 500 firms with substantial family involvement and that, in contrast to most studies, these firms actually provided higher returns for investors, even after controlling for industry segments.

Other researchers have tried to explain this phenomenon. They looked at finance and family business from several vantage points: families as financiers, families and the agency problem, the conditions that favor family ownership, how families affect ownership structures, and, in general, families as sources of economic value. These other sources of economic value include the proclivity toward active management, long-term commitments, their role as substitutes for regulation and stability, providers of human capital, and even their political connections. Discussion of family business has even crept into an age-old financial debate about what should and does determine how firms determine their capital structure.

The rest of this chapter is built along the lines of the aforementioned vantage points for value creation. It offers no new empirical or theoretical insights but provides a summary of the change in views among economists about the significance of family business.

FAMILIES AS FINANCIERS

For much of history, family institutions were one of the few that provided finance, especially financing across long distances and cultures. Some of the most important work in this area has been done by economic historians. Sadly, economic historians are conspicuous in their efforts to integrate developments in financial theory, whereas financial theorists, in contrast, are conspicuous for their general lack of interest in the insights provided by history, unless history provides some direct verification of their theory.[1] Banking historians have understood the importance of families to banking in the early modern period for a long time, but several new books have linked their successes before 1914 with thoroughgoing discussions of the attributes of family banks as well as the absence of alternative institutions.

Niall Ferguson's majestic two-volume history of the Rothschild family as well as his latest book are full of anecdotal evidence about how

---

[1] See Mary O'Sullivan and Margaret B.W. Graham (2010). "Moving Forward by Looking Backward: Business History and Management Studies." *Journal of Management Studies*, 47(5): 775–90, about the importance of integrating theory into business studies, especially the study of family business. A quick review of many of the recent financial articles published since 2008 and cited here show no citing of Harold James' study of family firms (2006), whereas he cites many important financial studies.

clan ties contributed to the rise of the Rothschilds and the Warburgs. At a time when communication was vastly slower and more expensive, the Rothschilds built a financial empire that, at its peak, rivaled the economic power of several of our largest financial institutions combined. They not only influenced private individuals and companies to accept financial discipline and liberal ideals, but the brothers and later the cousins also cajoled governments to do the same. The close family ties allowed them to manage complex investments over vast distances, not just by speeding up communication, but, in large part, by making communication unnecessary because of their high degree of shared trust and values (Ferguson 1999). A recent study has demonstrated that the Rothschilds actually did much of their investing around the turn of the century in companies that they not only could control but whose markets they could easily control to produce steady, profitable returns. Their investments were clustered in companies that could be organized into cartels. They deliberately avoided companies and sectors, and whole economic regions such as the United States, that they could not "restructure" (López-Morell and O'Kean 2010).

As another eminent economic historian has pointed out the advantages of families in banking – basing his observations on those of the nineteenth-century economist Walter Bagehot, "In Banking, connections count. That means family, continuity, good marriages, dynastic succession" (Landes 2007: 8). Family banks not only served to instill confidence in their own institutions, but they were also the major actors in London's, by and large, self-regulating investment banking community. Before hostile takeovers and huge size became feasible tools for competitive advantage, intermarriage and progeny were essential parts of business development and management continuity, even among public banks (Cassis 1994).

During the so-called first period of financial globalization, family banks played a key role between creditor and debtor nations, especially between the United States and Europe. Cross-border investment into the United States, the largest debtor nation and emerging market, needed strong intermediaries. Before the second half of the twentieth century, for many reasons, joint stock companies were ill equipped to play this role. Regulation and technology restricted head-office control. With weak regulation, investors demanded active management by trustworthy agents, a role that, for the most part, only family banks could play around the turn of the century. J.P. Morgan and his father were only one of many family combinations that lured funds from Europe, especially England, to the United States, with the promise of active, on-the-scene control.

The legendary New York investment bankers of the day, Kuhn, Loeb (Warburg), Speyers, and Seligmans, did not owe their importance to local deposits or investors, but rather to their international family connections. Indeed, Ferguson and others claim that the relative decline of the Rothschild banking house was due to its inability to find a family member to go to the largest emerging market of its day, the United States. Even the large joint-stock banks relied on family ties for much of their international business.

Only when American and other regulators substituted other forms of governance and limited the ability of banks to earn above-normal rents did family-private banks lose their preeminent investment-banking role between the United States and Europe. As technology and regulation wiped out most of these family advantages in international finance, today, only in a few financial segments, such as private equity, do the virtues of family financial institutions in cross-border and domestic capital flows and governance still predominate. Kobrak (2009) told a story about two aspects of family banks that are not usually emphasized. First, their actual raison d'être was governance. They sold their competence to govern distant investments, a competence that, in some sectors, is still in demand. Second, they lost their competitive advantage in this area not because of a lack of successors or other explanations often invoked to explain family business failures, but rather because of change in the regulatory and, more general, political environment in which they worked.

FAMILIES AND THE AGENCY PROBLEM

One of the few areas of finance in which the study of families seemed to be a natural fit is agency theory, but the potential of family business reducing agency costs is only a recent contribution to this area. Like some later contributions to financial theory, such as behavioral finance, agency theory did not represent a complete rejection of the advantages of publicly held companies and large capital markets. But its development came at a time of increasing recognition that many of these companies were underperforming their risk-adjusted costs of capital and that capital markets were, perhaps, not as frictionless as hoped, both phenomena that mainstream financial theory, which includes the core ideas of the Capital Asset Pricing Model, Efficient Market Hypothesis, and Modigliani and Miller, had difficulty explaining.

Beginning in the 1970s, several financial theorists began to focus on the financial costs of different ownership structures and modes of control

(Jensen and Meckling 1976). Like Berle and Means before them, financial advocates of agency theory are focused on the cost of separation of ownership and control, not on the role of families in addressing the agency problem. Managers have their own agendas, which are not necessarily tied to those of shareholders. Diffuse ownership increases the unit costs of control and creates a free-rider problem. Michael Jensen and others argued that the separation of ownership and control implied some direct and indirect costs that influenced financing decisions. These direct costs included the cost of monitoring and financial reporting. The indirect costs included over- and underinvestment. Minority shareholders are not sufficiently incentivized to take on the monitoring chores, because, if they succeeded, other shareholders would reap the benefits of much of their work. Companies with diffuse ownership structures had an additional incentive to pay high dividends and incur debt, because the debt served as an economic check on the actions of managers.

Although Jensen was an early advocate of private equity and the reprivatization of firms, he and most other financial theorists did not connect this to family business, an odd omission considering the number of U.S. companies that are still small and family run. Private companies, family or others, reduce agency costs by better allocating the costs of monitoring with the rewards. Until very recently, insofar as families played a role in the agency literature, they were seen a siphoning-off value from the firm. For him and others, family firms played a key role in the restructuring of American companies in the 1980s, but the nature of the business is ignored. Although Jensen lists family firms as the big players expediting restructuring and control, families entering governance to create effective monitoring by actively managing management and finances are, for him, more like Japanese *keiretsu*, or groups of enterprises, rather than institutions held together and whose competitive advantages (or lack thereof) come from kinship (Jensen 2000: 64–5; James and Kobrak 2004). In short, in many discussions of the agency problem and governance, explicit recognition of the role of families in monitoring the business is omitted.

In 2000, Mark Roe, a Harvard law professor, whose first work in governance introduced a historical dimension to the literature and whose large presence in debates illustrates the interdisciplinary nature of the field, put a new twist on this thinking by adding a larger social element without focusing exclusively on families. For Roe, agency costs are higher in social democracies. He postulated that social democracies tend to discourage diffuse shareholding because the normal agency problems are harder to work out. By its nature, social democracy weakens the ties between managers and shareholders. All the normal agency problems are there, plus there are legal and social constraints on managers, who themselves are more socialized to think of the social rather than shareholder good. Block shareholding (largely families) persists as a counterweight to managers and other social groups, such as workers.

He supports his hypothesis with two arguments. The first is a clever deductive hypothesis. Imagine a company with strong supervision and projected earnings of 50 million euros. The family wants to sell. An investment banker capitalizes the earnings at a 10 percent rate, leading to a potential sales price of 500 million euro, if the underwriters can sell the shares on diffuse capital markets. But there is fear that, without the strong supervision, the projected earnings will fall to 40 million euros, because of the added relative power of other stakeholders. There is no clear way of bolstering a new board to replace the strong supervision of the strong owners who were there. To save the 100 million euros of value, the family holds on to the firm.

The second part of the argument involves more general historical comments and cross-cultural comparisons. He cited several studies that confirmed large drops in shareholder value as Germany strengthened its co-determination rules, one of the major pillars of German corporate governance that gives workers a large say in determining the corporate policy in that country. If increasing worker power as a counterweight to shareholder power reduces shareholder value, his assumption of lost value without strong shareholders becomes more credible. Roe also cited the high correlation between social democracy and concentrated ownership, and the absence of many aspects of corporate governance designed to protect diffused shareholders, such as transparent accounting, incentive compensation, and hostile takeovers. Although Roe's argument has struck a chord with many corporate governance theorists, his somewhat imprecise use of terms such as social democracy and dispersed shareholding, as well as his failure to capture the potential added social and economic value that a more cohesive society might bring to companies, has limited its influence.[2]

In the past decade, agency literature has begun to distinguish different types of agency costs and the effect of families on them. There is increasing recognition that the classic shareholder–manager conflict described

[2] Mark Roe, *Stanford University Law Review*, 2000. This article has been cited 257 times, a huge amount of citations but not nearly as high as most of his other pieces. The article was reprinted in the volume cited here (2003).

by Berle and Means (1932) and Jensen and Meckling (1976), "agency problem type I," is mitigated in a family firm because ownership and control are typically entwined, as the family with a dominant ownership stake often participates in management and policymaking. As the shareholders and managers are the same, it provides great incentives for the manager of a family firm to maximize the firm value for the interest of shareholders. However, in a family-controlled firm, another type of conflict of interests may arise, that is, the controlling shareholder–minority shareholders conflict, "agency problem type II." The activity by which a controlling shareholder (a family) extracts private benefits at the expense of minority shareholders is often called "tunneling" (Johnson et al.). The private benefits of control are expected to be large in countries in which formal institutions, especially the legal protection for investors, are poor (Burkart, Panunzi, and Shleifer 2003). Bertrand and Schoar (2006) use the cultural explanation that strong family values may inefficiently push business organizations toward family control. However, as admitted by these authors, their macro-level empirical evidence was simply suggestive.

Since the year 2000, numerous articles have explored the multifaceted effect of family businesses on a wide range of agency issues. Some recent studies provide evidence showing that the divergence of the cash-flow rights and control rights held by dominant shareholders is associated with lower firm value (Claessen et al.). Family firms with a large ownership stake, however, tend to reduce the expropriation risk. As a consequence, a positive association between cash-flow rights and firm valuation is observed (Claessen et al. 2002). Other recent studies cast doubt on the expropriation's view. Almeida and Wolfenzon (2006), for example, created a rigorous model showing that the ability to use the retained earnings of existing group firms allowed the controlling family to design its investment strategies across the group more efficiently. Although this study did not reject the expropriation hypothesis outright, it instead proposed an alternative hypothesis to explain the cross-sectional negative impact on a firm's value. Using the agency problem type I and type II distinction, Villalonga and Amit (2006) found that family ownership of the U.S. Fortune-500 firms creates value if the founder stays on to serve as a CEO or as a chairman of the firm even with a non-family CEO. But firm value is destroyed when a descendant serves as a CEO.

Some have even begun to delve into families, the agency problem, and financing issues. Theoretically, the role of family ownership on a firm's leverage is unclear. On the one hand, Jensen and Meckling (1976) and Jensen (1986) argued that debt constrains managerial expropriation by imposing fixed obligations on corporate free cash flows. Consistent with this view, in the context of family firms, the disciplining role of debt should limit expropriation by the controlling shareholder. This predicts that a high divergence of cash flow and control rights would be associated with lower leverage. On the other hand, Stulz (1988) and Ellul (2009) support the argument that debt allows controlling shareholders to control more resources without diluting their control.

Anderson, Mansi, and Reeb (2003) investigated the role of a founding family on the agency costs of debt in the United States. They found that the presence of a founding family is associated with a lower cost of debt financing for the firm. They argued that founding family firms have strong incentives to reduce agency conflicts between equity and debt claimants because of the family's interest in the firm's long-term survival and the family's concern for the firm's (that is to say, the family's) reputation.

Other studies have started to refine their conclusions. Ellul, Guntay, and Lel (2009) argued that the impact of a family on debt agency costs depends on how market discipline is exercised. Using international bond issues from 23 countries, they showed that family firms in high-investor-protection countries benefit from lower debt costs compared to non-family firms. However, family firms in low-investor protection countries suffered from higher debt costs. The results are consistent with the view that, in a high-investor-protection country, a family can mitigate debt costs through its undiversified investments, intergenerational presence, and concerns for the survival of the firm. In contrast, in a low-investor-protection country, a family can exacerbate debt costs because of its unique power position to extract private benefits, leading to a higher risk of bankruptcy, at the expense of the debt holders.

Some of the studies have been regional in scope. Bunkanwanicha, Gupta, and Rokhim (2008) studied the relationship between the ownership structure of family firms and the leverage of listed firms from Thailand and Indonesia. They found that firms with higher expropriation risk (lower cash-flow rights and lower ratio of cash-flow to control rights) have higher debt levels. They conjectured that the ownership structure with high risk of expropriation provides incentives for a controlling family to control more resources than it can expropriate.

Others have tried to gather data from a large number of firms, scattered over a broad range of countries. Ellul (2009) used the sample firms from thirty-six countries and found that family firms have higher leverage compared to non-family firms. The results are consistent with the view that debt offers a solution for family firms to obtain external finance without diluting corporate control. They also imply that debt should be used more where control is valued most. Consistent with this view, he found that family firms have even higher leverage in countries where minority shareholders are poorly protected. Faccio, Lang, and Young (2010) argued that a family-controlling shareholder chooses both a leverage and a pyramiding structure jointly. Consistent with Bunkanwanicha, Gupta, and Rokhim (2008), they found that, when creditor protection is weak, family firms with a high expropriation risk (lower ratio of cash flow to control rights) have higher leverage. In countries with strong creditor protection, family firms with a lower ratio of cash flow and control rights have lower leverage. These contrasting results based on the different level of creditor protection have been interpreted in terms of how risk is shared between the controlling and the minority shareholders.

OTHER FACTORS AFFECTING THE ECONOMIC VALUE OF FAMILY BUSINESS

Much of the evidence of the virtues of family involvement comes from outside the financial literature. Following up on the early aforementioned work of Robert Pollack, Harvey S. James Jr. argued that not only do family businesses help resolve the agency problem, but they also encourage long-term horizons for managers by providing loyal stakeholders, insurance, and stability. While recognizing that family investment imposed positive (low monitoring costs) and negative (lack of succession planning) tradeoffs, James posited that non-family firms might adopt some of the virtues of family businesses. The thrust of his paper is to outline the economic justification for family-owned firms. Indeed, he argued that instilling loyalty in times of economic insecurity, for example, might lead to higher employee retention and a long-term management orientation, important virtues for small- and medium-sized companies that make up large portions of many countries' economies, especially the growth sectors (James 1999).

In his recent book, the economic historian Harold James postulated that family businesses created economic value by providing trust and by acting as intermediaries. Unlike most financial arguments, he uses the anecdotal evidence of three families from three European countries. Drawing on these and other companies, he argues that the longevity of economic value creations, an area in which families have been very strong, should count too. Not only does he challenge the predominant view among social scientists that family business harmed economic value

(Landes 1949; Kindleberger 1964; Chandler 1977), but, accomplished historian that he is, James also distinguishes when and where, and for what kind of sectors, familiness contributed value. For example, he argues that the role of families is particularly important to markets that have suffered shocks or where capital market regulation is not well developed (James 2006).

Some papers that appeared only in the last few years have tried to go beyond the question of general family effects on value creation by examining the timing and modes of family exit or expansion more closely. Some have focused on particular cultures and others on different kinds of companies. Along these lines, Pérez-González (2006) and Bennedsen and colleagues argued that families exiting firms had a large negative causal impact on firm performance. Their findings were particularly dramatic in fast-growing sectors, industries dependent on a highly skilled labor force, and among relatively large firms. Mehrotra and colleagues found that a uniquely Japanese custom of adopting male heirs into business families allowed family firms in Japan to overcome the constraint of suboptimal succession faced by family firms elsewhere. They showed that heir-managed firms do not underperform non-family firms.

Several researchers go back to the importance of the legal or cultural context. Ellul, Pagano, and Panunzi (2010) showed how inheritance law that governed the division of the family's wealth among the family members affected the investment decisions of family firms. They found that stricter inheritance law is associated with lower investment in family firms owing to a reduction in the family firm's ability to pledge future income streams to external financiers.

But some researchers rediscovered that families are not identical in their makeup or economic impact. Bertrand and colleagues (2008) found that family structure shapes the organization of family businesses and their governance. They showed that the size of the family business group is positively associated with the number of sons. They also found that groups with more sons perform worse after family succession and also delay restructuring in response to a financial crisis. Along these lines, Bunkanwanicha, Fan, and Wiwattanakantang (2012) showed that the value of family-controlled public corporations is affected by the marriage of members of the controlling family. They found that a firm's stock price increases with the announcement that a member of the controlling family is marrying someone from a prominent business or political family. In contrast, marriages to celebrities or ordinary citizens were not associated with any abnormal stock price reaction.

UNTRAVELED ROADS

Despite the recent stream in the literature about the financial issues connected with the retention of family control, there is still a rich assortment of undeveloped research questions. As economic studies begin to reintegrate the importance of institutions, a better understanding of how and why families make decisions may help unlock some age-old questions in finance.

We still know painfully little about the corporate financing policy of family firms. Is dividend payout policy special for family firms? DeAngelo and DeAngelo (2000) used a clinical study of The Times Mirror Company, a NYSE-listed Fortune 500 firm controlled for more than one hundred years by the Chandler family, to cast doubt about the disciplinary role of corporate payout policy in a family firm. The evidence suggests that the payout policy of a firm with the presence of family as a controlling shareholder may not be consistent with the irrelevant propositions of Miller and Modigliani (1961), but is instead sometimes tailored to meet the preferences of the controlling family (Miller and Modigliani 1961: 195). The evidence is far from conclusive. More research should be done to understand the payout policy of family firms better, in detail, and the payout of firms with the presence of controlling shareholders, in general.

Very little has been done to understand why some family firms choose to use public equity markets and why some do not. The finance literature suggests that the company's size and the industry's market-to-book ratios increase the likelihood of an IPO (Pagano, Paletta, and Zingales 1998). However, anecdotal evidence appears to be inconsistent with the empirical findings in the finance literature. Many large corporations operating in a very high growth industry (e.g., retailing sector) are still privately held. A good example is the Swedish company IKEA, which is controlled by the wealthiest man in the country, Ingvar Kamprad (the founder). Another example is one of the largest discount supermarket chains, ALDI, owned by the Albrecht family, which is the richest family in Germany based on the Forbes' Billionaires ranking.

CONCLUSION

Although the number of studies by economists on the value creation of family business has risen greatly over the last decade, the evidence pointing to their financial contribution is still mixed. Several studies have contradicted the findings of Anderson and Reeb, at least for some countries and regions.[3] The evidence is still anecdotal about the ability of family firms to provide a useful corporate governance alternative in the face of weak formal institutions. Distinguishing between family firms with active family management – as opposed to those without – and determining the degree to which the family makes gains from the firm, directly or indirectly, is difficult.

We know that there are still some financial and other constraints to family firms. Shareholders are less liquid and minority shareholders often have little legal protection. Some management incentives are difficult to create. There are also public policy questions that arise from fears of unscrupulous use of political power and perceptions of social injustice in the absence of high inheritance taxes. Moreover, we still know very little about the effect of familiness on financing choices in various economic environments and in comparison with public companies.

The literature about family business has profited from the greater awareness of small firms as engines of growth in many countries, even the more developed ones such as the United States. As more and more emerging markets display their potential for growth based on alternative business structures, business theorists will probably continue to revise their judgments about the overall economic utility of kinship.

Revisionism about the value of families to enterprises is also likely to profit from the rather shaky performance of so-called market mechanisms for corporate governance in recent years. Shocked by unbridled corporate greed and the seeming indifference of many business leaders to the social significance of work, many regulators and the public at large are reconsidering the social responsibility of business and looking for ways to control its activities better. Not just banking, but many other sectors, including the so-called market for corporate control, with its virtually automatic incentives for aligning the interests of managers and shareholders, have failed to produce the desired results. Perhaps more importantly, a fundamental tenet of liberal capitalism – that of unbridled propriety rights and individual and corporate pursuits of their own interests – has been seriously shaken. For some social thinkers, the privileges accorded to the corporation of protecting shareholders from the economic and "moral" consequences of the use of their assets go to the heart of what ails our system. We should remember that much of Berle and Means' concern

---

[3] See Claessens et al. (2002) for Asian countries and Morck, Strangeland, and Yeung (2000) for Canada.

about the separation of ownership and control involved social, rather than purely economic, issues. The concentration of power, with little legal or social control, represented – for both them and many New Dealers – a political threat. Like Walter Rathenow and others in Europe, they feared the depersonalization of ownership. As they wrote in 1932, part of the justification of property rights was their contribution to the greater good:

> To him [the economist] property rights are attributes which may be attached to wealth by society and he regards them and their protection, not as an end in themselves, but as a means to a socially desirable end, namely, "a plentiful revenue and subsistence" for the people. (Berle and Means 1932: 299)

To be sure, family businesses have demonstrated their own capacity for political threats and an absence of social consciousness. But just as they served, in past eras, to bridge spaces in our regulatory frameworks, so today kinship qualities in business may represent a much-needed counterweight to the social costs of uncritical reliance on market corrections. At the very least, there are some signs that economists are beginning to broaden their approach to financial value creation to include a better understanding of the institutional dimensions to growth and stability, and a greater recognition of the dependence of financial markets on a healthy social and political "ecosystem."

References

Almeida, Heitor, and Daniel Wolfenzon (2006). "A Theory of Pyramidal Ownership and Family Business Groups." *Journal of Finance*, 61(6): 2637–81.

Anderson, Ronald C., Sattar A. Mansi, and David M. Reeb (2003). "Founding Family Ownership and the Agency Cost of Debt." *Journal of Financial Economics*, 68(2): 263–85.

Anderson, Roland C., and David M. Reeb (2003). "Founding-Family Ownership and Firm Performance: Evidence from the S&P 500." *Journal of Finance*, 58(3): 1301–28.

Bennedsen, Morten, Kasper Meisner Nielsen, Francisco Perez-Gonzales, and Daniel Wolfenzon (2007). "Inside the Family Firm: The Role of Families in Succession Decisions and Performance." *Quarterly Journal of Economics*, 122(2): 647–91.

Berle, Adolf A., and Gardiner Means (1932). *The Modern Corporation and Private Property*. New Brunswick, NJ: Transaction Publishers, 2002.

Bertrand, Marianne, Simon Johnson, Krislert Samphantharak, and Antoinette Schoar (2008). "Mixing Family with Business: A Study of Thai Business Groups and the Families behind Them." *Journal of Financial Economics*, 88(3): 466–98.

Bertrand, Marianne, and Antoinette Schoar (2006). "The Role of Family in Family Firms." *Journal of Economic Perspectives*, 20(2): 73–96.

Bunkanwanicha, Pramuan, Joseph P.H. Fan, and Yupana Wiwattanakantang (forthcoming). "The Value of Marriage to Family Firms." *Journal of Financial and Quantitative Analysis*.

Bunkanwanicha, Pramuan, Jyoti Gupta, and Rofikoh Rokhim (2008). "Debt and Entrenchment: Evidence from Thailand and Indonesia." *European Journal of Operational Research*, 185(3): 1578–95.

Burkart, Mike, Fausto Panunzi, and Andrei Shleifer (2003). "Family Firms." *Journal of Finance*, 58(5): 2167–201.

Cassis, Youssef (1994). *City Bankers: 1890–1914*. Cambridge: Cambridge University Press.

Chandler, Alfred D. (1977). *The Visible Hand: The Managerial Revolution in American Business*. Cambridge, MA: Harvard University Press.

Chandler, Alfred D. Jr. (1990). *Scale and Scope: The Dynamics of Industrial Capitalism*. Cambridge, MA: Harvard University Press.

Claessens, Stijn, Simeon Djankov, Joseph P.H. Fan, and Larry H.P. Lang (2002). "Disentangling the Incentive and Entrenchment Effects of Large Shareholdings." *Journal of Finance*, 57(6): 2741–71.

DeAngelo, Harry, and Linda DeAngelo (2000). "Controlling Stockholders and the Disciplinary Role of Corporate Payout Policy: A Study of the Times Mirror Company." *Journal of Financial Economics*, 56(2): 153–207.

De Long, J. Bradford (1991). "Did J.P. Morgan's Men Add Value? An Economist's Perspective on Financial Capitalism." In Peter Temin (ed.), *Inside the Business Enterprise: Historical Perspectives on the Use of Information*. Chicago: University of Chicago Press.

Ellul, Andrew (2009). "Control Motivations and Capital Structure Decisions." Working Paper, Indiana University.

Ellul, Andrew, Levent Guntay, and Ugur Lel (2009). "Blockholders, Debt Agency Costs and Legal Protection." FRB International Finance Discussion Paper No. 908.

Ellul, Andrew, Marco Pagano, and Fausto Panunzi (2010). "Inheritance Law and Investment in Family Firms." *American Economic Review*, 100(5): 2414–50.

Faccio, Mara, Larry H.P. Lang, and Leslie Young (2010). "Pyramiding vs. Leverage in Corporate Groups: International Evidence." *Journal of International Business Studies*, 41(1): 88–104.

Ferguson, Niall (1999). *The House of Rothschild*. New York: Viking.

Hannah, Leslie (2007). "The 'Divorce' of Ownership from Control from 1900 Onwards." *Business History*, 49(4): 404–38.

Hannah, Leslie (2011). "J.P. Morgan in London and New York before 1914." *Business History Review*, 85(01): 113–150.

James, Harold (2006). *Family Capitalism*. Cambridge, MA: Harvard University Press.

James, Harold, and Christopher Kobrak (2004). "Persistent Traditions: Family Business in Germany." Presented at Johns Hopkins, September 2004. In preparation for publication in volume edited by Lou Galambos and Caroline Fohlin.

James, Harvey S. Jr. (1999). "Owner as Manager, Extended Horizons and the Family Firm." *International Journal of the Economics of Business*, 6(1): 41–55.

Jensen, Michael C. (1986). "The Agency Costs of Free Cash Flow: Corporate Finance and Takeovers." *American Economic Review*, 76(2): 323–9.

Jensen, Michael C. (2000). *A Theory of the Firm: Governance, Residual Claims, and Organizational Forms*. Cambridge, MA: Harvard University Press.

Jensen, Michael C., and William M. Meckling (1976). "Theory of the Firm: Managerial Behavior, Agency Costs and Ownership Structure." *Journal of Financial Economics*, 3(4): 305–60.

Johnson, Simon, Rafael La Porta, Florencio Lopez-de-Silanes, and Andrei Shleifer (2000). "Tunnelling," *American Economic Review*, 90(2): 22–7.

Kindleberger, Charles P. (1964). *Economic Growth in France and Britain, 1851– 1950*. Oxford: Oxford University Press.

Kobrak, Christopher (2008). *Banking on Global Markets: Deutsche Bank and the United States, 1870 to the Present*. Cambridge: Cambridge University Press.

Kobrak, Christopher (2009). "Family Finance: Value Creation and the Democratization of Cross-border Governance." *Enterprise and Society*, 10(1): 38–89.

Landes, David (1949). "French Entrepreneurship and Industrial Growth in the Nineteenth Century." *Journal of Economic History*, 9(1): 45–61.

Landes, David (2007). *Dynasties: Fortunes and Misfortunes in the World's Great Family Businesses*. London: Viking.

La Porta, Rafael, Florencio Lopez-de-Silanes, and Andrei Shleifer (1999). "Corporate Ownership around the World." *Journal of Finance*, 54(2): 471–517.

La Porta, Rafael, Florencio Lopez-de-Silanes, Andrei Shleifer, and Robert Vishny (1998). "Law and Finance." *Journal of Political Economy*, 106(6): 1113–55.

Lopez-Morell, Miguel A., and José M. O'Kean (2010). "Seeking Out and Building Monopolies: Rothschild Strategies in Non-ferrous Metals International Markets (1830–1940)." Working Paper. Working Paper ECON 10.17 – Department of Economics Universidad Pablo Olavide.

Mehrotra, Vikas, Randall Morck, Jungwook Shim, and Yupana Wiwattanakantang (forthcoming). "Adoptive Expectations: Rising Son Tournaments in Japanese Family Firms." *Journal of Financial Economics*.

Miller, Merton H., and Franco Modigliani (1961). "Dividend Policy, Growth and the Valuation of Shares." *Journal of Business*, 34(4): 411–33.

Morck, Randall, David A. Stangeland, and Bernard Yeung (2000). "Inherited Wealth, Corporate Control, and Economic Growth: The Canadian Disease." In R. Morck (ed.), *Concentrated Corporate Ownership*. National Bureau of Economic Research Conference Volume. Chicago: University of Chicago Press: 319–72.

O'Sullivan, Mary, and Margaret B.W. Graham (2010). "Moving Forward by Looking Backward: Business History and Management Studies." *Journal of Management Studies*, 47(5): 775–90.

Pagano, Marco, Fabio Panetta, and Luigi Zingales (1998). "Why Do Companies Go Public? An Empirical Analysis." *Journal of Finance*, 53(1): 27–64.

Pérez-González, Francisco (2006). "Inherited Control and Firm Performance." *American Economic Review*, 96(5): 1559–88.

Pollack, Robert A. (1985). "A Transaction Cost Approach to Families and Households." *Journal of Economic Literature*, 23(2): 581–608.

Rajan, Raghuram G., and Luigi Zingales (2003). "The Great Reversals: The Politics of Financial Development in the Twentieth Century." *Journal of Financial Economics*, 69(1): 5–50.

Roe, Mark (2003). *Political Determinants of Corporate Governance: Political Context, Corporate Impact.* Oxford: Oxford University Press.

Stulz, René M. (1988). "Managerial Control and Voting Rights: Financing Policies and the Market for Corporate Control." *Journal of Financial Economics*, 20(1–2): 25–54.

Villalonga, Belén, and Raphael Amit (2006). "How Do Family Ownership, Control, and Management Affect Firm Value?" *Journal of Financial Economics*, 80(2): 385–417.

PART THREE

ENDOGENOUS DETERMINANTS

Inside the Black Box

9

The Women of the Family Business

Christine Blondel, with the collaboration of Marina Niforos

INTRODUCTION

Women have always been pillars of family business endurance, in many different ways, even though their contribution has, most of the time, hardly been visible or even recognized. The evolution of society, alongside the "professionalization" of family business leadership and governance, all contributes to the opening of new possibilities as well as increased visibility for women. This chapter explores this (r)evolution, from the historical roles of the "hidden giants," to that of visible leaders, and the challenges and opportunities that this evolution entails.

HISTORICAL ROLES: THE "HIDDEN GIANTS," OR WOMEN AS INVISIBLE PILLARS OF FAMILY BUSINESS ENDURANCE

Long-lasting family firms present numerous examples of the contributions of women to the sustaining of the business and the family legacy. The following example of a fourth-generation French family firm illustrates how the founder's spouse, and the women from the succeeding generations, have supported the family business from generation to generation (Blondel 2005, p.5):

The company was created after World War I. The founder's wife, although she did not work officially in the firm, had a great influence on its philosophy and values – for instance, by conveying her wariness of debts. The founder's son took over from his father. The daughters (the second generation of women in the family) became shareholders, albeit to a lesser extent than their brother; they did not usually work, but supported their brother and helped carrying out tasks in the firm during the war.

When time came for the third generation, one of the founder's grandsons took over the firm. At that time (the 1970s), women rarely worked out of choice, but often to cope with a "crisis" such as their husband's death or a divorce. That was the case for the CEO's sister; she joined the firm and took progressively a part as co-ordinator of the ownership group – in charge of all the family's patrimonial affairs, but also in a more informal way, of family cohesion. Thanks to her relational work, her brother could spend his energy on the management of the firm. He also liked to have her opinion on some of the corporate issues.

The CEO's daughter, a member of the fourth generation of family members, naturally started working after her university degree, but in another company. It was only after this first successful experience that she joined the family business. Whether she will walk in her aunt's steps or in her father's steps is still an open question, but she will probably have more options than her predecessors.

This particular example brings to the fore some classical elements of the contributions of women, such as the transmission of values, the care for family relationships and cohesion, and also their support in the business and in the handling of ownership matters. We note that the share the founder's daughters inherited was not equal to that of their brother (at that time, ownership was often linked to business leadership, which was predominantly masculine) and that, in the second and third generations, women joined the family business out of necessity – the need for a workforce in times of war and the need to work for personal reasons. The situation is different for the current CEO's daughter, now in her thirties: for her, having a career seems only natural – a career that she started outside before joining the family business on professional terms.

Supporting Wives and Business Partners

One of the most traditional roles that women played, and still play, in many family businesses is that of spousal support. Kaye (1999) reminds us that an index of a family firm's success can be found in the caliber of talent that it manages to attract and retain through marriage. In the 2007 American family business survey (Glavin, Astrachan, and Green 2007), business owners' spouses, both men and women, were presented as their most trusted advisors.

Even when they are not formally employed by the firm, spouses may have an influence in some key business decisions, for instance, the selection of executives. Blondel (2005) recounts the influence that the family leaders' spouses and daughters had in the recruitment of a family office CEO: three candidates had been short-listed for the position. Each of them, with his wife, met the "women of the family." The latter were able to have a sense of the candidates' values and attitudes when they interacted over lunch – their observations included the interactions of the candidates with their own wives – and influenced the final decision on the criteria of the best fit of values between the owning family and the future CEO.

Spouses can assume official or non-official functions in the company – often with little status or pay. In the Swedish Bonnier publishing "dynasty," which traces its origins back to 1804, Annelie Karlsson Stider (2001, p. 99) recounts that "The daughters of Albert Bonnier, founder of the Bonnier empire, and the wives of the following generations, helped their husbands to perform tasks of a purely publishing nature (e.g., assessing manuscripts)."

Curt Carlson, the founder of the Carlson Companies group, now one of the largest family businesses in the United States, acknowledged the support that he received from his wife at the very beginning of his venture (Carlock 1999, p. 89): "My wife was my only support because nobody knew what stamps were... in the shops, my wife wore the blue and golden uniform and sat at a table answering questions as the customers came in...."

Another direct contribution brought by wives to the business is financial: bringing in capital, or earning money for the family, and sometimes simultaneously working both in the family business and outside (Rowe and Hong 2000).

The Ambassadors and Enhancers of "Social and Cultural Capital"

A subtle and vital role played by women in enduring family firms was the cultivation and development of relationships and networks, in other words, of the social capital of the family and the family business. The role of "good marriages" as enhancers of connections is underlined by Landes in his study of dynasties (2007, p. 8, quoted by Kobrak and Bunkanwanicha in Chapter 8 in this volume): "In banking, connections count. That means family, continuity, good marriages, dynastic succession."

Annelie Karlsson Stider (2001, p. 83) describes the home as a "disregarded managerial arena." In her aforementioned study of the Bonnier family, she focuses on the role played by women, namely, in the development of the social network, that is, the relations with the major contacts of the company (pp. 98–101):

The wives of the first generations had access to the management arenas and processes of the home. They were not owners and were not employed by the firm, but, despite this, they associated with its leading men. They made their home, Manilla, the great meeting-place for family and company [...] they gave dinners for company associates in their homes [...]

The wife's role is to give business meetings a personal – even a private – air, and to strengthen the family's personal ties with potential customers and business associates (...). To disregard the home and the wives in the management process is to present an incomplete picture of management (...). Entertaining is thus not a private affair or a way of reproducing contacts with business associates. It is a strategy for converting social and cultural capital into financial gain.

The women of the family had an implicit responsibility to nurture the social capital (these notions were developed, in particular, by the French sociologist Pierre Bourdieu, 1979) that would be useful for the family and for the business. Not only did they contribute to its development, but they also transmitted it to the next generation, together with the "cultural capital," a notion developed by Bourdieu (1979).

Women as the Mothers of the Next Generation, Facilitators of Transmission, and "Emotional Leaders" of the Family

Endurance of the family business is possible only if it can be transmitted to the next generation: "The name of the firm must continue; and The family involvement in the firm must continue" (Sharma and Salvato, Chapter 2 in this volume). Belardinelli (2002) posits that the spirit and the virtues essential for building a financial enterprise are not produced automatically – they need to be cultivated.

Several scholars suggest that family business transmission starts before any successor joins the business. Garcia-Alvarez et al. (2002) propose two stages of early socialization: the first stage, for all descendants, comprises value transmission and training. The second stage, reserved to potential successors, is business socialization. Lambrecht (2005) posits that the transfer of family businesses is "a lifelong, continuous process, in which the family must address and foster the soft elements of the transfer process: entrepreneurship, freedom, values, outside experience, upbringing, and education." Christina Lubinski (2011) studied the period of "anticipatory socialization," prior to the successor's entering the business, and when social capital and cultural capital are transmitted (also referring to

Bourdieu). Education, values, and early socialization are typically transmitted by both parents, independently of whether they work in the firm or not, and, most of all, by the one most present at home – traditionally, the mother. Agulles, Ceja, and Tàpies (Chapter 10 in this volume) identified generosity, humility, and communication as values of enduring family firms, values that are typically transmitted at home from the earliest years of life.

The development and transmission of social capital and cultural capital do not just support the longevity of the family business; this "family capital" can also support new ventures started by family members, another route for the sustainability of the business family (Anderson, Jack, and Drakopoulou Dodd 2005; Rodriguez, Tuggle, and Hackett 2009; Steier 2009).

During the leadership transmission itself, mothers and wives can play the important role of conciliators, especially between father and son. In a striking illustration of this phenomenon, the fifth-generation male leader of a multibillion-dollar company introduced – at a conference – the moderator who had facilitated the transition between his father and himself: those present were treated to the surprise of seeing his mother come on stage. More generally, women often assume the role of emotional leaders of the family. When the "matriarch" dies, the resulting emptiness and void can be felt.

In summary, women take part in the creation of capital for the family firm in various ways: as business partners, they support their husbands, contribute to vital functions in the business, and bring in financial capital, directly or indirectly; as spouses, they contribute to the development of the social, cultural, and symbolic capital through relationships with different stakeholders; as mothers and as "matriarchs" in charge of family cohesion, they develop the human and emotional capital. Because these roles are key, but nonetheless often not acknowledged, we call them the "hidden giants." Using the three-circle model developed by Tagiuri and Davis (1982), we can position their numerous possible contributions (Figure 9.1).

Challenges for the "Hidden Giants"

As mentioned, these roles have largely been played in the shadow. Even wives in "co-preneur" couples (couples starting businesses together), have often been perceived as subalterns to their husbands (Hollander and Bukowitz 1990).

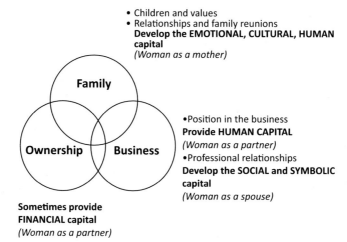

- Children and values
- Relationships and family reunions
Develop the EMOTIONAL, CULTURAL, HUMAN capital
(Woman as a mother)

•Position in the business
Provide HUMAN CAPITAL
(Woman as a partner)
•Professional relationships
Develop the SOCIAL and SYMBOLIC capital
(Woman as a spouse)

Sometimes provide FINANCIAL capital
(Woman as a partner)

FIGURE 9.1. The roles played by the "hidden giants." (Adapted from Blondel 2005, 2011.)

The invisibility of women in support roles was documented in a more general setting by Rosabeth Moss Kanter. In her book, *Men and Women of the Corporation* (1977), she analyzed the role of women in business. Similarly to what we have seen in family firms, she described the role of executive spouses who worked indirectly for the company by supporting their husbands and participating in the receptions of the partners of the firm. She also noted that this role had an implication for women working in the company: the secretaries acted as invisible forms of support within the company, and any women who endeavored to make a career suffered from being assimilated to these supportive roles. More recently, Joyce K. Fletcher (1999 and 2001) has explained how women often carry out a necessary, yet often hidden, task within the companies: namely, relational practice. She defines relational practice as a means of achieving the objectives and tasks by using talents such as listening, mutualism, reciprocity, and sensitivity to the emotional context, and states that "most people have a (largely female) network of people supporting their so-called individual achievement" (Fletcher 2001, p. 2).

A challenge that some spouses may be faced with is that of being seen by others as such – and confined to this role in its most restrictive sense. Their own professional achievements or qualities may be ignored. Women who have had a successful career can suffer from feeling belittled. Some can have the feeling that they only count as their husbands' shadows or as the successors' mothers.

TRADITIONAL SUCCESSION PATHS: TRANSPARENT DAUGHTERS

Daughters Transparent for Their Parents and Brothers

Until recently, daughters were often overlooked in succession paths, and the pioneers in the study of female successors qualified them as "invisible" (Dumas 1989, p. 39: "The invisible successor," Hollander and Bukowitz 1990). Dumas (1989, p. 39) states that the fifteen fathers whom she interviewed for her study all said that they had not considered their daughters as viable successors, either before or after they had joined the business. But also, "Similarly, all the daughters interviewed had never even considered entering the family business, let alone becoming manager or successor, until a crisis or unforeseen circumstances had forced them to consider the family business as a source of employment."

We have to keep in mind that the evolution of the role of women in family businesses mirrors their evolution in society and business at large. As recounted by Gillis-Donovan and Moynihan-Bradt (1990, p. 154, also quoting Blau 1984),

Prior to 1940, the average American female worker was young and single. Middle-class values dictated that mothers (and most married women) could seek jobs only under conditions of economic hardship. A family's status was generally provided by the husband's employment; the husband would lose status for having a working wife. If a man appeared weak or a failure, his wife also lost status; a married woman's status was determined by her husband's level of success. These social norms created a net of respectable invisibility around women who could work in the family business but leave the titles, money, and credit to others.

These social norms applied to the spouses of the family business leaders (our hidden giants) and to their daughters. The authors mention the case of a wife who played a major, yet largely invisible, role in the business (which she contributed to finance): she did not consider her daughters to be successors but did consider her sons-in-law.

Culture clearly plays a key role in the consideration of daughters as potential successors (see Gupta in Chapter 6 in this volume, as well as Helkias et al. 2011) and the evolution, though real, is slow: "Gender splitting, in the form of expectations of family and society, still pushes women more than men into the role of caretakers, not only in their families but often in their careers as well" (Lansberg 1999, p. 158).

When it comes to considering roles in the family business, the transparency of daughters is still more frequent than one might expect in the twenty-first century. Recent MBA graduates made a striking discovery

(Blondel 2005, p. 12): "This experience has been a revelation on a question I had not thought much about up to now, i.e., the role my sister could have in the family firm. I think I had made the same assumption as most men in their company – i.e., that our sisters were not interested in getting involved."

This candid admission is interesting in that it reflects the fact that daughters are often not overlooked voluntarily. Assumptions that "they are not interested" are being made without even realizing that, if asked, they might have a different opinion. An instant survey done with voting devices at the Family Business Network Summit in Berlin[1] (2007) showed an interesting twist in perception: when asked about the likeliness of a woman becoming the next family business leader, 30 percent of the men in the room replied positively, compared to 50 percent of the women (in Blondel 2011).

Of the Risks of Leaving Out the Daughters in Family Firms

Today, with women studying even more than men (58.9 percent of university degrees in 2006, according to the EC Women and Decision-Making Report 2008, in Niforos 2010), excluding women from succession paths can deprive the company of human and financial resources, and even sometimes generate resentment toward both the family and the company.

Depriving the Company of Financial Resources. Traditionally, the daughters of the family were not to be involved in the firm: they would marry and join their husband's family. Thus, to protect them from the risks of the company, they did not receive any shares in the family firm, but received compensation, instead, in the form either of real estate or of other goods.

Excluding daughters from any shareholding compelled the family to find other resources to make it up for them. Sometimes, the family separated the business operations from the property, the latter (providing more stable income) being given to the girls and the business operations to the boys who were going to work in the company. But generally, these patterns deprived the company of certain resources: the money distributed to the girls could not be used to develop the business.

Hence, one of the very practical reasons for giving shares to daughters was to keep the money to develop the business: "We had to include women in the ownership for very practical reasons: we needed the money

[1] Survey conducted by the author, with voting devices, in an audience of about 500 members of business families, Family Business Network Summit, Berlin 2007.

for business expansion and could not afford to continue compensating daughters with cash for the fact that they were excluded from ownership" (in Blondel 2005, p. 17).

Depriving the Company of Human Resources. Excluding women from any shareholding removes them and their descendants from the family firm, be they men or women. A typical case is that of Steve (in Van der Heyden, Blondel, and Carlock 2005, p. 15):

This young executive with several years of successful management experience in a large multinational corporation was interested in exploring career opportunities in the family business. However, he never initiated the communication with his uncle about a potential career within the family business. Why? Because in the previous generation, women did not receive shares in the business, as was probably judged fair at that time. Ownership and employment were restricted to the male heirs bearing the family name. Unfortunately, the males of Steve's generation who had the "right" name lacked interest and preparation to management. Steve felt a particular attachment to his grandfather and wished to see the family legacy perpetuated. But he was not considered for the job. The business was ultimately sold: the consolidation of the industry was the primary reason, but one could wonder if the lack of successor was not another important consideration.

Nowadays, women are more and more frequently included as shareholders, at least in Europe. Another step is to consider them for management or governance positions, which may be seen as an opportunity to leverage the human capital of the family.

Generating Negative Energies. Not only can the exclusion of women deprive the company of important human and financial resources, it can also, in some instances, create resentment that will generate negative energy, conflicts, and frustration.

For instance, we mentioned earlier that it was rather common, until recently, to give shares from the firm to sons and to give the daughters other assets or real estate as compensation. Although this may have been fair at the time, perceptions of unfairness are sometimes observed in the following generations, after a different evolution of the respective values of the inheritance, or because some branches of the family find themselves excluded from the family business.

In some families, corrective actions have been taken: in the most generous instances, shares have been redistributed by men who wished to restore balance and peace in the family. Other families initiate new communication, recognizing the difference in treatment carried out in the past, and engage women in the family or business governance. These changes are not always easy to bring about, as they are highly dependent on the culture of the surrounding society/the culture in which they are embedded.

BECOMING VISIBLE: WIDOWS

A very old succession pattern is that of widows succeeding their husbands. In these cases, the invisible partner suddenly becomes visible. These women take over until their children are ready. This can be the occasion for them to uncover their talents and a great motivation for their role as leaders.

The Pivotal Role of Widows in Long-lasting Dynasties

Many business dynasties have been sustained thanks to the leadership of widows at some point in their history. The famous brand of champagne Veuve Clicquot (the "widow Clicquot") is named after the woman who, after having lost her husband at the age of twenty-seven in 1805, developed and transformed the business with a firm hand. She retired at the age of sixty-four but is said to have continued to follow the business closely (*Histoire d'entreprises*, 2008). Susanna Fellman mentions that the two women found in her study of leadership were both widows, and she mentions the "legendary figure in Finnish business history," Marie Hackman, wife of Johan Hackman, who, after the death of her husband in 1807, led the Hackman trading house with decisiveness for fifty years ("*Marie Hackman.*" *Suomen Kansallisbibiliografia*, Fellman, 2013, Chapter 11 in this volume). Widows held the reins in many long-lasting dynasties, such as Krupp, Haniel (James 2006), de Dietrich (Blondel 2008), and Wendel (Blondel and Van der Heyden 1999a, pp. 2–4):[2]

In the Wendel family, which bought its first ironworks in France in 1704, a woman, Marguerite d'Hausen, managed the ironworks during the French Revolution, as of 1789. During the unrest of the time, one of her children was condemned to death. Most family members chose to go into exile. Despite her age (she was sixty-nine in 1789), Marguerite d'Hausen remained in France to manage the ironworks, her son and sons-in-law having emigrated. She showed great tenacity, energy and courage on all fronts: in the ironworks to supervise the production as well as in Paris to get paid, so as to be able to pay the employees and their family.

---

[2] Please note that the following three paragraphs are not specific quotations from the authors, but summaries of the authors cited, hence the omission of inverted commas.

Two generations later, when her grandson died in 1825, he left the ownership of the forges to his wife, Josephine de Fischer de Dicourt. Becoming a widow at the age of forty-one, she lived for another forty-seven years. She managed the forges with her son and her son-in-law over a period that saw significant development of the business with the construction of railways and iron ships. New coal collieries were open, new forges built as well as schools, housing and churches for employees – the employment figures of the forges exceeded 10,000.

At the age of eighty-six, having lost her husband and her children, she organized the transmission of the ironworks' shareholding to her grandchildren. The articles of association of the company which she created in 1871 gave guidelines for the family firm, which are still very much alive in the twenty-first century. She had set the principles regarding the transfer of shares, the sharing of profits, and the roles of in-laws.

These women who, at first, thought they would act as a link between their deceased husbands and their young children, often found that they had a talent, even a passion, for the management of the firm.

Unusual Paths of Succession: Daughters as Widows

A striking succession path is that of Katharine Graham, a former leader of the *Washington Post*. Although she was the daughter of the owner, it is her husband who had assumed the leadership and who had the majority of the shares of the company. But he committed suicide and she succeeded him, as his widow, continuing her family legacy.

When her father appointed her husband as successor, she commented in her autobiography: "Far from troubling me that my father thought of my husband and not me, it pleased me. In fact, it never crossed my mind that he might have viewed me as someone to take on an important job at the paper" (Graham 1997, quoted in Smith and Epstein, 2001, p. 5).

Her husband ended his life in 1963, and Katherine Graham found herself with four children aged from 11 to 20 years old, as well as the responsibility to decide over the future of the company: "When my husband died, I had three choices. I could sell it. I could find somebody else to run it. Or I could go to work. And that was no choice at all" (Smith and Epstein, 2001, p. 5).

She very soon announced to the Board of Directors of the *Post* that the company would stay in the family and took over as president. "Madame Graham" led the *Washington Post* through two famous episodes in American journalism, the publication in 1971 of the Pentagon Papers and the Watergate scandal – which led to Richard M. Nixon's resignation as

President of the United States in 1974. Together with Benjamin C. Bradlee, the editor she had chosen to manage the information room, she changed the *Post* and its reputation. However, she was far from self-confident when she took over: "When I first took over The Washington Post Company in 1963, I seemed to be carrying inadequacy as baggage. What most got in the way of my doing the kind of job I wanted to do was my insecurity."

What a contrast with the mark that she left:

The nation's capital and our entire nation today mourn the loss of the beloved first lady of Washington and American journalism, Katharine Graham. Mrs. Graham became a legend in her own lifetime because she was a true leader and a true lady, steely yet shy, powerful yet humble, known for her integrity, and always gracious and generous to others. (President George W. Bush at her funeral in 2001, related by Smith and Epstein, 2001, p. 1)

Throughout her career, Katharine Graham knew how to find support, either from the managers of the newspapers, or from people from outside. Warren Buffet, for instance, joined her board of directors and often advised her.

THE REVOLUTION: THE INCREASED LEADERSHIP VISIBILITY OF WOMEN

The Evolution of Society and the Accession of Women to Business Leadership Roles

During the past decades, only a few women were visible in significant business positions, most of whom actually came from family firms. More women are now being appointed as CEOs of major firms. The evolution of women leadership in family firms seems to have surged in the recent years: if confirmed by further surveys, the numbers of the 2007 American Family Business Survey (among 650 respondents) show a substantial increase in the number of women in a CEO position in five years: from 9.5 percent in 2002 to 24 percent in 2007.

This evolution, in our view, can be linked to general trends both in society at large and in family businesses in particular, which challenge the traditional succession patterns: the evolution of the visibility of women in society, the rise of individualism, and the "professionalization" of family businesses.

TABLE 9.1. *The Evolution of Women Leaders in U.S. Family Businesses*

American Family Business Survey	1997 (%)	2002 (%)	2007 (%)
The present CEO is a woman	4.7	9.5	24
The next CEO could be a woman	25.4	34	34
At least a woman in the family is employed full-time	40.9	52.4	52
% of women among the family employees	19.2	26.6	40

Source: American Family Business Surveys, 1997, 2002, 2007.

The Evolution of the Visibility of Women in Society. The visibility of women is increasing in two ways: first, the number of women leaders is slowly increasing in the business world. Second, because this increase is still limited, what is, in fact, highly visible is the public debate around it. An illustration of this can be found in the adoption of quotas for boards of directors in several countries, forcing boards of directors to include a certain percentage of women. Although this kind of measure is not always appreciated, it forces businesses to look for these "less visible" women who can bring their competence to the boards. Another factor of visibility is the fact that institutions such as the World Economic Forum study and raise awareness of the "Gender Gap," through discussions and reports.

The most important determinant of a country's competitiveness is its human talent – the skills, education and productivity of its workforce. Women account for one-half of the potential talent base throughout the world and therefore, over time, a nation's competitiveness depends significantly on whether and how it educates and utilizes its female talent. [...] the gap between women and men on economic participation and political empowerment remains wide [...] The Global Gender Gap Reports also confirm the correlation between gender equality and the level of development of countries, thus providing support for the theory that empowering women leads to a more efficient use of a nation's human talent." (WEF Gender Gap report 2010, preface v)

Several actors contribute to raise awareness on the general issue of women leadership, issuing statistics, linking gender-balance to performance, or advising on the needed corporate culture change to foster women's presence in business (e.g., Simmons School of Management and its Center for Gender in Organisations, World Economic Forum, Catalyst, McKinsey, Goldman Sachs, The Conference Board of Canada, European Professional Women's Network).

The Rise of Individualism. Another trend that has an impact on the change in traditional succession patterns is the rise of individualism. Indeed, potential successors no longer consider themselves obliged to work in the family business, but look for a career that best fits their aspirations, be it in the family firm or elsewhere. We often witnessed this reflection (and hesitation) among the participants of the MBA course at the INSEAD Business School. When the eldest son of a family business decides not to join the family firm, contrary to what is expected of him, it can create unexpected challenges. In a traditional dynasty in which other family members were "very well trained not to put their hands on," and hence were not prepared at all, the refusal of the eldest son to join the business presented significant problems to the firm and the succession (Blondel and Van der Heyden 1999b).

The result of this quest for personal fulfillment is that the classical succession pattern is replaced with an opening to other talents in the family, creating opportunities both for younger sons and for daughters.

The Professionalization of Family Businesses. A related trend here is the professionalization of the "recruitment" into family businesses (see Chapter 11 by Fellman). Family businesses are increasingly considering competence and attitude rather than birth order when looking for the next leader of the business. Potential candidates can come from the overall family "talent pool," as well as from outside the family. To minimize conflicts, families are increasingly developing policies for family members joining the business as part of broader family constitutions or charters. These policies indicate the expectations set for family candidates, as well as the processes for selection. This further formalizes the move from "eldest son" to "most qualified."

Challenges of Daughters' Successions

Changing Family Relationships. Daughters accessing leadership roles challenge traditional family relationships. Although they seem to have better relationships with their fathers – the father–daughter succession is said to be easier than father–son or mother–daughter – their relationships with their mothers, as well as with their older brothers, can be more difficult, and these changes can be unsettling for some members of the family. Dumas (1989) used expressions such as "Daddy's little girl" and the "Snow White syndrome" to describe father–daughter and

TABLE 9.2. *Differences in Parenthood among Male and Female Senior Executives*

% of Senior Executives Who Have:	Among Women (%)	Among Men (%)
Delayed the time for having children	35	12
Decided not to have children	12	1
Children	65	90

Source: Catalyst, Families and Work Institute, and the Center for Work and Family at Boston College (2003). Joint survey entitled, "Leaders in a Global Economy, a Study of Executive Women and Men." Boston: The Center for Work and Family at Boston College.

mother–daughter relationships. Halkias et al. (2011) studied succession in diverse countries and cultures from the daughter–father perspective and confirmed the impact of culture but found that daughters seemed particularly cautious about preserving good relationships with their predecessors and within the family.

Work–Life Balance – Easier in Family Firms?. The discrepancy between the success of women as students and their entry level in companies, and their presence in executive offices and on boards, is due not just to the fact that women do not seek promotion or that companies have "gender stereotypes" that trap women in certain roles and styles. The business culture (long work hours, late meetings) was designed by men who had spouses at home to care for the family, and this culture is not adapted to employees who have outside responsibilities such as a family. Indeed, the female employment rate falls by 12.4 points when they have children, while it rises by 7.3 points for men with children, reflecting the unequal sharing of care responsibilities and the lack of childcare facilities and work–life balance policies. The percentage of female employees working part-time was 31.2 percent in 2007, four times higher than that for men. (Source: E.C. Women and Decision-Making Report 2008, in Niforos 2010.)

Men and women do not face the problem of making family life and professional life compatible in the same way. A recent survey of more than 1,000 senior executives shows the differences (Table 9.2).

Work–life balance is one of the issues reported by women in family firms as well (Cole 1997; Vera and Dean 2005). A family firm probably offers a more favorable environment to women than other enterprise forms. Indeed, despite the "transparency" effect, women in the family are natural candidates for management positions, and even more

TABLE 9.3. *Female Board Members in Publicly Traded Firms in France*

% of Women on Boards of Directors in 2010	Family Businesses (%)	Non-Family Businesses (%)
Small- and medium-sized firms	25	13
Intermediary firms	16	7
Large firms	14	8
"Giant" firms	16	12

Source: Gomez, Pierre-Yves, and Zied Guedri (2012). "20 ans d'évolution des conseils d'administration en France 1992–2010." Cahier de l'IFGE 2012 no. 3, October 2012.

so for positions on the board of directors. We have mentioned the widows who took up the leadership of the family firm in the eighteenth century. This would hardly have been conceivable in non-family firms such as the state factories of the time. Family firms give more opportunities to family members, women included. A recent study of boards of directors in French traded companies (Gomez and Guedri 2012) clearly evidenced the higher presence of women on family-business boards (Table 9.3).

Moreover, working for a family firm increases a member's motivation because it entails working for the family – in a broad sense. The family firm often offers more flexibility, which is an important factor for many women. Finally, the culture of the family firm is probably closer to what women are looking for.

In Europe, Marianne is the CEO of a very large family firm. She succeeded her father while being in "competition" with several men in the family. She frequently travels for work, is married and has four children. Her cousin is in charge of the relationships with the family shareholders, which enables Marianne to concentrate on the running of the company. She employs two persons at home to take care of the children and the house. When she joined the family firm, she asked for eighty percent of the proposed salary in order to be able to spend more time with her children. Notwithstanding this, her bonus is calculated according to her performance, regardless of her working hours. She has thus differentiated the pay relating to the "input" (the working hours) from the pay relating to the "output" (the results). For her, having more children is almost easier than having less: indeed, siblings are more easily self-sufficient. (Blondel 2005, p. 24)

Marilyn Carlson Nelson is one of the most visible and powerful women in the United States. She directed and now chairs the board of the travel and hotel company created by her father, Curtis L. Carlson. The company and its franchisees employ 170,000 people throughout the world. Marilyn Carlson Nelson is recognized as one of the world's most powerful women

(*Forbes* magazine) and one of America's best leaders (*U.S. News & World Report*) and has been keen to exercise and promote authentic leadership. The power given by her role has enabled her to change the corporate culture of the Carlson group and to encourage women to work and accept corporate responsibility. She has adapted her company to the needs of working parents, because she is convinced that it is a competitive edge for her company to be considered as an outstanding workplace by men as well as women. The actions taken to allow parents to work more easily included the creation of daycare in the company, flexible hours and the opportunity to work from home, twelve weeks of paid maternity leave (contrary to the common practice in the United States), supportive groups for parents, quick medical care, and so forth. To encourage women to take up corporate responsibilities, Marilyn Carlson Nelson has taken various initiatives, such as mentoring. The percentage of women among the executives with corporate responsibilities has increased from 5 percent to 40 percent.

Women in Need of "Hidden Giants"?. One of the problems of women is that they themselves rarely have an "invisible giant," such as a husband who supports them during their career. A recent survey of one thousand senior executives illustrated this point: 74 percent of the women in the survey had a husband working full-time, whereas 75 percent of the men had a wife without a full-time professional activity (Catalyst 2003). Thus, most women do not find as much support from their husbands as the husbands do from their wives. Moreover, their husbands may be expecting support from them.

But the broader family can also provide support to parents who have responsibilities in the family business, assisting in the upbringing of the children and in the transmission of values through the family meetings.

Toward the Recognition of the "Hidden Giants"

As we expect to see more women leaders in the coming years, the role of the "hidden giants" will probably also be more visible thanks to several factors. First, there is increasing literature on the role of women, on the one hand, and on the need for "family governance," whether by men or women, on the other. Second, the importance of "family capital" and "familiness" as key competitive factors, based upon the resource-based theory of the firm, will help the recognition of those who foster, develop, and transmit this family capital.

The Development of Literature on the Roles of Women in the Family Firm

The literature on women in the family firm has developed significantly from the early days of the 1980s and 1990s. Pioneers such as Colette Dumas, Joanne Gillis-Donovan, Matilde Sagalnicoff, Barbara Hollander, and Wendi Bukowitz have paved the way for a stream of research on this topic. Eleven years after Nelton's call for research (1998), Martinez Jimenez (2009) was able to review forty-eight articles and research works. Expressions such as "fundamental wives" (Marshak 1994), "spousal leadership" (Poza and Messer 2001), or "spousal commitment" (Van Aukjen et Werbel 2006) may contribute to putting a value on the contribution of spouses.

Beyond academic articles, books and conferences can raise awareness among family businesses. Several books dedicated to the topic of women in the family business have been published in recent years, by researchers and practitioners (Dugan et al. 2008; Gupta et al. 2008; Annino et al. 2009; Barrett and Moores 2009; Halkias et al. 2011). The Family Business Network organizes sessions in local chapters or in global summits on the topic of women in the family business.

The emphasis that practitioners place on the "professionalization of family and business roles" (e.g., Carlock and Ward 2010: 113) brings roles that traditionally were in the shadow very much to the fore.

The Development of the Notions of "Familiness" and Family Capital as Resources for the Business. The family as a factor of differentiation has been used by scholars applying the resource-based theory of the firm. Habbershon and Williams coined the term "familiness" (1999), while others used the term "family capital," consisting of the financial, human, and social capital brought by the family to the firm. This stream of research has been further developed by Sirmon and Hitt (2003), Hoffman et al. (2006), Danes et al. (2009), and Sorenson and Bierman (2009).

These management theories bring us back to the social capital developed by our "hidden giants" in the home and may contribute to a revaluation of this invisible work.

CHANGING DYNAMICS: FEMALE ENTREPRENEURS AND A NEW GENERATION

Women have also made their way in business by being the founding entrepreneurs. Although there are probably many more female entrepreneurs today, female entrepreneurship in previous centuries has been documented, as shown in the works of Alison Kay (2008) about female entrepreneurship in Victorian Britain, Angel Kwolek-Folland in the United States or Paloma Fernández Pérez in Spain. Founding and running small business enterprises was an important source to earn a living for both single and married women, and some have created famous businesses, such as Estée Lauder, Coco Chanel, and Mary Kay.

In their study of career choice intentions of adolescents, Schröder, Schmitt-Rodermund, and Arnaud (2011) found that girls showed a greater inclination to start a new company, rather than to be a successor in the family business, contrary to some previous studies.

Starting one's own company attracts more and more women. Why do women wish to create their own company? Women are looking for a consistency between their private and their professional lives, and the flexibility required to manage both. They are rather less attracted by power and money than men, both traits that are to be found in large organizations. During our interviews (Blondel 2005), we were struck by a recurring theme among women who had taken over a family firm and those who had created their own: to be oneself. It is probably this very strong need that has led many women to start their own company.

Marian Ruderman, a researcher at the Center for Creative Leadership, carried out a study of "performing" women. According to her, nowadays, women are not so much striving to prove that they are capable as much as looking for a balance, in order to build careers that are both fulfilling and meaningful. She identified five main themes stemming from these women's approach to their careers and their lives: to act with authenticity, to establish connections, to find the means to be autonomous, to be united, to be personally more clear-sighted.

In China, where the market economy has recently been legalized (in 1988), women owned a third of all small- and medium-sized companies in 2004 (*Financial Times*, 2004); among the companies owned by women, more than a fifth employ more than one thousand people, according to the female federation called the All-China Women's Federation.

By having a better understanding of the motivations of women, we can see how a family firm may meet their needs, more than a large anonymous firm, and why more and more women create their own companies. A survey of female executives and managers carried out by Korn/Ferry International confirms these analyses: 75 percent of women who are leaders and owners are happy on a personal level, whereas only 39 percent of non-shareholder female executives are.

In our research, we have met many female entrepreneurs born into entrepreneurial families. There is a great deal of interest in business creation, both for women and for men coming from family firms. Indeed, the persons concerned see it as a way of asserting themselves while keeping a corporate tradition. For the family firm itself, it can also be a way of diversifying, renewing itself and thus enduring.

Some families encourage their members to create companies. For instance, entrepreneurs may receive help from the family (in competition with other projects) in the form of starting capital and/or advice from more experienced family members. As for the creation of a company, family members develop talents that will be useful for the family firm, for instance, for governance positions. Moreover, the companies thus created can sometimes join the family group and enhance it.

The female entrepreneurs whom we have met often continue to play roles in the family firm, on the board of directors, and even, at times, managing the family holding. But they fulfill their dreams in their own company.

This, for instance, is the case with Elena, the daughter of an entrepreneur who created a very successful company (Blondel 2005, p. 39):

Elena has worked in the company for several years, together with her father and her brother, designated as the successor. She realized that by staying in the company she would fulfill the dream of family members, but not her own. She traveled while 'listening to her inner voice,' to fulfill her own destiny. Then, she created her own company, which promotes women writers. Her energy and enthusiasm are clear and when you meet her you can see that she is 'fulfilling her dream.' But she still takes part in the family board of directors. Thus, she has experienced the transition from being 'the daughter of . . .' to becoming 'the sister of . . . ,' and finally, herself. And she admits that being born into a family of entrepreneurs made such a development possible.

Grace, a member of the third generation of a family firm, summarizes the evolution of the role(s) of women, which she classifies by generation (Blondel 2005, p. 39):

The women of the first generation were invisible, unacknowledged spouses. I acknowledge the role of these women who were the main parts of the family unity: one year after my grandmother's death, the family split. The women of the second generation are daughters and in fact, their fathers, the entrepreneurs, often see future mothers in them, not directors of the company. Finally, as a third-generation woman, I created my own company and thus became a first-generation entrepreneur. In this activity, I do not feel any discrimination. I have to face up to the same hardships as men.

Her last comment, that she has to face the same hardships as men, brings us to the most recent trends, which are a sort of convergence of the aspirations of both men and women regarding their lives. Changing demographics and the transition of generations is having a strong impact on business culture, obscuring the lines about gender-specific preferences. According to "Bookend Generations," a study from the Center for Work-Life Policy (now called the Center for Talent Innovation) (Hewlett et al. 2008), "Gen Ys" want a balance of rewards. Instead of the traditional quest of prestigious title, powerful position, and high compensation, both men *and* women value challenging and diverse job opportunities, a collaborative workplace and flexible work options, and a commitment to corporate social responsibility initiatives, values that are typically classified as "female." With 89 percent of Ys affirming that flexible work options are an important consideration in choosing an employer, "Millenials view work–life balance as their right," observes Ron Alsop in *The Trophy Kids Grow Up* (2008, quoted in Hewlett 2011, p. 1). To obtain that balance, they are becoming "agents of change, pushing flexibility to the top of the workplace agenda" (Hewlett 2011, p. 1). Transposing this generational evolution in work ethics and culture to the family business, there is evidence of young women considering themselves to be the vectors of change in business and social norms, and thereby becoming champions within the context of their own family firm. Carolina states in her testimonial:

Since I came back in 2007, I have a vision of what I want this company to look like. We have 700,000 women working for us. This is a great opportunity to change the region and empower women. I want the company to set an example of doing good and doing business. (Niforos 2011, p. 278)

The young female successor perceives that her age has been much more of an impediment to her acceptance as a leader in the family firm than her gender (Niforos 2011, p. 280).

It's not just about gender, it is more about age: When a young person arrives, man or woman, it is very difficult. The leadership in a family business is there for a very long time, with no frequent transitions. The culture is entrenched. Having a young person take over is not easy for the older members of the firm. Being a woman is even harder, because we lead differently, we are more team-oriented, but the harder is the generation change.

In conclusion, our study of the women of the family business has allowed us to uncover many roles and dynamics at play in the family business. Several implications apply to both men and women, such as the importance of roles that may not be visible inside the business, the dangers of preconceived assumptions, and the difference that vibrant talents can bring to the family business. The evolution of the distribution of roles will open more areas for research, such as mother–daughter and mother–son succession (touched on by Kaslow 1998) and the future of the roles historically played by the "hidden giants."

References

Alsop, Ron (2008). *The Trophy Kids Grow Up: How the Millennial Generation Is Shaking Up the Workplace*. San Francisco, CA: Jossey-Bass.

Anderson, Alistair R., Sarah L. Jack, and Sarah Drakopoulou Dodd (2005). "The Role of Family Members in Entrepreneurial Networks: Beyond the Boundaries of the Family Firm." *Family Business Review*, 18(2): 135–54.

Annino, Patricia, Thomas Davidow, Cynthia Adams Harrison, and Lisbeth Davidow (2009). *Women in Family Business: What Keeps You Up at Night?* Charleston, SC: BookSurge.

Barrett, Mary, and Ken Moores (2009). *Women in Family Business Leadership Roles: Daughters on the Edge*. Cheltenham: Edward Elgar Publishing.

Belardinelli, Sergio (2002). "The Evolution of Family Institution and Its Impact on Society and Business." *Family Business Review*, 15(3): 169–73.

Blondel, Christine (2005). "Las Mujeres y la Empresa Familiar: Funciones y conclusion. Associacion Catalana de la Empresa Familiar y PricewaterhouseCoopers," (French version in INSEAD Working Paper 2005/64/WICFE).

Blondel, Christine (2011). "A Historical Perspective: From Hidden Giants to Visible Leaders? The Evolution of Women's Roles in Family Business." In Daphne Halkias, Paul W. Thurman, Celina Smith, and Robert S. Nason (eds.), *Father–Daughter Succession in Family Business, a Cross-cultural Perspective*. Farnham: Gower.

Blondel Christine, and Ludo Van der Heyden (1999a). "The Wendel Family: 'Affectio Societatis'." Case A, INSEAD case study, Fontainebleau.

Blondel, Christine, and Ludo Van der Heyden (1999b). "The Next Generation in Large Family Firms," Presentation at FBN conference, Stockholm, September 18, 1999.

Bourdieu, Pierre (1979). *La distinction, Critique sociale du jugement*. Paris: Editions de Minuit.

Carlock, Randel S. (1999). "Filling Big Shoes at the Carlson Companies: Interviews with Curt Carlson and Marilyn Carlson Nelson." *Family Business Review*, 12(1): 87–93.

Carlock, Randel S., and John Ward (2010). *When Family Businesses Are Best*. Basingstoke: Palgrave Macmillan.

Catalyst, Families and Work Institute, and the Center for Work and Family at Boston College (2003). Joint survey entitled, "Leaders in a Global Economy, a Study of Executive Women and Men." Boston, MA: The Center for Work and Family at Boston College.

Cole, Patricia M. (1997). "Women in Family Business." *Family Business Review*, 10(4): 353.

Danes, Sharon M., Kathryn Stafford, George Haynes, and Sayali S. Amarapurkar (2009). "Family Capital of Family Firms: Bridging Human, Social and Financial Capital." *Family Business Review*, 22(3): 199–216.

Dugan, Ann M., Sharon P. Krone, Kelly LeCouvie, Jennifer M. Pendergast, Denise H. Kenyon-Rouvinez, and Amy M. Schuman (2010). *A Woman's Place: The Crucial Roles of Women in Family Business*. Basingstoke: Palgrave Macmillan.

Dumas, Colette (1989). "Understanding of Father–Daughter and Father–Son Dyads in Family-Owned Businesses." *Family Business Review*, 2(1): 31.

Fernandez-Moja, Maria, and Rafael Castro-Balaguer (2011). "Looking for the Perfect Structure: The Evolution of Family Office from a Long-Term Perspective." *Universia Business Review*, Cuarto Trimestre 2011: 82–93.

Financial Times, June 24, 2004. Quoted in globewomen.com.

Fletcher, Joyce K. (1999). *Disappearing Acts: Gender, Power, and Relational Practice at Work*. Cambridge, MA: MIT Press.

Fletcher, Joyce K. (2001). "Invisible Work: The Disappearing of Relational Practice at Work," CGO Insights, Boston.

García-Álvarez Ercilia, Jordi López-Sintas, and Pilar Saldaña Gonzalvo (2002). "Socialization Patterns of Successors in First- to Second-Generation Family Businesses." *Family Business Review*, 15(3): 189–203.

Gillis-Donovan, Joanne, and Carolyn Moynihan-Bradt (1990). "The Power of Invisible Women in the Family Business." *Family Business Review*, 3(2): 153–67.

Glavin, Bill, Joe Astrachan, and Judy Green (2007). *American Family Business Survey*. Springfield, MA: Massachusetts Mutual Life Insurance Company.

Gomez, Pierre-Yves, and Zied Guedri (2012). "20 ans d'évolution des conseils d'administration en France 1992–2010." *Cahier de l'IFGE* 3.

Graham, Katharine (1997). *Personal History*. New York: Alfred A. Knopf.

Gupta, Vipin, Nancy Levenburg, Lynda L. Moore, Jaideep Motwani, and Thomas V. Schwarz (2008). *Culturally Sensitive Models of Gender in Family Business: A Compendium Using the GLOBE Paradigm*. Hyderabad, India: ICFAI University Press.

Habbershon, Timothy G., and Mary L. Williams (1999). "A Resource-based Framework for Assessing the Strategic Advantages of Family Firms." *Family Business Review*, 12(1): 1–25.

Halkias, Daphne, Paul W. Thurman, Celina Smith, and Robert S. Nason, eds. (2011). *Father–Daughter Succession in Family Business: A Cross-cultural Perspective*. Farnham: Gower.

Hewlett, Sylvia Ann (2011). "Ys just want to have fun (and flexibility)." HBR blog, 2011. http://blogs.hbr.org/hbr/hewlett/2011/06/ys_just_wanna_have_fun_-_and.html (accessed April 2013).

Hewlett, Sylvia Ann, Maggie Jackson, Laura Sherbin, Peggy Shiller, Eytan Sosnovich, and Karen Sumberg (2008). "Bookend Generations: Leveraging Talent and Finding Common Ground." Available at: http://www.worklifepolicy.org/index.php/section/research_pubs (accessed April 2013).

Histoires d'entreprises (2008), 6, interview with Cécile Bonnefond, pp. 37–43.

Hoffman, James, Mark Hoelscher, and Ritch Sorenson (2006). "Achieving Sustained Competitive Advantage: A Family Capital Theory." *Family Business Review*, 19(2): 135–45.

Hollander, Barbara S., and Wendi S. Bukowitz (1990). "Women, Family Culture, and Family Business." *Family Business Review*, 3(2): 139–51.

James, Harold (2006). *Family Capitalism: Wendels, Haniels, Falcks and the Continental European Model*. Cambridge, MA: Belknap Press.

Karlsson, Stider Annelie (2001). "The Home – A Disregarded Managerial Arena." In Sven-Erik Sjöstrand, Jörgen Sandberg, and Mats Tyrstrup (eds.), *Invisible Management, the Social Construction of Leadership* (pp. 98–101). London: Thomson Learning.

Kaslow, Florence W. (1998). "Handling Transitions from Mother to Son in the Family Business: The Knotty Issues." *Family Business Review*, 11(3): 229–38.

Kaye, Kenneth (1999). "Mate Selection and Family Business Success." *Family Business Review*, 12(2): 107–15.

Lambrecht, Johan (2005). "Multigenerational Transition in Family Businesses: A New Explanatory Model." *Family Business Review*, 18(4): 267–82.

Lansberg, Ivan (1999). *Succeeding Generations, Realizing the Dream of Families in Business*. Cambridge, MA: Harvard Business School Press.

Lubinski, Christina (2011). "Succession in Multi-generational Family Firms. An Explorative Study into the Period of Anticipatory Socialization." *Electronic Journal of Family Business Studies* (EJFBS), 5(1–2): 4–25.

Martinez, Jimenez Rocio (2009). "Research on Women in Family Firms, Current Status and Future Directions." *Family Business Review*, 22(1): 53–64.

McCollom Hampton, Marion (2009). Book Review. India: ICFAI University Press. *Family Business Review*, 22(4): 366–9.

Moss Kanter, Rosabeth (1977). New edition 1993. *Men and Women of the Corporation*. New York: Basic Books.

Nelton, Sharon (1998). "The Rise of Women in Family Firms: A Call for Research Now." *Family Business Review*, 11(3): 215–8.

Niforos, Marina (2010). Lecture at the Women in Leadership Conference, Barcelona Chamber of Commerce.

Niforos, Marina (2011). "A Case Study of Family Business Succession in Peru." In Daphne Halkias, Paul W. Thurman, Celina Smith, and Robert S. Nason (eds.), *Father–Daughter Succession in Family Business, a Cross-cultural Perspective* (pp. 278–9). Farnham: Gower.

Rodriguez, Peter, Christopher S. Tuggle, and Sean M. Hackett (2009). "An Exploratory Study of How Potential 'Family and Household Capital' Impacts New Venture Start-Up Rates." *Family Business Review*, 22(3): 259–72.

Rowe, Barbara R., and Gong-Soog Hong (2000). "The Role of Wives in Family Businesses: The Paid and Unpaid Work of Women." *Family Business Review*, 13(1): 1–13.

Ruderman, Marian N., and Patricia Ohlott, Center for Creative Leadership (2002). *Standing at the Crossroads: Next Steps for High-achieving Women*. San Francisco, CA: Jossey-Bass.

Sagalnicoff, Matilde (1990). "Women in Family Businesses: Challenges and Opportunities." *Family Business Review*, 3(2): 125–37.

Schröder, Elke, Eva Schmitt-Rodermund, and Nicolas Arnaud (2001). "Career Choice Intentions of Adolescents with a Family Business Background." *Family Business Review*, 24(4): 305–21.

Sirmon, Davis G., and Michael A. Hitt (2003). "Managing Resources: Linking Unique Resources, Management, and Wealth Creation in Family Firms." *Entrepreneurship Theory and Practice*, 27(4): 339–58.

Smith J.Y., and Noel Epstein, 2001. "Katharine Graham Dies at 84." *Washington Post*. Available at: www.washingtonpost.com/wp-dyn/content/article/2005/08/04/AR2005080400963.html (Accessed April 2013).

Sorenson, Ritch. L., and Leonard Bierman (2009). "Family Capital, Family Business and Free Enterprise." *Family Business Review*, 22(3): 193–5.

Steier, Lloyd (2009). "Where Do New Firms Come From? Households, Family Capital, Ethnicity, and the Welfare Mix." *Family Business Review*, 22(3): 273–8.

Tagiuri, Renato, and John A. Davis (1982). "Bivalent Attributes of the Family Firm." Working Paper, Harvard Business School, Cambridge, MA. Reprinted 1996, *Family Business Review*, 9(2): 199–208.

Van der Heyden, Ludo, Christine Blondel, and Randel Carlock (2005). "Fair Process, Striving for Justice in the Family Business." *Family Business Review*, 18(1): 1–21.

Vera, Carolina F., and Michelle A. Dean (2005). "An Examination of the Challenges Daughters Face in Family Business Succession." *Family Business Review*, 18(4): 321–45.

World Economic Forum (2010). Gender Gap Report, written by Ricardo Hausmann (Harvard University, Cambridge, MA), Laura D. Tyson (University of California, Berkeley, CA), and Saadia Zahidi (World Economic Forum). Geneva: World Economic Forum.

The Role of Values in Family-Owned Firms

Remei Agulles, Lucia Ceja, and Josep Tàpies

INTRODUCTION

The present book is a manifestation of the continued interest in the endurance of family-owned businesses around the world. Sharma and Salvato (Chapter 2 in this volume) demonstrate that perpetuating the *essence* – the values that drive all that happens in both the family *and* the business – is key to the longevity of family-owned businesses. In this sense, families in business, which last across generations of family and business life cycles, are masterful at preserving their core focus on the values and purpose of the owning family, while embracing change with regard to the tasks, products/services, or markets of the family business, or to how it is organized, controlled, managed, or governed. In other words, flexibility and adaptation to changing societal needs flourish in family-owned businesses in which the owning family actively commits itself to a clear set of values.

Belief in the importance of values in family-owned firms inspired collaboration on this chapter among the disciplines of management, psychology, and philosophy. The goals of the chapter are threefold: to define the concept of values and provide a classification and a hierarchy of values from a philosophical perspective; to examine the espoused values underpinning the world's largest family-owned and non–family-owned corporations; and to examine critically the values that are characteristic of family-owned firms.

WHAT ARE VALUES?

WHAT ARE VALUES?

Before building a definition of "value," it may be interesting to examine how values appear in the Mission Statements of companies.[1]

Values in Mission Statements: The Differences among Vision, Mission and Values

In most corporations today, people no longer know – or even care – what or *why* their companies are. [. . .] Strategies can engender strong, enduring emotional attachments only when they are embedded in a broader organizational purpose. (Bartlett and Ghoshal 1994: 81, italics in the original)

Mission Statements have been used in different forms throughout the twentieth century. However, they became common during the 1980s, and, in the 1990s, they were considered a preferred strategic tool by both companies and the literature. Some studies – the work by Pearce and David (1987) is considered to be the first – have even attempted to link higher performance to a more comprehensive Mission Statement. This is still a contested issue, however.

Mission Statements have a range of styles, from a short motto or quotation from the founder to a long, complex explanation. Sometimes they appear under a title such as "our culture" or "our identity," and they are often broken down into "vision," "mission," and "values." This threefold structure does not always provide clarity, because these terms are not used consistently. For instance, if we examine "values," our main subject, we may instead find vision declarations[2] ("Create a more affluent lifestyle for humanity" or "Make a positive difference to our community"), elements of the mission ("Deliver exceptional vacation experiences"), and even social claims and commitments ("More women in the workforce").

Using the dictionary, Senge (1998: 17, italics in the original) defines *mission* as "'purpose, reason for being.' *Vision*, by contrast, is 'a picture or image of the future we seek to create' and *values* articulate how we intend to live as we pursue our mission." We understand "vision" as a future scenario for the company itself or for society, a desideratum. "Mission" is the specific task of the organization – what the company

---

[1] We will follow Fairhurst, Jordan, and Neuwirth (1997, endnote 1) in using capital letters for the Mission Statement, which includes, in turn, vision, mission, and values.

[2] These examples have been taken from real firms.

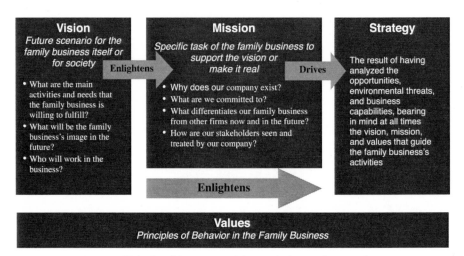

FIGURE 10.1. Relationship among vision, mission, values, and strategy.

does or commits itself to do – to support the vision or make it real. "Values" are the principles of behavior in the company. In other words, the people in the organization must *believe in* and *live according to* a set of shared values and *carry out* the mission, while always *aiming at* the vision.[3] As Figure 10.1 demonstrates, the vision inspires both the mission and the corporate, competitive, and functional strategies; the strategy is designed to carry out the mission; and all three components – vision, mission, and strategy – must be consistent with corporate values.

In Table 10.1, we provide a few examples of clear-cut distinctions among vision, mission, and values, according to how we have defined them here.

The question "What falls under the category of *value*?" is not easy to answer. Indeed, in actual Mission Statements, a whole conceptual world made of behaviors ("quick response"), virtues ("integrity"), beliefs ("continuous improvement"), character strengths ("leadership"), or objects ("our brand") appears under this label. In one extreme, there are excessively self-evident value statements ("freshness of our products" for a grocery chain, or "making beds well" for a hotel chain). In the other, some formulations lack an essential ingredient, which is "goodness" (e.g., "competition," "solution," "profit," or "stakeholder relations," which

---

[3] See also Tàpies (2009: 51–57).

TABLE 10.1. *Examples of Vision, Mission, and Values*

Vision:	"To be the Urban Resort of Reference in Europe." (Hotel Rey Juan Carlos I, Barcelona)
	"Our purpose is to be the global leader in nourishing people." (Cargill)
Mission:	"To attract and attain customers with high-valued products and services and the most satisfying ownership experience in America." (Toyota USA)
	"Sometimes, to move forward you need to take a step backwards. That is just what Fiat has done recently, by returning to the company's original mission, namely to build cars with attractive styling and exciting engines, cars that are accessible and improve the quality of everyday life." (Fiat)
Values:	"Integrity First, Service before Self, Excellence in All We Do." (U.S. Air Force)
	"Honesty: we respect; Entrepreneurship: we act; Responsibility: we care; Quality: we deliver." (ISS Facility Services)

should read, for example, "fair competition," "customized solutions," "profit sharing," and "good stakeholder relations").

The Notion of Value

A Definition of Value. Most often, in everyday language, *value* refers to desirability, importance, usefulness, or monetary worth. [...] When used as a verb, *to value* can neutrally mean more or less the same as *to assess* or *to rate*, but when expressing a high regard it can also mean to respect and to esteem. (Koiranen 2002: 176, italics in the original)

The term "value" exceeded its economic meaning in the nineteenth century, when philosophers such as Rudolf Hermann Lotze, Friedrich Nietzsche, and Karl Robert Eduard von Hartmann introduced it in their works. In the twentieth century, authors such as John Dewey, and especially phenomenologists such as Max Scheler or Dietrich von Hildebrand, dedicated a great part of their philosophical work to values. Given the relevance of values to human action, axiology (the theory of values) was subsequently cultivated in the fields of anthropology (Clyde Kluckhohn), sociology (Max Weber), and psychology (Milton Rokeach, Shalom H. Schwartz). The attempted definitions of values have been consistent in some basic elements (Koiranen 2002), such as the desirability of values, their being held by individuals or groups,[4] and their being criteria for judgment. Two examples in which we emphasize these elements are the following: "a *conception*, explicit or implicit, distinctive of an individual or characteristic of a group, *of the desirable* which influences the *selection* from available modes, means and ends of action" (Kluckhohn 1951: 395) and "beliefs concerning desirable *modes of conduct* or desirable *end-states of existence*" (Rokeach 1973: 7).

Shalom H. Schwartz, in his well-known search for basic human values, provided a definition that synthesizes and completes previous efforts. This is the definition that we have chosen to build on in this chapter. As it appears in Schwartz and Bilsky (1990: 878; Schwartz 1992: 4), it reads: "Values (a) are concepts or beliefs, (b) pertain to desirable end states or behaviors, (c) transcend specific situations, (d) guide selection or evaluation of behavior and events, and (e) are ordered by relative importance."

Given that some objects – or entities – may be considered values (e.g., "riches," "the brand," "our employees"), we have added this item to the definition. Likewise, what is evaluated according to the criteria of values may be not only events and behavior, but also objects, things. Therefore, the definition we will use is:

- Values (a) are concepts or beliefs; (b) pertain to desirable *objects*, end states or forms of behavior; (c) transcend specific situations; (d) guide selection or evaluation of behavior, *objects*, and events; and (e) are ordered by relative importance.

We will now comment on this definition item by item.

With regard to (a), values are concepts or beliefs. In actual practice, some values declarations start with the phrase "we believe in." They are in the realm of ideas, and their influence is mainly tacit, although we can define them, list them, and make them explicit through reflection. It has been said before that they are "principles," which means that they are "at the origin" or "on the basis" – the two philosophical meanings of "principle." Thus, values (c) "transcend specific situations": they are generic and universal, they apply to any case, and, in organizations, cannot change if the organization's identity does not change. In (d), these principles "guide

---

[4] "Values can be either personal values (of somebody) or shared values of a group (like a family or a family business, for example)" (Koiranen 2002: 180). If most of an organization's members do not share certain values, the organization as a whole cannot claim to possess them.

selection or evaluation of behavior, objects, and events." In other words, we evaluate – judge – things, events, and behaviors; and we select things and decide according to the criteria of our values. This is the reason why values are so strongly linked to an individual's or an organization's "identity" or "idiosyncrasy."

As for the first part of (b), it should be noted that, as far as it is perceived as something "good," a value is "desirable." Values that we lack are to be (personally) pursued and (socially) promoted; others must be nurtured or educated; values that we already possess should be enjoyed and preserved; and so on.

The second part of (b) – values refer to "desirable objects, end states or behaviors" – opens the possibility of classifying them, depending on where desirability or "goodness" lies. Doing a valuable synthesis, and expanding on the work of Rokeach (1973), Meglino and Ravlin (1998: 353) provide a classification that is consistent with the definition that we are endeavoring to explain, claiming that there are basically two types of value:

- "Value that an individual places on an object or outcome (e.g., the value one places on pay)."
- "A second type of value is more likely to be used to describe a person as opposed to an object."

Meglino and Ravlin (1998) subdivide this second type into two additional categories:

- Terminal values: "Self-sufficient end-states of existence that a person strives to achieve (e.g., a comfortable life, wisdom). [. . .] They are pursued for their own sake." Following Rokeach (1973), we call them "end-state values."
- Instrumental values: "Modes of behavior (e.g., honesty, helpfulness) rather than states of existence. [. . .] [I]nstrumental values describe behaviors that facilitate the attainment of terminal values." We call them "behavioral values."

To summarize, people value objects or outcomes ("our brand," "our employees," "the environment," "a product of quality") as well as other items that refer to people, including desirable end-states ("customer satisfaction/happiness," "success," "prestige") and desirable modes of behavior ("integrity," "quick response") – which, at the beginning, were called ethical standards of behavior. We can call all these different items "values," and each one depends on where we find "desirability" or "goodness."

Meglino and Ravlin (1998: 353) note that research has mainly focused on "behavioral values." They "have more in common with values as they are used by researchers and practitioners to describe an organization's culture (Schein 1985)." Most values in firms' Mission Statements belong to this category – but they are not all the same. Regarding behavior, people place value on the following items:

- *Positive attitudes*[5]: An attitude is the way in which we approach something (event, person, object). Positive attitudes are often considered to be values. Examples of these are "optimism," "responsibility," "we care," and "we are customer-driven."
- *Technical values or skills*: The acquired ability (habit[6]) to perform a task or produce something (technically) well, correctly. For example: "ability to negotiate," "communication."
- *Moral or ethical values*: Connecting with a philosophical tradition that goes back to Greek classical thinkers, Scheler (1973) calls moral values "virtues." They are also called "habits of character" (Snook and Khurana 2004; Yepes 1996). They are the habits of acting morally well or acquired dispositions to do well, for example, "honesty" and "generosity."

Figure 10.2 provides a general summary of what has been said to this point.

The Hierarchy of Values. We have left the last part (e) of the definition – values "are ordered by relative importance" – for discussion in a separate subsection. Is there an objective criterion for this order? Before answering this question, we must address another: Is there any objectivity in values?

There is an intimate connection between something being desirable (a value) and the act of appraising or appreciating (valuing) it. But the order of this connection is not clear *a priori*. Do we value something because it is worthy, desirable, or useful? Or, on the contrary, is it because we deem it valuable that it becomes a value for us? In some ways, both are true.

---

[5] Although "values" and "attitudes" are conceptually distinct (Rokeach 1973; Koiranen 2002), what we mean here is that people do value positive attitudes as good standards of behavior.

[6] We are using "habit" in its classical meaning of "stable acquired disposition" (in Latin, *habitus*). Therefore, here it does not mean "custom."

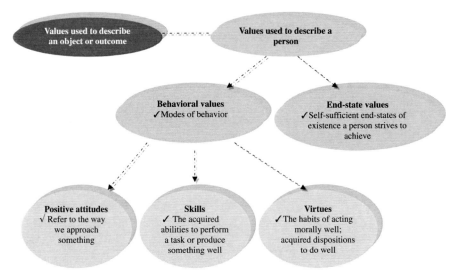

FIGURE 10.2. Types of values.

There have been many relevant works in the field of organizational culture with a focus on values, their classification, the relationship between culture and predominant values, and so on, all from a cross-cultural point of view (Hofstede 1980; Hofstede et al. 1990; Schwartz and Bilsky 1990; Schwartz 1992; House et al. 2004).[7] We decided to investigate here what philosophy – especially the disciplines of ethics and philosophical anthropology – has to say regarding the question of whether there is a universal foundation for values and their hierarchy.

This issue has concerned many philosophers throughout history. For example, Max Scheler (1973) defended the idea that values are objective, although subjectively perceived. Bain, Kashima, and Haslam (2006) state that our views of the nature of things, and mainly of human nature, influence our set of values. This explains how someone could consider a value something that is actually a disvalue (e.g., "the superiority of one race or sex over the others") or how someone might rank values in a distorted way (e.g., "profit" over "honesty"). However, Scheler (1973: 88) links the objectivity of values to their essence; thus, some goods are always – that is, independently from subjective views – more valuable than others. Hence, some values – which refer to objects, end-states,

---

[7] Two examples applied to family businesses: Gupta (Chapter 6 in this volume) and Distelberg and Sorenson (2009).

or behaviors – are higher than others on the scale of values. In other words, there are values that refer to objects that will always be superior to others ("persons" or "family" vs. "money"); likewise for end-state values ("happiness" vs. "pleasant food") and behavioral values ("humility" vs. "readiness").

Representatives of the theory of values, such as von Hartmann, von Hildebrand, or Scheler, have attempted to classify values. We take, as an example, Scheler (1973), who, as we stated, bases the objectivity of values on characteristics of the essence of values, such as extension, endurance, or depth. He proposes five ranks of values, from more to less important: values of the holy, values of the spirit (which includes moral, aesthetic, and intellectual values), values of life and the noble, values of pleasure, and the values of utility. Referring to this hierarchy, Scheler (1973: 88, emphasis in the original) states: "He who 'prefers' the noble to the agreeable will end up in an (inductive) experience of a world of goods very different from the one in which he who does not do so will find himself."

Given that the objectivity of values ultimately arises from the idea of "goodness," Scheler's order of values is reminiscent of the Aristotelian senses of "good," taken from Aristotle's *Nicomachean Ethics*, and this is the thread that we propose here. Although Aristotle's *Ethics* focuses on virtue and neither he nor any other ancient Greek philosopher talks about values, both ethical views are based on the concept of "good" as "desirable." Aristotle's thesis is that things are deemed good as far as they are useful, pleasurable, or noble (in the sense of "good in itself" or "honest").[8] We do not see any objection to considering what Scheler (1973) calls the "values of the holy" and the "values of the spirit" as part of what, in Aristotelian terms, is "noble." These values rank highest because they refer to the deepest sense of "integrity": a person with integrity behaves according to the most complete good. It does not mean that nobility excludes pleasure or utility; rather, in reference to human

---

[8] See Aristotle (*Nic. Eth.* II, 1104 b 30 ff; *Nic. Eth.* VIII, 1155 b 15 ff). He also applies these concepts to friendship (*Nic. Eth.* VIII, 1156a 5 ff), understood as the mutual exchange of goods. In the short term, relationships based on pleasure and utility might seem more rewarding, but they are short and perishable. The noblest friendship is that which seeks mutual good, and it turns out that these friends are maximally useful and pleasant for each other, because they always seek the good of the other. We use the term "honest" (or "noble") in the archaic sense of "honorable" or "upright," not simply "frank." In Latin, it is *bonum honestum. Bonum utile* and *bonum delectabile* are the equivalent Latin terms for the other two. Aristotelian tradition can be traced across the Middle Ages, mainly in the works of Thomas Aquinas (see *Summa Theologiae* I, q.5, a.6).

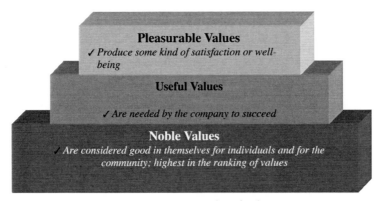

FIGURE 10.3. Hierarchy of values.

behavior, the two latter kinds of values are subordinate to the former, because they point to some aspect of goodness for the agent, whereas integrity points to what is "integral" – that is, what is good for the agent as a whole (as a person).

If we apply Aristotle's criteria to a firm's Mission Statement, we can consider that a firm has the goal of making a profit; but this is not the only goal or, at least, the ultimate goal. According to Aristotle (*Nic. Eth.* I, 1096a 5 ff), "Wealth[9] [. . .] is merely useful and for the sake of something else." Current trends regarding corporate social responsibility (CSR) – if they are to be taken seriously and not viewed as a fad – point out that, as a human organization, a firm must have an end (noble) goal beyond profit: the common good. This is why firms elaborate on their Mission Statements.[10] "Useful" values will clearly be present in the values declaration, but they should be accompanied by "noble" values. It will be less common to find "pleasurable" values in Mission Statements, such as "Have fun at work" or "Be a great place to work."

Figure 10.3 illustrates what has been said on this point, with the *caveat* that we do not consider the three kinds of values to be mutually exclusive.

Values and Habits: The Enactment of Behavioral Values. Behavioral values are values that describe certain behaviors. We previously found three kinds of behavioral values: positive attitudes, skills, and moral habits

---

9 In this passage and in the *Nicomachean Ethics* in general, when Aristotle talks about "wealth" – *ploutos* – he refers to material possessions.

10 This is the dark side of Mission Statements: they might become a platitudinous mask of simple greed and other anomalies (see Fairhurst, Jordan, and Neuwirth 1997).

or virtues (see Figure 10.2). Although holding certain values does not necessarily mean acting according to them (for values are conceptual), it does imply endeavoring to conform one's behavior to these standards. This is what we mean by "enacting values," which, in each case, is performed differently, although what they have in common is that, as Meglino and Ravlin (1998: 354) state, when it comes to behavior, desirability is "oughtness": "Values specify an individual's personal beliefs about how he or she 'should' or 'ought' to behave."[11]

The way in which we approach reality – *attitude* – depends on our personality traits and our system of basic beliefs. It can be modified as far as our character allows – that is, depending on our temperament, previous experience, and *acquired habits*.

Although modern psychology has made important developments regarding the mechanisms and development of habits and conduct, the conceptual roots of these aspects of human life go far back. We agree with Alasdair MacIntyre (1984) that Aristotelian theory of human action has much to say to contemporary people and organizations. In Aristotle's theory, although their natures are diverse, both *skills* and *virtues* are *habits*, which are learned through training, not theoretically (*Nic. Eth.* II, 1103a 30)[12]; they both require instruction and, above all, the actual repetition of certain actions. On the other hand, "in matters of conduct," there is no list of precepts, instructions, or rules of thumb to be learned by heart and then applied: "the agents themselves must in each case consider what is appropriate to the occasion" (Aristotle, *Nic. Eth.* II, 1104a 10). In this training, it is very important to watch others acting – learning by example from role models – especially for moral training.

Values, in general, are really principles of action, but this is truer in the case of those values that are also habits. In fact, there is a mutual influence between behavior and values. Acquired habits provide a certain way of judging our own actions. In the case of *skills* (e.g., negotiation

[11] We disagree, however, with their putting, at the root of this "oughtness," what is socially desirable. Values may refer to what is *socially* as well as *personally* acceptable (Kluckhohn 1951; Rokeach 1973; Koiranen 2002). Although values are socially learned, an individual may hold principles about what is desirable that diverge from what is socially considered desirable (e.g., about the death penalty as a just solution, or about slavery or polygamy). In consequence, "guilt," "shame," and the feeling of acting against social expectations are not always synonymous, as they seem to be to Meglino and Ravlin (1998). Reducing the reason for similarities and differences within values to the factors of biology and socialization does not account for the examples above. In brief, we will see that every single choice shapes (reinforces or shakes) one's value system.

[12] Here, we are using "skill" for what Aristotle calls *techné*, which is sometimes translated as "art." The examples Aristotle gives in this text are those of builders and lyre players.

skills), depending on how complete and correct the previous training has been, the solution applied to a certain problem will either be the correct one or it will not be – in this case, we have a "technical error." This is so because skills enable the correct execution of a certain task or action. Skills are ordered to a certain "result" (the performance of a task or the production of an object).

Otherwise, the object of *virtues* is acting morally well, not simply "correctly" (Aristotle, *Nic. Eth.* II, 1106a 20). If these moral habits are negative (i.e., disvalues), the order of preferences will be distorted, as the choices will be. As Aristotle explains, "Therefore it is evident that it is impossible to be practically wise[13] without being good" (*Nic. Eth.* VI, 1144a 35). Virtues are also called "habits of character" (Yepes 1996; Snook and Khurana 2004) because each of our decisions leaves on us a mark that, over time, becomes a habit, and this habit shapes our character and our subsequent choices. Ordinary language reflects this idea: "a person with values" is the same as "a person of character," and both mean "a person with moral principles," which are shown in certain behaviors.

To conclude, if we apply the hierarchy of values to behavioral values, we see that skills are in the domain of what is useful or pleasurable, whereas virtues are in the sphere of what is noble or honest. Therefore, virtues are the values at the summit in any human organization. With regard to whether there is an internal hierarchy among virtues, interestingly enough, Aristotle (*Nic. Eth.* VI, 1144b 30 ff) considers that values are all interconnected and mutually required, and that it makes no sense to position two virtues against each other (e.g., sincerity vs. loyalty, or prudence vs. bravery).

If we are to consider that "values are the underpinning of human actions" (Sharma and Nordqvist 2008: 82), families aiming to establish or to revise their own values and those of their businesses must have a clear vision of what values are, their different types, the order existing within them, and some ideas for developing and transmitting them. These have been the issues addressed in Section 2. In the empirical section (Section 3), we will have the opportunity to relate our findings to all of them.

FAMILY BUSINESS VALUES IN PRACTICE

To present the applicability of the theoretical framework outlined in Section 2, we now turn to an empirical approximation regarding the differences and the similarities of the values espoused by the top 100 of the

---

[13] "Practical wisdom": for the Greek *phrónesis*, more commonly translated as "prudence."

world's largest family-owned firms and the top 100 non–family-owned businesses. Through a detailed analysis of these values, we will arrange the most frequently mentioned values according to their typology and hierarchical order. Likewise, we will conduct a fine-grained analysis of the top two values that are characteristic of some large family-owned firms. With the aid of psychology, we will provide insights into the consequences of practicing these values and suggest different ways of cultivating and transmitting them over time.

The empirical approximation mentioned in the preceding text[14] consists of a sample of the values formally stated on the websites of the world's top 100 largest family-owned businesses, listed in *Family Business Magazine* for the year 2010, and the world's top 100 largest non–family-owned businesses, listed in the Fortune 500 company rankings for the year 2008. From the overall sample (200 corporations), we collected a total of 832 values (427 from family-owned businesses and 405 from non–family-owned businesses). Once we had the complete list of values, we ranked them according to the number of times each value was mentioned on the companies' websites. From this ranking, we focused on the top-23 values that were mentioned most frequently in both family-owned companies and non-family organizations (see Table 10.2).

Table 10.2 describes the values that were most frequently mentioned by the world's largest corporations. Interestingly, the top-three most mentioned values are the same for both family-owned businesses and non-family businesses (i.e., "integrity," "respect," and "customers"). Several authors identify "integrity" and "respect" as core business values, along with "truth," "reputation, "honesty," and "responsibility" (e.g., Cavanagh 1998; Van Lee et al. 2005). Hence, it is not surprising to find "integrity" and "respect" as top values in both types of organizations. Similarly, without customers, a company could not exist; hence, it should be expected to find the value of "customers" occupying the third position in the ranking for both types of businesses.

To study further the most characteristic espoused values, we created a ranking with the most mentioned values in family-owned businesses that were less mentioned in non-family businesses. To appreciate the difference better, we calculated a ratio representing the distance between the values on both lists by dividing the number of times a value was mentioned in

---

[14] To learn more about the methodology used in this empirical section, see Ceja, Agulles, and Tàpies (2010).

TABLE 10.2. *Number of Occurrences of Core Values Identified in the Sample*

Values Mentioned in Non-Family Firms	Total	Values Mentioned in Family-Owned Firms	Total
Integrity	39	Integrity	36
Respect	25	Respect	23
Customers	23	Customers	20
Innovation	21	Quality	16
Teamwork	17	Responsibility	15
Responsibility	13	Excellence	14
Performance	12	Teamwork	11
Trust	12	Care for people	10
Diversity	9	Innovation	10
Care for people	9	Employees	9
Employees	8	Community involvement	9
Environment	8	Passion	8
Community involvement	8	Creativity	6
Openness	8	Diversity	6
Commitment	7	Entrepreneurship	6
Excellence	7	Shareholders	6
Leadership	7	Communication	6
Passion	7	Generosity	5
Quality	7	Honesty	5
Transparency	7	Humility	5
Ethical behavior	7	Continuous improvement	5
Honesty	6	Service	5
Professionalism	6	Fairness	5

family-owned businesses by the number of times that same value was mentioned in non-family businesses. We focused on those values that present a distance ratio > 2. Five values were found to be most characteristic of family-owned businesses: "generosity" (was not mentioned by non-family firms), "humility" (distance ratio = 5), "communication" (distance ratio = 3), "service" (distance ratio = 2.5), and "quality" (distance ratio = 2.3). Hence, our analyses show that specific values are mentioned frequently by family-owned businesses, whereas they were seldom stated or not stated at all by non-family businesses. We briefly analyze the top-two values showing the highest distance ratios (i.e., "generosity" and "humility") in the subsections that follow. However, we first focus on the practical application of the theoretical framework presented in Section 2 to categorize each of these values according to its typology and hierarchical position.

Putting Theory into Practice: Respecting the Typology and Hierarchy of Values

Our aim was to examine the top-23 most mentioned values on the websites of the world's top-100 largest family-owned firms and non-family businesses, as well as those values more characteristic of family-owned businesses, in terms of their type and place in the natural hierarchy of values. We used the theoretical framework developed in Section II to create a matrix in which values can be ordered according to the principles stated in our theoretical approximation (see Figure 10.4).[15]

In Figure 10.4, all the values listed in Table 10.2 are ordered according to their type and place within the proposed hierarchy (see Section 2). For instance, "integrity" and "respect," which were among the top-three most mentioned values in both family-owned businesses and non-family companies, are classified as behavioral values, and, within this category, they are placed in the "virtues" frame (i.e., habits for acting well). Moreover, "integrity" and "respect" are noble values (i.e., those values that are good or honest in themselves), meaning that they are among the highest values in the natural hierarchy of "good" according to Aristotle. It is important to note that some values can occupy more than one place within the natural hierarchy of values, depending on how the organization defines such values. In other words, the boundaries presented in our matrix become fuzzy, depending on how the organization defines a specific value. For instance, the values of "customers" and "employees" can be regarded as noble if the company considers its employees and customers as good in themselves. However, if the company perceives their employees and customers as something that it needs in order to be successful (i.e., as simple resources), the values should be placed within the useful category.

In our view, families in business, as well as other practitioners and academics in the field of family businesses, could benefit from the simple exercise of placing the values which they are working on in the matrix presented in Figure 10.4, according to their type and hierarchical place. This task should be a positive way of helping families in business to reflect on their values and should ensure that there is a correct integration of noble, useful, and pleasurable values in their daily activities.

---

[15] In Figure 10.4, the values that were found to be more characteristic of family-owned businesses are emphasized with boldface and italics.

HIERARCHY OF VALUES			TYPES OF VALUES		
Noble	Useful	Pleasurable			
customers, employees, environment, shareholders, excellence	employees, customers, **quality,** excellence, performance, environment, shareholders	quality	Object/Outcome values		
happiness		happiness	End-state values		
respect, responsibility, care for people, trust, diversity, **service,** community involvement, transparency	innovation, entrepreneurship, openness, commitment, transparency, professionalism, continuous improvement	innovation, passion	Attitudes	Behavioral values	
	teamwork, **communication,** creativity, leadership	creativity	Skills		
integrity, respect, **humility, generosity,** ethical behavior, honesty, fairness			Virtues		

FIGURE 10.4. Hierarchy and types of values.

Analysis of the Values Most Characteristic of Family-Owned Firms

The five values that are more characteristic of family-owned firms include "generosity" and "humility," which are noble values because they are good or honest in themselves and, at the same time, virtues. Moreover, the value of "communication" can be classified as a skill and is placed within the useful frame. The value of "service" can be considered to be an attitude and could be placed within the noble or useful frame. Finally, "quality" is an outcome value and can be classified as useful or pleasurable. More specifically, these values concern positive traits – "generosity," "humility," "service," "communication," "quality" – that contribute to the fulfillment of the organization's members; thus, they appear as fundamental and people-oriented. Likewise, they emphasize collectivity and have a stakeholder perspective.

Given the scope and space restraints of this chapter, we analyze in detail the top-two values showing the highest distance ratio (i.e., "generosity" and "humility"), emphasizing their link to family-owned firms as well as their consequences. The forthcoming analysis is based on the assumption that the entwined nature of family-owned firms (i.e., overlap among three subsystems: family, ownership, and business[16]) implies that strong values, which are held by the founding or owning family, are likely to be transferred and maintained in the business system (Denison, Lief, and Ward 2004; Sharma and Nordqvist 2008). Hence, our analysis is based upon the link between values and the owning family, as well as the effects of pursuing such values at individual level (individual family members and employees) and group level (families in business and the company as a whole).

Generosity. "Generosity" can be defined as the "common orientation of the self toward the other" (Peterson and Seligman 2004: 326). Family-owned businesses are known for their commitment to being generous, socially responsible, and good members of the community (Breeze 2009). Their distinct commitment to long-term stewardship, stability, and continuity means that an orientation toward generous behavior is frequently embedded in their businesses.

For instance, one family-owned business, a leader in communications, media, and automotive services, posts the value of "generosity" as a key

---

[16] Tagiuri and Davis (1996).

corporate principle[17]: "We believe it's good business to serve through volunteerism and financial support."[18] Likewise, a family-owned firm engaged in various business sectors defines "generosity" as a core corporate value: "We try to play a role in non-governmental organizations, in services and activities for the benefit of society and the public."[19] Family-owned firms often manifest the value of generosity through philanthropic activities; indeed, in America, Europe, and Asia, family businesses dedicate an important part of their patrimony to philanthropy (Amit and Liechtenstein 2009). For instance, a managing director of a family-owned multinational conglomerate in which philanthropy plays a major role in its thinking observes: "I find it very energizing to be able to go to work to earn profits by being more efficient and decent about the way of doing business [. . .] I do the job because 30–40% of the profit is going back to help other people. That's why we do the job."[20]

Likewise, the founder of a family-owned firm that is one of the world's largest fashion distributors created a foundation whose object is to promote activities in the fields of culture, education, research, social action, social welfare, and science. The founder expresses the value of generosity in his reasons for creating a nonprofit organization:

It is my belief that societies improve through the work and contributions of all their members. [. . .] My true and simple desire is that, through the strategies and activities of the Foundation, the results of my life experience, both personal and professional, may reach all those members of the society who might be in special need of backing and encouragement.[21]

These examples show that the value of generosity, channeled through philanthropic activities, can generate positive ripples of empathy and social responsibility among communities and stakeholders. According to psychological research (e.g., Wheeler, Gorey, and Greenblatt 1998; Musick, Herzog, and House 1999; Van Willigen 2000), the practice of generosity can have positive consequences for society (e.g., economic benefits, increased global well-being) and for benefactors (e.g., longevity, psychological well-being, satisfaction with life, personal fulfillment).

[17] All the examples included in this section are based on the public image transmitted through different media channels by the companies espousing specific values.
[18] Available at: http://www.coxenterprises.com (Accessed March 2010).
[19] Available at: http://www.sabanci.com (Accessed March 2010).
[20] *The Guardian*, Thursday, March 27, 2008.
[21] Available at: http://www.faortega.org (Accessed November 2010).

Humility. "Humility" can be defined as the disposition to view oneself as an equal to any other person, regardless of objective differences such as physical beauty, wealth, social status, intelligence, or other resources (Emmons 2000; Tangney 2000). Far from having a low opinion of oneself, being humble means having an accurate assessment of oneself and keeping one's talents and accomplishments in perspective (Richards 1992); having a sense of self-acceptance; and having the ability to acknowledge one's limitations, mistakes, and imperfections (Clark 1992). Likewise, humility is linked to the appreciation of the value of people and things, openness to new ideas, and the disposition to recognizing that one is but a part of the universe; several psychologists call this becoming "unselved" (Tangney 2000). In the context of families in business, the value of humility represents an important source of balance, well-being, and competitive advantage. For example, a family-owned firm that is one of the world's largest furniture retailers expresses "humility" as one of its core corporate values:

The stone wall is a powerful symbol for the grit and determination of the people of Småland, and it helps us [. . .] to remember our humble origins. The harsh conditions that Småland folk have traditionally had to struggle with [. . .] have forced the people in this part of Sweden to live on their wits. It has made them determined and tenacious, but also humble.[22]

From this example, we can see clearly that, for this family-owned business, the value of humility resonates with the family firm's origin. The humble spirit of the founding generation is present, along with the uniquely close relationship that the company has with the local community's culture. This value is likely to be transmitted across generations through mythical accounts centered on the founders, who attained astounding success for the company by enacting fundamental values.

The ability to keep one's accomplishments in perspective, a key element of humility, is reflected in the comments that the president of a family-owned multinational conglomerate made after he was awarded Businessman of the Year recognition. After the presenter said, "You have become a star," the president replied:

I am deeply [. . .] honored to have been awarded this honor. It's something that I will carry with humility because I believe all I have been doing in my small way is my own job. And I think I have a sense of great sensitivity to the fact that this is being recognized by you. So, thank you for giving me this recognition and for all the people who have made this happen.[23]

---

[22] Available at: www.ikea.com (Accessed March 2010).
[23] Available at: http://ibnlive.in.com June 20, 2007.

Moreover, the ability to acknowledge one's limitations, mistakes, and failures, an important element of humility, is represented in the words of the president and founder of one of the world's leading family-owned supermarkets: "On my way, I've made wise moves, but I've also committed many mistakes; the key is having the courage to get up after each failure and having a great team that has made it possible to be the company we are today."[24]

Being open to new ideas and recognizing the value of other people are essential elements of humility. In the words of a president of a large family-owned business: "To be a good president it is vital to have the capacity to listen to everybody, be open to new ideas and think carefully in order to get your decisions right."[25]

The value of humility represents wisdom. A family-owned business that has gained a sense of humility is no longer at the center of its own world. Rather, its focus is on the larger community, of which it is a part. This can give family-owned firms strong roots in their home communities, creating opportunities to strengthen the business, the family, and the community in which it operates.

CONCLUDING REMARKS

The definition and classification of values, the empirical approximation regarding the differences and similarities of the values espoused by the world's top-100 largest family-owned and non–family-owned businesses, and the link between these values and family-owned businesses – as well as the consequences of enacting these values – examined in this chapter have important practical implications for communicating, discussing, and putting into practice the values that are important to family-owned businesses.

We conclude this chapter by offering some practical tools to help families formulate both their own values and their companies' values to make a difference in society and to help them view their businesses as vehicles for more community involvement, personal meaning, and social contribution.

1. **Values that really are values.** Families in business must be certain that what they are expressing as values are really values: that is,

---

[24] *Expansión*, November 20, 2010.
[25] *Expansión*, November 20, 2010.

that they are clearly distinct from vision and mission, and that they point to any of the entities that we have defined here as values, including desirable objects or outcomes, desirable end-states, and desirable behaviors.

2. **Respecting the hierarchy of values.** It is important that the chosen values respect the natural hierarchy of values: first, honest or noble values; second, useful values; and, finally, pleasurable values. In any case, at least some of the first and second types of values must be present and in this order in the Mission Statement.

3. **Values that fit the family's values.** It is crucial for the family business to define the values that best fit with the principles and beliefs that sustain the family's culture. It is easy to appeal to standard or commonplace terms that are accepted by everyone but that say nothing; the challenge is to find the words that capture the differentiating traits of the family business.

4. **Consistency with values.** Values in a Mission Statement must be the actual principles of action for all the people involved in the business. Here, it is crucial that "espoused values" are "values-in-use" or "lived values" (Argyris 1976; Schein 1985). Inconsistency between official statements and actual behavior in an organization is a source of cynicism, internal demotivation, lack of trust, and even unethical behavior. In this sense, the best way to transmit values is through example.

5. **Revising values.** It is advisable to establish a periodic examination of the Mission Statement and its elements, such as during each generational transition or when enlarging the business. The main goal of the review is to check compliance.

6. **Learning values.** Communicating values frequently is vital. Governance structures, such as the family office, the family council, and the family assembly, are excellent spaces for reflecting upon personal, familial and organizational values. Likewise, the exercise of writing the values in the family constitution can yield very powerful results. The family constitution should clearly state how to apply each of the corporate and family values to everyday practice.

References

Amit, Raffi, and Heinrich Liechtenstein (2009). *Benchmarking the Single Family Office: Identifying the Performance Drivers*. The Wharton Global Family Alliance. IESE Business School, Barcelona, Spain.

Aquinas, Thomas. *Summa Theologiae*. Fathers of the English Dominican Province, trans. Westminster, MD: Christian Classics, 1981.

Argyris, Chris (1976). "Single-Loop and Double-Loop Models in Research on Decision Making." *Administrative Science Quarterly*, 21(3): 363–75.

Aristotle (1941). *Nicomachean Ethics*. In R. McKeon (ed.), *The Basic Works of Aristotle*. New York: Random House, pp. 972–1112.

Bain, Paul G., Yoshihisa Kashima, and Nick Haslam (2006). "Conceptual Beliefs about Human Values and Their Implications: Human Nature Beliefs Predict Value Importance, Value Trade-Offs, and Responses to Value Rhetoric." *Journal of Personality and Social Psychology*, 91(2): 351–67.

Bartlett, Christopher A., and Sumantra Ghoshal (1994). "Changing the Role of Top Management: Beyond Strategy to Purpose." *Harvard Business Review*, 72(6): 79–88.

Breeze, Beth (2009). *Natural Philanthropists: Findings of the Family Business Philanthropy and Social Responsibility Inquiry*. London: Institute for Family Business/Community Foundation Network.

Cavanagh, Gerald F. (1998). *American Business Values*. Upper Saddle River, NJ: Prentice-Hall.

Ceja, Lucía, Remei Agulles, and Josep Tàpies (2010). "The Importance of Values in Family-Owned Firms." Working Paper D-875-E. IESE Business School, University of Navarra, Barcelona, Spain.

Clark, Alice T. (1992). "Humility." In Daniel H. Ludlow (ed.), *Encyclopedia of Mormonism*. New York: Macmillan.

Denison, Daniel, Colleen Lief, and John L. Ward (2004). "Culture in Family-Owned Enterprises: Recognizing and Leveraging Unique Strengths." *Family Business Review*, 17(1): 61–70.

Distelberg, Brian, and Ritch L. Sorenson (2009). "Updating Systems Concepts in Family Businesses: A Focus on Values, Resource Flows, and Adaptability." *Family Business Review*, 22(1): 65–81.

Emmons, Robert A. (2000). "Personality and Forgiveness." In Michael E. McCullough, Kenneth I. Pargament, and Carl E. Thoresen (eds.), *Forgiveness. Theory, Research, and Practice*. New York: Guilford Press, pp. 156–173.

Fairhurst, Gail T., Jerry Monroe Jordan, and Kurt Neuwirth (1997). "Why Are We Here? Managing the Meaning of an Organizational Mission Statement." *Journal of Applied Communication Research*, 25(4): 243–63.

Hofstede, Geert H. (1980). *Culture's Consequences: International Differences in Work-Related Values*. London: SAGE.

Hofstede, Geert H., Bram Neuijen, Denise Daval Ohayv, and Geert Sanders (1990). "Measuring Organizational Cultures: A Qualitative Study Across Twenty Cases." *Administrative Science Quarterly*, 35(2): 286–316.

House, Robert J., Paul John Hanges, Mansour Javidan, Peter W. Dorfman, and Vipin Gupta, eds. (2004). *Culture, Leadership and Organizations. The Globe Study of 62 Societies*. Thousand Oaks, CA: SAGE.

Kluckhohn, Clyde (1951). "Values and Value-Orientations in the Theory of Action: An Exploration in Definition and Classification." In Talcott Parsons and Edward A. Shils (eds.), *Toward a General Theory of Action*. Cambridge, MA: Harvard University Press, pp. 388–433.

Koiranen, Matti (2002). "Over 100 Years of Age but Still Entrepreneurially Active in Business: Exploring the Values and Family Characteristics of Old Finnish Family Firms." *Family Business Review*, 15(3): 175–87.

MacIntyre, Alasdair (1984). *After Virtue*, 2nd ed. Notre Dame IN: University of Notre Dame Press.

Meglino, Bruce M., and Elizabeth C. Ravlin (1998). "Individual Values in Organizations: Concepts, Controversies, and Research." *Journal of Management*, 24(3): 351–89.

Musick, Marc A., A. Regula Herzog, and James S. House (1999). "Volunteering and Mortality among Older Adults: Findings from a National Sample." *Journal of Gerontology: Psychological Sciences and Social Sciences*, 54B(3): S173–S180.

Pearce II, John A., and Fred David (1987). "Corporate Mission Statements: The Bottom Line." *Academy of Management Executive*, 1: 109–15.

Peterson, Christopher, and Martin E.P. Seligman (2004). *Character Strengths and Virtues. A Handbook of Classification*. New York: Oxford University Press.

Richards, Norvin (1992). *Humility*. Philadelphia, PA: Temple University Press.

Rokeach, Milton (1973). *The Nature of Human Values*. New York: The Free Press.

Schein, Edgar H. (1985). *Organizational Culture and Leadership. A Dynamic View*. San Francisco, CA: Jossey-Bass.

Scheler, Max (1973). *Formalism in Ethics and Non-Formal Ethics of Values: A New Attempt Toward the Foundation of an Ethical Personalism*, Manfred S. Frings and Roger L. Funk, trans. Evanston, IL: Northwestern University Press. (Original German edition: *Der Formalismus in der Ethik und die materiale Wertethik*), pp. 1913–16.

Schwartz, Shalom H. (1992). "Universals in the Content and Structure of Values: Theoretical Advances and Empirical Tests in 20 Countries." In Mark P. Zanna (ed.), *Advances in Experimental Social Psychology*, Vol. 25. New York: Academic Press, pp. 1–65.

Schwartz, Shalom H., and Wolfgang Bilsky (1990). "Toward a Theory of the Universal Content and Structure of Values: Extensions and Cross-Cultural Replications." *Journal of Personality and Social Psychology*, 58(5): 878–91.

Senge, Peter M. (1998). "The Practice of Innovation." *Leader to Leader*, no. 9: 16–22.

Sharma, Pramodita, and Mattias Nordqvist (2008). "A Classification Scheme for Family Firms: From Family Values to Effective Governance to Firm Performance." In Josep Tàpies and John L. Ward (ed.), *Family Values and Value Creation. The Fostering of Enduring Values within Family-owned Businesses*. Basingstoke: Palgrave, pp. 71–101.

Snook, Scott, and Rakesh Khurana (2004). "Developing 'Leaders of Character.' Lessons from West Point." In Robert Gandossy and Jeffrey Sonnenfeld (eds.), *Leadership and Governance from the Inside Out*. New York: John Wiley & Sons, pp. 213–233.

Tagiuri, Renato, and John A. Davis (1996). "Bivalent Attributes of the Family Firm." *Family Business Review*, 9(2): 199–208.

Tangney, June Price (2000). "Humility: Theoretical Perspectives, Empirical Findings and Directions for Future Research." *Journal of Social and Clinical Psychology*, 19(1): 70–82.

Tàpies, Josep (2009). Empresa familiar: Ni tan pequeña ni tan joven [Family Business: Not So Small nor So Young]. Barcelona: Fundación Jesús Serra, Grupo Catalana Occidente.

Van Lee, Reggie, Lisa Fabish, and Nancy McGaw (2005). "The Value of Corporate Values." *Strategy and Business*, 39: 1–14.

Van Willigen, Marieke (2000). "Differential Benefits of Volunteering over the Life Course." *Journal of Gerontology: Psychological Sciences and Social Sciences*, 55B(5): S308–S318.

Wheeler, Judith A., Kevin M. Gorey, and Bernard Greenblatt (1998). "The Beneficial Effects of Volunteering for Older Volunteers and the People They Serve: A Meta-Analysis." *International Journal of Aging and Human Development*, 47(1): 69–79.

Yepes Stork, Ricardo (1996). *Fundamentos de antropología. Un ideal de la excelencia humana*, [Fundamentals of Anthropology. An Ideal of Human Excellence]. Pamplona, Spain: EUNSA.

Managing Professionalization in Family Business

Transforming Strategies for Managerial Succession and Recruitment in Family Firms in the Twentieth Century

Susanna Fellman

POINT OF DEPARTURE

Two opposing discourses on family businesses and owner managers persist in the scholarly literature. One presumes that owner managers are, on average, less qualified than salaried ones. Family firms are also susceptible to problems in relation to succession, are slow to adapt to changes in the economic and institutional environment, and are less inclined to grow. As a result, family firms are prone to being short-lived and less successful than those led by salaried managers.[1] This view, that family firms are predestined to fail, has been controverted, however, by the prevalence and persistence of both successful and long-lived family firms in various modes of capitalism. The other discourse is, in turn, based on a positive, nearly romanticized, view of family firms and their owners. Family firms are seen as durable, more responsible toward their employees, and inclined to stand for values other than pecuniary ones. This view is based on assumptions that family managers, as a rule, are oriented toward long-time planning and are guided by strong, positive family values and the feeling that they have a legacy to preserve (Rose 1995; Colli 2003; Colli and Rose 2008).

The origins of these contradictory views are rooted in several factors, which I do not address in depth here. There is extensive literature on family businesses and their management from a historical perspective. However, the overtly positive view of family firms and their managers

---

[1] Mike Burkhart et al. make a basic assumption that "a professional is a better manager than an heir," when constructing a model for succession in family firms (Burkhart et al. 2003).

is, in part, related to the fact that studies of family businesses are usually based on specific examples of successful family firms. The negative view of the family-led firm has, again, been nourished by the chandlerian claim (Chandler 1990) that the persistence of "personal capitalism" in the United Kingdom has been one reason behind the country's weaker economic performance in comparison to the United States and Germany since the late nineteenth century. Clearly, both views have their flaws and are, to some extent, built on assumptions that in-depth empirical research has been unable to support.

There also appears to be some kind of cyclicality in how the family firm is conceived. Today (2012), the image of the family business seems to be particularly positive. Family business has come to be seen as a possible solution to the faceless global capitalism of the new millennium and the investors' focus on the following quarter. The current financial crisis has enforced the positive image of family firms. Visible, active owners and long-standing family firms are considered to be the solution to the faceless market forces and irresponsible investors who look only for short-term profits and thus cause instability. The family business lobby has been quick to respond to this trend, and today a common slogan among many family firms is that their "quarter is 25 years."[2] Such slogans aim to give the impression that family firms represent long-term planning combined with a strong commitment to the local community and a more responsible form of capitalism.[3] The family-firm lobbies have grown strong and influential in many countries, to the extent of being able to affect matters such as taxation (Fernández Pérez and Puig 2009).

Although studies have proved that the family-firm model is not a relic of the early stages of capitalism, they have also shown that family businesses are susceptible to certain problems, and that by no means have

---

[2] "Rettigs kvartal är 25 år." Interview with Cyril von Rettig in *Hufvudstadsbladet* October 20, 2010. The Rettig Group Ltd. is a group of family-owned companies involved in four business areas: hydronic and electrical heating and indoor climate regulation, shipping, limestone-based products, and real-estate development and rental. See http://www.rettig .fi. Originally, the Rettig Company started in tobacco manufacturing.

[3] According to the Finnish association of family business "[f]amily enterprises are not only stable, they are also competitive and renewing, they follow developments in the market, create added value to the economy and create new entrepreneurship for their own part. Family enterprises also play a major role in regional and local economies. They bring stability and permanence to their regions. The owners do not very easily change their place of residence and thus the domicile of the enterprise often remains the same." Available at: http://www.perheyritystenliitto.fi/files/FINFamilyBusinessReport_2006_English.pdf.

all owner managers been up to their task. Succession in top management and the transition from owners to salaried managers is also an "Achilles heel" of family firms. Owners of family firms have themselves considered that the most significant, and, at the same time, the most difficult, questions that they face are how to cope with succession in top management and how to relate to managers coming from outside the family (Chua, Chrisman, and Sharma 2003; Colli 2003). Although many possess a positive view of the family firm, there is a tendency to view them as slow to change and inclined to underperform. As Alex Stewart and Michael Hitt (2011) note, there is an underlying idea that family firms should benefit from being a little more like a non-family firm.

Consequently, instead of resorting to simplified views and assumptions, more detailed empirical research is needed.

THE AIM OF THE CHAPTER

The topic of this chapter is how family firms have managed and responded to the professionalization of management and how this process has affected recruitment and succession in top management in family firms. When, why, and to what extent has this process led to the recruitment of outsiders? When management was transferred to outsiders, who and from where were these outsiders recruited? Or, if outsiders were not recruited, how was the education and preparation of the family heirs to the business transformed in response to the professionalization process? As many owner-led firms have been both resilient and successful over time, it is evident that owners have been able to find solutions and develop new strategies to respond to the challenges arising from the growing demand for skill and experience among top managers and professional experts. I am particularly interested in how the professionalization process has been reflected in the managerial profile and how the family firm has responded to the demands for "professionalism."

Furthermore, the chapter also aims to examine company-level discourses on professionalization, recruitment strategies, managerial selection, and managerial training. We know a great deal about the discourses of so-called management intellectuals, which discuss the need for management training and how to promote "professionalism" in companies in modern society. However, we know much less about how the owners at the company level reacted to these issues. To what extent have the owners of family business taken the professionalization process into account when they have prepared for succession?

Finally, the concept of the "professionalization of management" is also discussed and problematized. It is a complex concept that is seldom clearly defined (Fellman 2001; Hall and Nordqvist 2008; Galambos 2010). The professionalization of management has, for instance, often been equated with the transition from owner managers to salaried managers. This is a significant aspect of the concept, but, when studying the process in detail, it becomes evident that the professionalization process also includes other factors.

These questions are addressed empirically by studying top managers in Finnish family firms, including the changes in their educational and career backgrounds and the transformation in recruitment patterns and succession strategies. These topics are also put in a comparative context to show divergences and similarities and to reveal continuities and discontinuities. Nevertheless, there are some problems in carrying out comparisons. There are extensive long-term data about the transformation of the "managerial profile" in various countries, but these prosopographic studies of the transformation of the profile of the business élite surprisingly seldom distinguish between owner and salaried managers. It is true that there are also some investigations from other countries that address this matter and these studies, including the, by now, classical works by Mabel Newcomer (1955a) and Hartmut Kaelble (1980), which are acknowledged here. Also, of interest is a recent book dealing with entrepreneurship and entrepreneurs in a comparative historical perspective, which uses bigger samples of entrepreneurs and also touches on the role of the family, family networks, and owners (Garcia-Ruiz and Toninelli 2010).

The Finnish material covering the period from 1900 to 1975 consists of a sample of 324 managing directors (*verkställande direktör*) or directors with the equivalent position in 66 large-scale manufacturing firms during the period. The personnel data were collected from various sources, primarily registers of divergent types, and are investigated principally by cohort analysis. The managers have been divided into three cohorts both according to year of birth and year of appointment as managing director. In the case of analysis by year of appointment, the number of managers rises to 347, as 23 managers had been managing directors in more than one of our example firms. The material from the later period concerns the largest companies in all sectors of the economy and is not directly comparable to the earlier period, although the overwhelming majority of the firms included in the data set from these periods are, in fact, also to be found from the manufacturing industry. I often use the somewhat vague concept of the "top manager" in the text. Here, "top manager" means the managing directors or chief executive officers (CEOs).

This investigation thus focuses mainly on large-scale firms, both listed and unlisted, which to some extent limits the ability to generalize from the results. The overwhelming majority of the family firms are small and medium sized. On the other hand, questions related to professionalism, succession, and the relationship between family members and outside directors are relevant for all types of family firms, irrespective of size or industry.

INDUSTRIALIZATION AND THE "PROFESSIONALIZATION OF MANAGEMENT"

Industrialization, technological development, and the emergence of large firms had a profound effect on management. Managing a large business required new skills and a new approach to the managerial task. This led to an influx of professional experts at various levels and in various positions in growing companies. Gradually, top management positions were also taken over by a new cadre of managers with a formal education and ample experience. To an increasing extent, this new generation of managers consisted of salaried employees, without ownership in the firm or a family connection to the owners. The transition was a process best characterized as a "bottom up" change, in which, at first, junior management and expert positions were offered to candidates from outside the family, and then gradually positions higher up in the hierarchy were taken over by outsiders.

It has been thought that the shift from owners to salaried managers led to – in the chandlerian vocabulary – a "managerial revolution" in which old, ad hoc–based systems of management were replaced by systematic approaches to the managerial task (Chandler 1980). Thus, it was to be seen as a significant part of the modernization process. According to Chandler, there were, more or less, no limits to what these professional managers could do (Galambos 2010). On the other hand, it was also quickly observed that there could be negative effects from the dispersion of ownership and the transition toward salaried managers. These salaried managers lacking ownership in the firm might have goals other than those of the owners (see Berle and Means 1932, Book I, Chapter V). Moreover, empirical research on management in family firms could show that owner managers can be extremely competent, have an extensive professional education, and maintain a professional attitude, while salaried managers can both lack a formal education and act "unprofessionally."

The transition from owners to salaried managers and the changes it brought about has been a central issue in economic and business-history research, particularly since Alfred D. Chandler's book *The Visible Hand*. However, the matter had already been discussed much earlier. The transformations in top management, which occurred as a consequence of the industrial and corporate change, were easily visible in the interwar period in, for example, the United States, and, as a result, there was an extensive body of literature before Chandler that deals with various aspects of the phenomenon For instance, the books by F.W. Taussig and C.S. Joslyn (1932) and by William Miller (1962) are classical works. In *The Big Business Executive*, based on a detailed investigation of three cohorts (1900, 1925, 1950) of top managers in big U.S. corporations, Mabel Newcomer (1955a) gave a detailed account of how industrialization, the growth of big business, and the transformation in the educational system led to changes in both the backgrounds of business executives and their approach to the managerial task. Newcomer (1955b) also showed that industrial and corporate development not only had been marked by a transition toward selecting managers from outside the owning family, but had also been affected by parallel developments that were inseparable from this transition and that had profoundly transformed the profile of the big-business executive. Among other things, the amount of formal education had increased and managerial recruits had to spend increasingly long years before reaching top positions. Moreover, management became a full-time task and managers became more closely tied to the firm. The last notion could be seen as resembling "professional ethics," commonly associated with liberal professions. In fact, Newcomer (1955a: 143–4) observed an aspect, which is also interesting from today's perspective when demands for more responsible managers are increasingly at the fore, namely, that the professionalization of the big business executive was also accompanied by a prominent position in relation to the surrounding society and that this position required high moral values. Big business in the United States had obligations to contribute to "the community chest." In 1960, a contemporary analyst, Thomas Imse (1960), emphasized that a professional status for managers should include a greater responsibility toward both employees and customers.

This development has, from time to time, raised the question of whether management can be regarded as a profession in the same way as a traditional liberal profession. This debate was particularly lively in the 1960s and 1970s, when the debate on the "professionalization of everyone," as described by Harold Wilensky (1964), was also to the fore. During these decades, belief in the development of a management science and management education, which would provide the kind of skills necessary to lead any kind of firms, irrespective of size or industry, was also at its height. It was occasionally emphasized that management was a "specialist function" that required specialization irrespective of whether the manager was an owner or a salaried outsider. Thus, as Thomas Imse (1960: 38) argued, it was not surprising that "thoughts of professionalization of this occupation should arise." "Professional managers" have sometimes even been equated with managers with a management education, that is, those with an MBA or equivalent. For example, in 1966, R.A. Gordon (Gordon 1966: 318) defined professional managers as "salaried experts, trained by education and experience in the field of management."

At the time, these ideas were already widely refuted whereas today there is a widespread agreement among scholars that the professionalization of management did not signify the transformation of management into a full-fledged profession, for which a certain type of education was required, or that managers could be seen as forming a professional group. No single type of education or educational group has been able to monopolize the managerial function either, as managerial competence is highly dependent on the organization and the context.

However, the discussion has continued. One reason for this is that scholars naturally aim to understand what the "professionalization of management" might signify when it is not equal to management becoming a profession. For example, Michael Reed and Peter Anthony (1992) have argued that managers could be considered as a prototype of an "organizational profession." Managers have a knowledge base that can provide some resistance toward intrusion from competitor groups, although this control is much more limited than for a traditional profession. Although managers clearly do not form a professional group, they do possess techniques and languages that others do not have (for a discussion, see Wilson and Thomson 2006: 173).

Scholars have also discussed other dimensions that could be seen as indicators of professionalism among managers. Professionalism could, for instance, be observed in the introduction of meritocratic values, routinization and the systematization of procedures, and a formalization of structures (for an overview, see Stewart and Hitt 2012). These aspects are important both in family firms and in firms managed by salaried experts, but it is often assumed that family firms, in particular, suffer from nepotism and from a lack of meritocratic values and formalization. The concept is complex, but, as shown in the following section discussion of family firms can help illuminate the concept and its various aspects.

"THE PROFESSIONALIZATION OF MANAGEMENT" AND FAMILY BUSINESS RESEARCH

In family business literature, discussions on "the professionalization of management" have often focused on the separation of ownership and management. The concept has occasionally even been equated with the shift from owners to salaried managers. Professional managers are, then, the same as "full-time salaried managers."[4] This must be considered a very simplistic view of the concept, however. Moreover, as Annika Hall and Mattias Nordqvist (2008) stress, this means that owner managers, *by definition*, cannot be "professional." As they conclude, this must be seen as a very questionable argument.

W. Gibb Dyer (1989) recognized three characteristics that could signify the professionalization of management in family firms: the professionalization of the family members, the professionalization of existing employees, and the appointment of professional managers from outside the firm. In this extended, multidimensional view, professional experts in the family firm are seen as forming an inseparable part of the expanding and developing firm. Although family members could be as competent and as dynamic as the salaried managers, they could not manage without salaried managers. This is also a prominent feature in the process under investigation here.

As mentioned earlier, Newcomer had already observed that there are many aspects to "the professionalization of management" other than the ownership aspect. One is the competence aspect. For instance, in her empirical investigation of managing directors/CEOs in the Finnish manufacturing industry, Susanna Fellman (2000) showed the significance of the competence aspect for being considered as a "professional manager," and this issue is equally important to owner managers – an issue that is

---

[4] For example, Raveendra Chittor and Ranja Das have defined professionalization of management as "the succession of management from a family member to non-family professionals" (Chittor and Das 2007). For a recent discussion on the problems with this definition, see, for example, Galambos (2010).

returned to in detail later on. Moreover, she noted – in line with New-comer's work – that managers had to show a certain attitude toward the managerial task and toward succession. Management in big business also became a full-time job. This development occurred irrespective of the managers' ownership in the firm (Fellman 2000: 43).

According to Hall and Nordqvist (2008), the managing of family firms also requires a certain sociocultural sensitivity, which has to be included as an aspect of "professional management." They stress that this "cultural competence" is highly significant for successful management, especially in family firms. By cultural competence in family firms, they mean an "understanding of the family's goals and meanings of being in business, that is, the values and norms underlying the reason for being in business" (Hall and Nordqvist 2008: 58). Clearly, cultural competence is also nec-essary in other types of firms. All firms have norms and values for being in business, although such norms are, perhaps, particularly prominent in family firms. Other scholars have stressed that the family often has signif-icant tacit knowledge about the firm and its management, which salaried "outsiders" lack, which gives them some inherent strengths that cannot be acquired by formal training and career paths (Rose 1998).

Hall and Nordqvist conclude that family business research has tended to be overtly focused on the static, inherent status of "being" professional, when professionalism is primarily a question of "acting" professionally. In the discussions elaborated on here, the importance of "acting" profes-sionally will also be highlighted, for example, by pointing to an increas-ing awareness of the challenges of professionalization and a growing preparedness to react to transformations in the environment of family firms.

ONE ASPECT OF PROFESSIONALIZATION OF MANAGEMENT: THE SEPARATION OF OWNERSHIP AND MANAGEMENT

Although the professionalization of management is not just the separation of ownership and management, it is unquestionably a notable element of the process. Thus, an analysis of the transition toward professional management in family firms inevitably has to deal with this issue.

In Table 11.1, the managing directors/CEOs in large-scale manufac-turing industries in Finland during the period 1900–75 are viewed with regard to firm ownership. According to the figures in Table 11.1, there was a rapid shift from owner managers to salaried managers in the twen-tieth century, and up until the 1970s. In the last recruitment cohort, the

TABLE 11.1. *Breakdown of Owner and Salaried Managers, by Year of Appointment as Managing Director/CEO*

Year of Appointment	Owner N	Salaried managers N	Total N	Owners %	Salaried Managers %	Total %
1856–1900	29	12	41	70.8	29.2	100.0
1901–20	45	41	86	52.3	47.7	100.0
1921–40	24	59	83	29.0	71.0	100.0
1941–60	22	53	75	29.3	70.7	100.0
1961–75	11	51	62	17.8	82.2	100.0
Total	131	216	347	37.8	62.2	100.0

Source: Fellman (2000: 46).

firms that were still owner-led can be classified as traditional family firms, owned by famous entrepreneurial families such as the Hackmans, Fazers, Ahlströms, and Rettigs. Outsiders were occasionally appointed as managing directors in these firms, but, as a rule, a family member took over again after a few years. Although the CEOs in several of these family firms today (2010s) are outsiders, the owning families are still very visible.

The table also shows that the shift appears to have been particularly rapid in certain periods. The "first wave of professionalization" took place in the first two decades of the twentieth century, with a second wave beginning in the 1960s. These periods were also marked by other significant changes in the managerial background, for instance, a rapid increase in the level of education of managers (see later section 6).

Since the 1970s, the development appears to have slowed (see Table 11.2). The data in Table 11.2 are not directly comparable to the material in Table 11.1, as the data in Table 11.2 consist of the 50 largest firms at certain benchmark years and include companies from all industries. Nevertheless, some conclusions can be drawn. The slowdown in the overall trend toward a greater share of salaried managers was an obvious consequence of the fact that the overwhelming majority of the managing directors in large Finnish firms were salaried managers by 1975. However, although a sell-out of several family firms occurred in the 1980s, and some of the traditional family-owned firms were no longer to be found in the "top-50" firms by 2004, some of the old family firms continue to remain both family owned and family led. Furthermore, some firms founded by "new" entrepreneurs emerged, which grew rapidly in the 1960s and 1970s. Armas Puolimatka's Armas Puolimatka Oy is a good

TABLE 11.2. *Educational Background of Managing Directors/CEOs in Top-50 Finnish Companies 1974–2004 and Number of Degrees*[a]

	1974	1984	1994	2004
Engineering (university level)	17	17	20	18
Business school	18	18	18	27
Law degree	8	7	3	4
Other higher education.	4	8	7	7
Lower technical training	1	1	0	0
Business institute	2	2	1	0
No formal professional training	2	1	1	2
Unknown	1	0	3	0
Total amount of degrees	53	54	53	58
Number of owner managers	6	8	4	4

[a] Several managers had two university-level degrees, which is quite typical in the Finnish educational culture. As a result the number of degrees exceeds 50.
Source: Data collected by the author, based on personal information about managers in the top 500 firms in Finland. A list of the top-50 firms has been published by the weekly business magazine *Talouselämä* since 1973.

example. Puolimatka was a self-made man in the construction business, who gained his wealth partly by taking advantage of the Soviet markets and the opportunity for Finnish exports there. However, in the 1980s, the heirs sold the family business. Another "new entrepreneur" is the banker Björn Wahlroos, a symbol of personal financial capitalism in Finland. The success of Wahlroos occurred during the last decade of the twentieth century, when the Finnish economy went through an extensive transformation that opened a window of opportunity for entrepreneurial talent. Wahlroos, the head of, and a minority owner in, the Sampo Group, has come to personify this transition and the new opportunities that it created. His success in the financial business originated in the prosperous private bank, Mandatum, that he was able to acquire as a compensation for having to leave Suomen Yhdyspankki (SYP Bank) in 1992.[5] The return of family ownership can also be observed in the early twenty-first century, when high-profile entrepreneurs and entrepreneurial families have invested in some significant Finnish listed companies. The Paasikivi family is a good example here; they are, through their company Orasinvest, important shareholders in Kemira Oyj, a former state company.[6]

[5] In the 2010s, Wahlroos has become influential also in Nordea Bank as a result of Sampo Group's growing stake in Nordea.

[6] Kemira became in the 1990s a listed company, in which the state was the major shareholder. The state gradually sold out its shares, while the Paasikivi family has invested

Finnish development was very similar to that of other countries, although the trend began later than in, for example, the United States: Newcomer (1955a: 102–3) showed that the share of managers who had either inherited or invested in the company was 25 percent in the 1900 cohort, and had declined to around 21 percent in the 1950 cohort.

The role of family-owned and family-led firms in big business has generally been more significant in Europe than in the United States. For instance, Italy and France have strong traditions of family management and this is also true in the United Kingdom. But, in Europe, too, the transmission of top management to salaried managers has been undisputable. In the United Kingdom, the origins of what John F. Wilson and Andrew Thomson term as the "slow transition to professional management" (Wilson and Thomson 2006: 45) were at least partly to be found in the persistent tradition of family managers in British firms. Today, U.K. firms have a higher percentage of salaried managers than French firms, although management and ownership have, to an increasing extent, been separated also in French firms, particularly since the 1990s (Maclean, Harvey, and Press 2006: 67). The rapid transition in Britain over the past few decades was partly a result of a growing public concern in the 1980s about the weak performance and poor attitude of the country's managers, which in turn led to the implementation of professionalization and competence development programs (Reed and Anthony 1992; Wilson and Thomson 2006: 173).

So who were the first outsiders? Studies have shown that the first non-family member was seldom a complete "outsider"; more commonly, the position was given to a trusted professional employee. According to Mary Rose (1998), the first outside managers in traditional family firms were often recruited from within an "extended family," that is, from among professionals and acquaintances whom the family could trust and who had been working in the company for a long time. This was one way of coping with the risk that outside recruitment posed for the family. This view has received support in my research. For example, the first outsider in A. Ahlström Oy was Bengt Rehbinder, appointed in 1962, who had been the company's chief lawyer and legal expert for two decades. Another example is Marcus Nykopp, who was appointed managing director of W. Rosenlew & Co Ab in 1963 for a transitional

---

heavily in the company. Today, the state is only a minority shareholder. The Paasikivi brothers are self-made men, having started out in Oras Ltd., a successful company producing, among other things, water taps.

period until the heir, Gustav Rosenlew, was considered old enough to take over. Nykopp had been an executive at Rosenlew for a long time and, like Rehbinder, was the legal expert in the company (see, further, Fellman 2003).

Nevertheless, exceptions can also be found. In Yhtyneet Paperitehtaat (United Paper Mill), the aging Juuso Walden was replaced by a complete outsider on the initiative of the CEO of the company's main financier, Kansallis-Osake-Pankki, in 1969. However, this was a case of a company in crisis and it spelled the end of the era for the Walden family in Yhtyneet. Nor were "insiders" always a successful choice. The first manager outside the owning family at Söderström's publishing house was a long-time employee, Guido Hornborg, who had been the office manager. He was selected because the two owning families could not agree on who should take over the daily management of the firm. However, the appointment turned out to be a disaster, for he plunged the firm into a crisis by disappearing with a considerable sum of money that he had embezzled from the company, leaving the firm virtually bankrupt. After this débâcle, the family kept the top management firmly in their own hands (Stjernschantz 1991: 26, 67–8).

Family firms have also adopted various strategies with regard to "outsiders" in top management. In some firms, the day-to-day management was transferred to outsiders at an early stage, while the family concentrated on controlling the company through board membership. In others, the family has maintained the tradition of the managing director/CEO being a family member to this day. This was the case in the Björnberg family (Myllykoski Ab) and the Rettig family, where the first outsider in top management arrived only in the early 2000s.

In a similar way, owning families can implement diverse strategies to keep control of the firm. In the two largest Swedish family dynasties, Bonnier and Wallenberg, there have been divergent strategies for maintaining control and, at the same time, avoiding conflict between family lines. In the case of Wallenberg, full control was kept in the family hands by dividing the top positions primarily between family members, while the independent subsidiaries had non-family members as CEOs. The top management positions were commonly divided between two sons in the close family circle. In the Bonnier family, the general rule was to divide all top management positions between family members, which meant that several family members were involved in the company. However, the Bonnier group was smaller than the Wallenberg empire and less diversified (Larsson, Lindgren, and Nyberg 2008).

Systems with dual management have not been uncommon in Finnish family firms. One example of such a model would be when the managing director was a family member and the deputy managing director (*vice verkställande direktör*) was an outsider. This was a way of handling the growing importance of salaried managers and, at the same time, of keeping the control firmly in the family. A model of dual management was occasionally also used in firms in which there were competing family lines. For example, in Rosenlew, the position as chairman and the position as managing director were divided between representatives of the two owning families, the von Frenckells and the Rosenlews (Fellman 2003). This seems to have worked fairly smoothly in the Rosenlew case, but we can also find examples in which this model caused problems. In the famous Schenker family in Austria, two main families shared the management, but this caused severe internal tensions and, in the interwar period, the family era came to an end. This "dual model" was seen as one of the reasons behind the demise of the family control (Matis and Stiefel 1995: 322–4). Clearly, the aforementioned strategies can in no way cover all the approaches, and, according to Colli, Fernández-Pérez, and Rose (2003), control strategies also seem to appear to vary between countries.

MANAGING PROFESSIONALIZATION IN FAMILY FIRMS I: INCREASING LEVEL OF EDUCATION

One of the most distinct features of the professionalization process was the increase in educational levels of managers. Industrial development clearly required managers with new skills. The emergence of technical and commercial education in the late nineteenth century also provided the opportunity to receive an education that was considered useful in the corporate sector. The persistent idea that managerial skills were innate also gradually began to fade. Moreover, in modern professional society formal education would increase the status of managers and legitimize their positions as leaders in big corporations. This development also made family firms think about how to educate their heirs.

Although the increase in the level of education of managers is a more or less universal phenomenon, clear national differences can be seen both in the level and type of education, and in this pace of the process. This fact has been demonstrated by Youssef Cassis (1997), for instance. Cassis shows a rapid increase in the educational level of managers in the United Kingdom, Germany, and France in the course of the twentieth century, but both the level of education and the type of education varied between these three countries, where French managers, in particular, had a considerably higher level of education than their British colleagues. A recent study of entrepreneurs and entrepreneurship has shown that the level of education among Italian entrepreneurs was high throughout the last two centuries (Tortella, Quiroga, and Moal 2010). Interestingly, Spanish entrepreneurs, on the other hand, seem to have had a somewhat lower level of education – in some respects, even lower than the average Spaniard. However, when looking at big business, the level of education of managers was significantly higher (Garcia-Ruiz 2010).

U.S. managers are sometimes assumed to have had less formal training than their European counterparts. According to the study by Mabel Newcomer (1955a: 68), 25 percent of top U.S. executives in her 1900 cohort had only completed grammar school, but the educational level also rose in the United States: in the 1950 cohort, nearly half of the youngest managers had completed a university degree. In the largest corporations, as many as 82 percent of the big business executives had obtained a university degree (Newcomer 1955a: 72).

These differences can be explained not only by different development paths and industrial structures, but also by cultural factors that have influenced recruitment traditions and educational patterns among top managers. The general assumption is that managers tend to be better trained in, for instance, countries where formal training is held in high esteem and formal credential are important in recruitment in society at large. Here, Britain is commonly given as an example of a country in which an enduring gentlemanly, but amateurish, culture survived long into the twentieth century. This resulted in British managers having less formal education than their French and German colleagues, for example. On the other hand, Cassis' results also show that British managers were by no means the "amateurs" that they are sometimes considered to be, and their level of education rose considerably in the twentieth century (Cassis 1997: 135; see also Maclean et al. 2006: 119). Moreover, managers in late but rapidly industrializing countries also tend to have a high level of formal education. Investment in human capital is often seen as important in these countries.

In international comparison, Finnish managers seem to have had a high level of formal training. The high level of education among Finnish managers was, for example, noted in an international comparison in 1971. This was considered surprising because the country was still a latecomer in the industrial development at the time (de Bettignies and Evans 1971).

In Table 11.3, the educational background of managing directors/ CEOs in large Finnish manufacturing companies between 1900 and 1975 is presented. The high level of education can be noted. Moreover, the level of education among the managing directors rose rapidly during the first half of the twentieth century. At the beginning of the century, there were still a considerable number of managers without formal education, whereas more or less all top managers in big business had a higher education by the postwar period. One explanation for the rapid rise in the level of education of managers in the early twentieth century was a rapid increase in the supply of higher education, both in general and for business life. Moreover, in the mid-twentieth century, Finland was a typical example of a late industrializing country, experiencing a rapid catching up. In the Finnish case, cultural factors also influenced the pattern: formal education was an important selection mechanism and higher education enjoyed high esteem.

At the end of the twentieth and the beginning of the twenty-first centuries, the basic education of the Finnish CEOs was much the same as per previous cohorts (see Table 11.3). This is because practically every top manager had completed a higher education by the 1970s – many even had two university degrees – and it was difficult to raise the level of formal education any higher. Furthermore, the significance of management training grew rapidly in the 1990s and early 2000s (Fellman 2007).

In spite of some differences in the level of education and in the pace of development, it seems clear that the trend has been similar in all countries: the professionalization of management meant a rise in the educational level of managers. However, the focus of this chapter is on family managers. But how did the educational background of family managers differ from that of the salaried managers? And how did the education of heirs and owner managers change in the twentieth century?

There has been a general assumption that family managers are less educated than salaried managers. Empirical studies have also shown that family/owner managers tend to have less formal education than salaried managers. Heirs to family businesses do not have to legitimize their positions and/or show their competence through formal credentials. This assumption has also formed the basis for the claim that family managers are less competent and less "professional" than their salaried colleagues.

As previously mentioned, few of the investigations that provide a historical perspective on the educational background of top management distinguish between owner managers and salaried managers. However,

TABLE 11.3. *Educational Background, by Highest Degree, of Top Managers in the Finnish Manufacturing Industry, 1900–75*

| Year of Birth | 1829–74 | | | | 1875–1904 | | | | 1905–40 | | | |
| Education | Owners | | Salaried | | Owners | | Salaried | | Owners | | Salaried | |
	N	%	N	%	N	%	N	%	N	%	N	%
Doctoral or licentiate degree	3	5.9	1	2.6	5	8.8	4	4.8	1	–	6	8.5
Higher technical education	11	21.6	12	30.7	18	31.6	43	51.2	6	–	38	53.6
Law degree	4	7.8	3	7.7	3	5.3	4	4.8	5	–	7	9.8
Business school, higher	–	–	–	–	3	5.3	4	4.8	6	–	13	18.3
Forestry degree	–	–	–	–	1	1.7	3	3.6	1	–	1	1.4
Agricultural degree	–	–	–	–	2	3.5	1	1.2	–	–	1	1.4
Military academy	2	3.9	3	7.7	1	1.7	1	1.2	–	–	–	–
Other higher	1	1.9	1	2.6	3	5.3	5	5.9	–	–	5	7.0
Total, higher education	21	41.1	20	51.3	36	63.2	65	77.5	19	–	71	100.0
Vocational technical	3	5.9	1	2.6	3	5.3	–	–	–	–	–	–
Vocational commercial school	6	11.8	5	12.8	5	8.8	5	5.9	–	–	–	–
Other vocational training	2	3.9	2	5.1	2	3.5	6	7.1	1	–	–	–
Total, vocational training	11	21.6	8	20.5	10	17.5	11	13.0	1	–	–	–
No professional training	19	37.3	9	23.1	10	17.5	5	5.9	2	–	–	–
Unknown	–	–	2	5.1	1	1.7	3	3.6	–	–	–	–
Total number of managers	51	100.0	39	100.0	57	100.0	84	100.0	22	–	71	100.0

Breakdown of owner managers and salaried managers by year of birth.
Source: Fellman (2000: 115).

the scattered empirical evidence that does exist shows that the difference in the level of formal education between the owner managers and the salaried managers was less than was previously assumed, and that the difference has decreased over time. From Table 11.3, it can be observed that Finnish owner managers had, as a rule, less formal education than salaried managers, but also that owner managers were by no means poorly educated. If Table 11.3 is compared with Table 11.1, it can be observed that the increase in formal education to a large extent coincided with the shift from owner managers to salaried managers. The increase in the level of education was not, however, due solely to the growing share of salaried managers, as the level of education rose in both groups.

Newcomer (1955a: 77) noted a similar phenomenon in the U.S. data. In the 1950 cohort, the wealthy sons and heirs to firms held a university degree to a much greater extent than in the 1900 cohort. In Germany, as Hartmut Kaelble (1980) has pointed out, it was in fact the level of education of owner managers that rose particularly rapidly in the early twentieth century, with the share of owner managers with higher education increasing from 32 percent in 1907 to 51.5 percent in 1935. Among salaried managers, the level of education rose only slightly. On the other hand, it had already been at a much higher level in 1907.

One factor that seems to accentuate the differences in the level of education between salaried managers and owner managers is that the founding entrepreneurs, in particular, tended to have less formal training. In the first cohort in my data, a total of fifteen owner managers could be classified as founding entrepreneurs, and only five of them had completed higher education.

However, the second generation in a family business was usually already better educated. The owners of family business realized that their heirs had to be properly educated to be able to manage the family business and to legitimize their position.

Another obvious and simple reason for the lower level of formal education among family managers was that many heirs had studied at an institute of higher education, but they had never completed a degree. Family managers had less need for a formal degree. In her study, Mabel Newcomer (1955a: 68, Table 34) distinguished between those who had attended college or university and those who had a degree.

The type of education acquired by owner managers varied also to a greater extent than that of salaried managers (Table 11.3), who already at an earlier stage had often completed an education intended for a business career. The family manager did not have to show his competence with formal credentials, but another simple reason for the more varied types of education among heirs was that the intended successor had died young and it was the second or the third oldest son who took up the family business.

Over the course of time, however, there was convergence in the educational backgrounds of the two groups. This was a consequence of the professionalization process: irrespective of ownership relation to the firm, managers had to acquire a profound professional competence. Moreover, the growing awareness of this can, in fact, be considered as an increasingly "professional attitude" among the owning families and as a strategy with which to respond to the challenges of the professionalization process.

Some owner managers were, in fact, better educated than their salaried colleagues, and the older generation often planned the education of their sons (and later their daughters) carefully. As the owners of large businesses often had both the financial means and the required contacts, they could send their sons to the best educational institutions available, both at home and aboard. Many attended the most prominent primary and grammar schools, and later went on to attend what were seen as the best universities. These, wealthy, cosmopolitan families often sent their sons and daughters abroad during the summer from a fairly young age. In these schools and educational institutions, the heirs also formed important networks within the same social circles and occasionally found their future spouses. For instance, the most prestigious Swedish-language student union at the University of Helsinki was considered a place where the sons and daughters of business (and other well-off) families could meet. One sharp-eyed observer characterized the student union as a place where "a saucepan [a Hackman] can marry a refrigerator [a Rosenlew]" (Mazzarella 1981: 8).

A sound education, preferably in the right environment, was something that the influential Wallenberg dynasty considered to be of particular importance (Lindgren 2007: 34). In the Wallenberg family, military training was highly valued and, as a result, for example, the young Jacob Wallenberg, who later became head of the family bank, went to naval officer training school. His parents had great expectations for him, of which he was well aware. He entered officer training school and took up service as a marine officer for a few years. When his father asked him to resign his commission in the navy to take up a position at the bank, he agreed without much hesitation. He knew what was expected of him. However, according to his biographer, Håkan Lindgren, he still felt unhappy about the turn of events as he felt he had been given no choice. After leaving the navy, Jacob's education concentrated on preparing him for his future task, and he began his studies at the Stockholm School of Economics (Lindgren 2007: 60–4).

In Finnish family businesses, too, the educational paths of heirs were often planned in detail to allow them to compete with other family lines or with salaried professionals. In the wood-processing industry firm Oy Kemi Ab, situated in the north of Finland, one of the two founders, K.A. Snellman, planned the education of his son, August, very carefully. August was trained in various commercial tasks that were considered important for the exportation of sawn goods and pulp and paper. Later on, the Snellman family also controlled, Uleå Ab, another forest industry firm in the north. Uleå was led by Reinhold Weckman, who was the son-in-law of the second founder of Kemi, A.O. Snellman. Weckman was very ambitious and, in turn, planned the education of his two sons, with the goal of making one, Björn, the managing director of Uleå, and the other, Stig, the managing director at Kemi. Both sons were to become engineers: Björn, an expert on sawmilling, and Stig, a chemical-technical engineer, that is, a pulp and paper expert (Virtanen 1993: 188–9).

In the 1960s and 1970s, management education began to become more common among Finnish managers. In particular, the growing international orientation in Finnish business made the business élite interested in management training. Interestingly, it appears that, in family firms in particular, this awareness came early. For instance, Gustav Rosenlew had studied at the Harvard Business School and Gustaf Serlachius at the Centre d´Etudes Industrielles in Geneva. One reason for this was that these family firms were, in many cases, internationally oriented companies in the export sector. As mentioned previously, these families also had the financial means to send their sons aboard to study (Fellman 2003, 2007).

So far, the discussion has concerned changes in the formal education only of top managers. Until the latter part of the nineteenth century, the supply of education for those intending to pursue a business career was generally quite limited, and the acquisition of necessary and useful skills had to be taken care of in other ways. The business community actually made a virtue out of this necessity, and, for a long time, upheld the idea that managers "were born and not made." Furthermore, if some education was needed, it was best acquired through practical work, study trips, and apprenticeship periods, not by formal studies.

Influential corporate dynasties often developed their own ways of training their future successors. One such way was that of long study periods abroad. Indeed, this was an international phenomenon, with the *grand tour* being the traditional way of educating the sons of the business élite throughout Europe. This spell abroad was often quite long and could include extensive apprenticeship periods and on-the-job training and learning. Thus, even though the heirs to family firms did not necessarily have a high level of formal education, one should not conclude that they lacked the skills and knowledge required for managing a large firm. Moreover, as Mary Rose (1998) has pointed out, this was an important way of building business networks.

Although informal, even this form of education training was, in general, planned in detail, and, as a result, the young heirs received both an in-depth and a versatile education, in which study and apprenticeship periods were seamlessly interwoven during their early careers to constitute a totality of all the aspects of company management, from the production process to commercial skills. For instance, Henning von Rettig (born 1866), the managing director of the tobacco producer P.C. Rettig & Co Ab (today, the Rettig Group Ltd.) from 1914 to 1924, was sent on a *grand tour* of Europe as a young man. This study period lasted for four years, during which he studied languages and worked in a German tobacco firm. Henning became acquainted with both the production process and the purchase and trading of raw tobacco. After returning home, he started work at the family firm, where he first performed various tasks and worked in various departments, both in production and at the office (Bahne 1950: 260). In some family firms, these educational traditions remained unchanged over generations. Thus, although there were families in which every generation had an academic degree, there were other families in which the heirs were educated primarily through apprenticeship periods and study trips. The latter was the case for the Rettig family.

MANAGING PROFESSIONALIZATION II: CAREERS AND
SUCCESSION PLANNING IN FAMILY FIRMS

It has often been stressed that succession in top management is a watershed in a firm's life. The transition can bring about positive effects, but problems can also occur. Whatever the case, it is a significant occurrence. In family-business research, it is repeatedly claimed that family firms are especially prone to problems when power and management are transferred to the next generation. For instance, the intended successor

might be unsuited to the task or might be incompetent, the older generation might have difficulties in delegating power and relinquishing control
to the younger generation, and conflicts might arise between different
family branches (Handler 1994; Colli 2003).

In family firms, the transfer of top management from the family to
a salaried manager has been considered a particularly demanding task.
Consequently, to avoid problems related to succession, it is important to
have a strategy for the transition of top management and to prepare for
it well in advance. However, where managerial succession is a particular
problem for family firms, firms with a dispersed ownership and managed
by salaried managers are by no means spared from succession problems.
Moreover, empirical research has shown that family firms are actually
well aware of the problem (Astrachan, Pieper, and Jaskiewicz 2008).

Succession in top management in family firms – and the managing
of this process – is closely related to the question of professionalization of management, as it is often at such transitions when outsiders
are appointed. Moreover, this incidence can reveal attitudes toward the
recruitment of outsiders. In this section, the changes in recruitment and
selection of managers and managerial candidates in family firms are examined. First, changing recruitment patterns are discussed, after which the
focus will shift to how succession was prepared for, both in respect to
transferring top management from one generation to the next and from
family members to outsiders.

Table 11.4 presents data on whether top managers were recruited
externally or internally. Internal recruitment was more common in owner-
led firms than in firms with salaried managers. This is self-evident, as
family managers tend to have most of their career in-house, but salaried
managers were also recruited primarily internally. Interestingly, however,
owner managers were occasionally recruited externally. One explanation
for this is that some family managers had a career outside the firm before
taking over the family business. For example, the successor was not originally intended as the leader of the family firm, and, as a result, he had
pursued a career elsewhere. Furthermore, the family strategy was sometimes to encourage the heir to acquire ample experience in various tasks
in other companies before he was employed in the family firm.

Similar features can be observed in other countries. According to Newcomer (1955a: 97 Table 44), working outside the family firm seems to
have become more common among U.S. managers over time: in her study,
94.1 percent of heirs to family firms had worked solely within the family

TABLE 11.4. *Industrial Managers According to Form of Recruitment*

Year of Recruitment	1856–1918			1919–45			1946–75		
Form of Recruitment	Owners	Salaried	Total	Owners	Salaried	Total	Owners	Salaried	Total
Internal	27	16	43	19	26	45	18	52	70
External	11	26	37	11	40	51	8	41	49
Founder, recruited at foundation or change of ownership	30	5	35	5	7	12	2	2	4
Unknown	–	–	–	–	1	1	–	–	–
TOTAL	68	47	115	35	74	109	28	95	123

Number of managers according to year of appointment as managing director/CEO. Breakdown of owners and salaried managers according to year of recruitment.

Source: Fellman (2000: 179).

business in the 1900 cohort, whereas, in the 1950s cohort, the share was lower at 77.4 percent. Nevertheless, according to Newcomer (1955a: 98), the intended heir was required to work in the family firm for at least part of his career. This also seems to hold true in the Finnish case. When heirs had gathered experience in other firms, it was usually early on in their careers. In Britain, where there was a deep-rooted tradition of family ownership, family managers were often first employed outside the family firm to learn the trade (Stanford and Giddens 1974).

Those family managers in Finnish companies who spent the whole, or a significant part, of their careers in the family firm usually started in expert positions or in administrative positions at the head office. However, they advanced generally quite rapidly to middle management and/or line management position (see further Fellman, 2003).

During earlier periods, it was considered important to gain experience in both administration and production. For instance, R. Erik Serlachius in G.A. Serlachius Ab (GAS) began his career at the Mänttä paper mill – which was the main plant of GAS and also the location of the head office – but, after a few years, he was transferred to the Kangas mill, a subsidiary of GAS, where he worked as plant manager for three years. After the period at Kangas, he was moved back to Mänttä, where he became plant manager of the mill and deputy managing director of the whole company.

In the 1960s and 1970s, when a fashion for "general managers" became more pronounced, experience from production units became less significant as a way to the top in the manufacturing industry. This development is reflected in the career paths of both salaried and family managers. Neither Gustaf Rosenlew, managing director of Rosenlew, 1969–87, nor Gustaf Serlachius, managing director of G.A. Serlachius Ab, 1969–86, worked for any considerable length of time in production. For instance, Maarit Toivanen-Koivisto, currently CEO of the Finnish family-owned firm Onvest Ltd., has worked in various functions and departments in the family firm in the course of her career. She feels this has provided the most important experience for acquiring competence.[7]

In the course of the twentieth century, the career paths of family managers also became more similar to those of salaried managers (Table 11.5). This can be seen as a reflection of the professionalization process. Both

7 "Onvest Oy and Maarit Toivanen-Koivisto." *FBN News* No. February 2, 2010. Available at: http://www.fbn-i.org/feb-10/article1.html (Accessed October 2010). Onvest is a family firm that started out in plumbing wholesale, but that today is a significant provider of services within the HEPAC industry, delivering services and material for the construction business and real-estate sector.

TABLE 11.5. *Number of Managers Who Had Passed Certain Managerial Hierarchies during Their Careers Prior to Appointment as Managing Director/CEO*

Level	1829–74		1875–1904		1905–40	
	Owners N	Salaried N	Owners N	Salaried N	Owners N	Salaried N
Head of department	11	13	21	54	12	53
Factory manager, plant manager	6	13	14	23	2	11
Senior executive	8	4	9	21	10	35
Deputy managing director	1	1	6	19	12	28
Total number of managers in each cohort	51	39	57	84	22	71

Breakdown of owners and salaried managers according to the year of birth.
Source: Fellman (2000: 174).

heirs and managerial recruits without ownership had to climb similar career ladders through the hierarchy of the large organization. Although the career ladders of owner managers were still somewhat shorter than those of salaried CEOs in the 1970s, the kind of "fast tracks" to the top found among heirs in the early cohorts had disappeared by 1975 (Fellman 2000: 195–6). Similar features were noted by Newcomer (1955a: 96) in the United States, and by Stanworth and Giddens (1974: 87) in the United Kingdom. In the 1970s, the majority of the chairmen in British companies who also had ownership in the firm had spent nearly thirty years before becoming chairmen. Only a handful of the chairmen had reached a top position in a decade or less.

If actual succession is more closely examined, the most common pattern that emerges is one in which the owner chose the intended successor at an early stage, often, although not necessarily, the eldest son. The role of the older generation in the selection process was clearly much more pronounced in family firms than in firms led by salaried managers. In family-led firms, it was more or less expected that the owner picked the successor – for better or for worse. The fact that the successor was chosen at an early stage enabled him to be well trained and prepared for task, which was an advantage (Fellman 2003).[8]

---

[8] For examples of this in the United States, see Newcomer (1995: 110).

In less-successful cases, the older generation "bet on the wrong horse." In the history of family firms in Finland, it is easy to find examples of successors who were incompetent, lacked interest in management, or did not enjoy the trust of the other family members or the financiers.

When various branches of the family were involved in the business, there could also be conflicts, but, as was stated earlier, this could also lead to a "division of labor" between branches of the family, as was the case in the Wallenberg dynasty, where power and control was very selectively allocated. Nevertheless, conflicts between owner groups were not uncommon, either. For instance, in the Finnish firm Oy Kemi Ab, there was a prolonged tug-of-war between the two main family branches over the management of the company. The special education of the two Weckman sons was a conscious strategy adopted by Reinhold Weckman to gain the upper hand in an ongoing power struggle (Virtanen 1993: 153). However, as a result of these continuous conflicts, the two families gradually lost control of the company.

As stated previously, the position as deputy managing director was occasionally a position for the salaried manager, while the position as managing director was reserved for the heir. This was a way of handling the growing need for salaried employees, without ceding the family control of the day-to-day management. However, the position as a deputy managing director was often used as an important running-in period for the intended heir before promoting him or her to the top position, and thus was a sign of better preparation of the transfer of power from one generation to another. As can be seen in Table 11.5, a growing number of managers in the last cohort had passed this position on their way to the top.

FAMILY VALUES AND PROFESSIONALIZATION

Dyer argued that one aspect of professionalization in family businesses was to professionalize those employed in the firm. According to Hall and Nordqvist, it also entailed a demand to internalize the values of the family firm. The identification and selection of talent among young recruits is a challenge in any firm, and, when cultural factors and the norms and values of the family business are criteria for professionalism, it becomes a particularly challenging task. There have been various methods used to tackle this issue. For example, in the Finnish family-owned, Ahlstrom Corp., young professionals are sent on a two-week course called JUMP, which is held at the old firm's former head-office in Normarkku (about 10 kilometers from Pori, in southwest Finland), where Ahlström originally started. In this traditional mill community, the company's long history is still highly visible. Besides providing a thorough introduction to the activities and business areas, one of the aims of the course has been to introduce the young employees to the core values and goals of the family company.[9] This supports the view of Hall and Nordqvist that professionalism in family firms is related to the adoption of certain norms and values, and that some family firms still continue to cherish such values today.

In the Swedish Wallenberg family, competence was the core value. Larsson et al. (2008) have emphasized that ability was a "badge of honor" in the Wallenberg companies, and this was an explicit requirement for all concerned. Everyone, from the salaried managers who took care of the company's subsidiaries to the firm's inventors and professionals, required the family's whole-hearted confidence before they were allowed to develop their ideas further. But in the event that the production plant or the line of business was not profitable, a change of leadership was usually the first alternative suggested.

FEMALE SUCCESSORS IN FAMILY BUSINESSES

The discussion to date has concerned only men. In the data on managing directors for 1900–75, only two women can be found. They were both widows of two founding entrepreneurs, who managed the family firm during a period of transition. The role of top female managers in big industrial companies has been negligible, even in Finland, a country that has been a pioneer in the promotion of equal opportunities for men and women.

Nevertheless, there have been well known women in big business, although they were not included in this sample of managers. For example, Marie Hackman, wife of Johan Hackman, is a legendary figure in Finnish business history. After the death of her husband in 1807, she led the Hackman trading house adroitly for fifty years.[10] A more recent figure was Hanna Paviainen of Joh. Parviainen & Co, a sawmill and plywood company. From 1925 to 1936, Hanna Parviainen managed the business

---

[9] Interview with vice president of human resources in Ahlstrom Corp. Tarja Takko. December 3, 2010.

[10] "Marie Hackman." Suomen Kansallisbibiliografia. Available at: http://artikkelihaku .kansallisbiografia.fi/artikkeli/493 (Accessed December 2010).

that her father, Johan Parviainen, had founded. In contrast to many other young women of the time, she was educated with the aim of her having a role in the family business. She attended good schools at home and in Geneva and completed her education by studying at a commercial school in Stockholm. She started as the firm's accountant but gradually received more responsibilities and took over the whole company after the death of her brother Walter in 1925.[11] Her education did not differ much from that of her male colleagues of the time.

Although few in number, it appears that it was easier for a woman to reach the top in a family business than for a woman without ownership in publicly traded companies with dispersed ownership. Furthermore, women have also made their way in business by being founding entrepreneurs. As Alison Kay (2008) demonstrates in her book on female entrepreneurship in Victorian Britain, founding and running small business enterprises was an important form of livelihood for both single and married women. Angel Kwolek-Folland (2002) has highlighted similar patterns in the United States. Moreover, according to Kwolek-Folland (2002: 25), in more traditional family firms, it was often seen as the duty of wives and daughters to participate in the family business. As Therese Nordlund has shown (2012), many of the wives in Swedish family businesses were responsible for maintaining networks and for other important, but often invisible, tasks. This is also addressed in this volume in Chapter 9 by Blondel and Niforos, who refer to the wives in family firms as "hidden giants." They could also be de facto partners and were important for connecting significant entrepreneurial families through marriage (Colli and Rose 2008). In the Finnish family firms studied here, women were often important shareholders and also often board members exercising both covert and overt influence.

The role of women in big business clearly grew in the course of the twentieth century, but this growth was painfully slow. Even today, women in top management in big business are a small minority. In the data sample for the top fifty companies in Finland, which forms the basis for Table 11.2, just one woman, Maarit Toivanen-Koivisto in Onvest Ltd., can be found. However, this is clearly a very small sample – the "top of the top" – which clearly makes it difficult to draw any

[11] Maritta Pohls, "Parviainen, Hanna (1874–1938). Joh. Parviaisen tehtaat Oy:n toimitusjohtaja, lahjoittaja, kauppaneuvos." Biographical portrait in Kansallisbiografia. Available at: http://www.kansallisbiografia.fi.libproxy.helsinki.fi/kb/artikkeli/4797 (Accessed January 2011).

definite conclusions. Maarit Toivanen-Koivisto succeeded her father, Erkki J. Toivanen, in 2001. Although she was well educated, received in-depth experience in both various tasks and various departments in the family firm, and worked as her father's "right-hand," it was neither easy nor self-evident that she would take over the company. In an interview, she revealed that she had felt lost when she was asked to take over as CEO, and felt that she had not received, during her early career, enough hand-on instruction from her father on how to manage a firm. It seemed to her that her father had never really accepted her as his successor[12]:

My father allowed me to work in the business but never encouraged me to think of myself as the potential leader. He was of the generation that went through World War II and had quite traditional views on the place of women. He never told me very much about the business that he led for over 40 years....

The day after my father died, I sat in his office with my mother and we knew that we faced a huge challenge. At that point, I had not even been a director. I had to learn a lot and learn it quickly. I soon realized that quick decisions could lead to costly mistakes. But we learnt to live with the situation and manage it.[13]

There is an extensive body of research on the relationship between fathers and sons in family business, and recently the various problems that daughters experience and the various roles they develop as successors in relation to their fathers have also been the focus of research. Colette Dumas (1989) has characterized the role of female heirs, as experienced by Toivanen-Koivisto while her father was alive, as the "silent voice" – that is, daughters in family business rarely speak with their own voice about the business as long as their fathers are in charge.

The story of Antonia Ax:son Johnson, who at the age of thirty-two took over the large Swedish conglomerate the Axel Johnson Corporation in the 1960s, is very different from that of Toivanen-Koivisto. Even when she was in her early twenties, her father took her on business trips and business meetings in order for her to learn the business. She was, from the start, prepared as the intended successor.[14]

---

[12] "Maarit Toivanen-Koivisto." Biographical portrait in Kansallisbibliografia. Available at: http://www.kansallisbiografia.fi/talousvaikuttajat/?iid=3691 (Accessed December 2010).

[13] "Onvest Oy and Maarit Toivanen-Koivisto." *FBN News* No February 2, 2010, p.1. Available at: http://www.fbn-i.org/feb-10/article1.html (Accessed October 2010).

[14] "Månadens person: Antonia Ax:son Johnsons koncept: Förvärva, ärva och förädla:" *Forum för ekonomi och teknik* no 12. December 1999. Available at: http://www.forum-fet.fi/dec99/manpers1.html (Accessed October 27, 2010).

CONCLUDING REMARKS

The aim of this chapter was to highlight the various aspects of the professionalization of management using a long-term perspective and with a particular focus on family firms. I have dealt with the changes in "managerial profile" in big business, which occurred as a consequence of the professionalization process. I have discussed what professionalization meant in family firms and how the owners of family businesses adapted and related, both consciously and unconsciously, to this development.

The overall trend has been quite similar in most of the industrialized world, but, by looking at the process in greater detail, it has also varied depending on the economic and institutional context. For instance, in countries where higher education was held in high esteem, family managers often also had a high level of education. Nevertheless, family traditions, or even the personality of individual owners, have affected the path. Moreover, long-standing family firms often developed distinct traditions for education and recruitment.

Significant transformations in the profile of top management occurred throughout the period under investigation and this concerned both owners and salaried managers. There was a shift from owner managers to salaried managers, the level of education rose, and the significance of management education grew. The careers of owner managers and outsiders became more similar.

I have also demonstrated that it is false to claim that family managers were poorly educated and badly prepared for their task. Throughout the period studied, the heirs in family firms often received the best education available. They went to élite schools, participated in the most prominent MBA and executive programs, and traveled abroad to refine their skills.

The educational "package" was also often very target oriented and their career paths well plotted. Succession and recruitment became better planned. A routinization of the selection and recruitment of managers and experts – in the sense that the system became characterized by standardized procedures – also developed in family business. Skill development became increasingly important. The planning of the transition of power from one generation to the next generation increasingly became the center of attention in family firms.

Although top management was kept in the hands of the family, the growing use of professional experts was seen in all family firms. The ability to select and utilize skilled professionals as colleagues could actually also be seen as a sign of professionalism. For example, one of Gösta

Serlachius' (GAS) abilities as a manager was his skill in finding and employing competent professionals (Fellman 2003). In the Wallenberg family, Marcus Wallenberg Jr. is reputed to have kept a notebook labeled "Possible CEOs" (Larsson et al. 2008).

Even though succession in family firms gradually became better prepared for, it does not mean that successions were poorly prepared for during earlier periods. Then, too, the education and careers of intended heirs were often carefully planned. However, it appears that, as time progressed, the owners of family businesses became more aware of the demands placed on them by the professionalization process and responded to them in a proactive way. This growing awareness of the challenges of succession, and the more systematic planning resulting from this, must, in itself, be seen as a sign of professionalism.

The role of internalizing – even strengthening – the values and norms of the family business came to be seen as an important part of professionalism in family firms. Managing the family firm required not only a systematic approach to the managerial task, skill and competence, but also sensitivity toward the company and its norms, values, and culture. This seems to have been the case in many of the firms studied here.

The professionalization of management in family business cannot be equated with the rise of salaried managers, nor can it be seen as referring to managers with management education, or any other type of education. Rather, it is the complex combination of expertise and competence leading to a systematization of management, on the one hand, and sensitivity to the values and goals of the firm and the owners, on the other. Moreover, professionalism among owners and managers in family business can be observed in their growing readiness to react and respond to both internal and external changes. However, there was a significant variation in the way this readiness translated into action. The "variety" of family firms is as large as that of firms in general.

References

Astrachan, Joseph, Torsten Pieper, and Peter Jaskiewicz (2008). "Introduction." In Jonathan Astrachan, Torsten Pieper, and Peter Jaskiewicz (eds.), *Family Business* (pp. xiv–xix). The International Library of Critical Writings on Business and Management. Cheltenham: Edward Elgar Publishing.

Bahne, Erik (1950). P.C. Rettig & Co. 1845–1945. Ett blad ur tobaksindustriens historia i Finland. Åbo: Rettig Ab.

Berle, Adolf C., and Gardiner C. Means (1932). *The Modern Corporation and Private Property*. New York: MacMillan.

Bettignies de, H.C., and P. Lee Evans (1971). "Europe Looks North at the Scandinavian Business Elite." *European Business*, 31 Autumn: 59–69.

Burkhart, Mike, Fausto Panunzi, and Andrei Schleifer (2003). "Family Firms." *Journal of Finance*, 58(5): 2167–2201.

Cassis, Youssef (1997). *Big Business: The European Experience in the Twentieth Century*. Oxford: Oxford University Press.

Chandler Alfred D. Jr. (1980). *The Visible Hand: The Managerial Revolution in American Business*. Cambridge, MA: Belknap Press.

Chandler, Alfred D. Jr. (1990). *Scale and Scope. The Dynamics of Industrial Capitalism*. Cambridge, MA: Harvard University Press.

Chittor, Raveendra, and Ranja Das (2007). "Professionalization of Management and Succession Performance – A Vital Linkage." *Family Business Review*, 20(1): 65–79.

Chua, Jess H., James J. Chrisman, and Pramodita Sharma (2003). "Succession and Non-Succession Concerns in Family Firms and Agency Relationship with Nonfamily Managers." *Family Business Review*, 15(2): 89–107.

Colli, Andrea (2003). *The History of Family Business, 1850–2000*. New Studies in Economic and Social History. Cambridge: Cambridge University Press.

Colli, Andrea, Paloma Fernández-Pérez, and Mary B. Rose (2003). "National Determinants of family firm development. Family firms in Britain, Spain and Italy in the nineteenth and twentieth century." *Enterprise & Society*, 4(1): 28–63.

Colli, Andrea, and Mary B. Rose (2008). "Family Firms." In Geoffrey Jones and Jonathan Zeitlin (eds.), *The Oxford Handbook of Business History* (pp. 194–218). Oxford: Oxford University Press.

Dumas, Colette (1989). "Understanding of Father–Daughter and Father–Son Dyads in Family-Owned Business." *Family Business Review*, 2(1): 31–6.

Dyer W. Gibb Jr. (1989). "Integrating Professional Management into a Family Owned Business." *Family Business Review*, 2(3): 221–35.

Fellman, Susanna (2000). *Uppkomsten av en direktörsprofession – Industriledarnas utbildning och karriär i Finland 1900–1975*. Bidrag till kännedom av Finlands natur och folk nr. 155. Helsingfors: Finska Vetenskaps-Societeten.

Fellman, Susanna (2001). "The Professionalisation of Management in Finland – The Case of the Manufacturing Sector, 1900–1975." *Scandinavian Economic History Review*, 49(3): 5–27.

Fellman, Susanna (2003). "The Role of Internal Labour Markets and Social Networks in the Recruitment of Top Managers in Finnish Manufacturing Firms, 1900–75." *Business History*, 45(3): 1–21.

Fellman, Susanna (2007). "From Consolidation to Competition – The Development of Modern Management Education in Finland, 1958–2000." *Nordiske Organisasjonsstudier*, 9(3): 1–38.

Fernández-Pérez, Paloma, and Nuría Puig (2009). "Global Lobbies for a Global Economy: The Creation of the Spanish Institute of Family Firms in International Perspective." *Business History*, 51(5): 712–33.

Galambos, Louis (2010). "The Role of Professionals in the Chandler Paradigm." *Industrial and Corporate Change*, 19(2): 377–98.

García-Ruiz, José L. (2010). "Education and Entrepreneurship in Twentieth Century Spain." In José L. García-Ruiz and Pier Angelo Toninelli (eds.), *The Determinants of Entrepreneurship: Leadership, Culture, Institutions* (pp. 161–84). London: Pickering & Chattoo.

García-Ruiz, José L., and Pier Angelo Toninelli, eds. (2010). *The Determinants of Entrepreneurship: Leadership, Culture, Institutions*. London: Pickering & Chattoo.

Gordon, Robert A. (1966). *Business Leadership in the Large Corporation*. Berkeley, CA: University of California Press.

Hall, Annika, and Mattias Nordqvist (2008). "Professional Management in Family Business: Toward an Extended Understanding." *Family Business Review*, 21(1): 51–69.

Handler, Wendy C. (1994). "Succession in Family Business: A Review of Research." *Family Business Review*, 2(2): 133–57.

Imse, Thomas P. (1960). "Evidence of Professionalization among Managers of Business Enterprise." *The American Catholic Sociological Review*, 21(1): 37–43.

Kaelble, Hartmut (1980). "Long-Term Changes in the Recruitment of Business Elites: Germany Compared to the U.S., Great Britain and France since the Industrial Revolution." *Journal of Social History*, 13(3): 1404–23.

Kay, Alison (2009). The Foundations of Female Entrepreneurship. Enterprise, Home and Household in London, c. 1800–1870. Routledge International Studies in Business History. London: Routledge.

Kwolek-Folland, Angel (2002). *Incorporating Women. A History of Women and Business in the United States*. New York: Palgrave.

Larsson, Mats, Håkan Lindgren, and Daniel Nyberg (2008). "Entrepreneurship and Ownership: The Long Term Viability of the Swedish Bonnier and Wallenberg Family Business Groups." In Susanna Fellman, Martin Jes Iversen, Hans Sjögren, and Lars Thue (eds.), *Creating Nordic Capitalism. The Business History of Competitive Periphery* (pp. 75–103). Basingstoke: Palgrave-Macmillan.

Lindgren, Håkan (2007). *Jacob Wallenberg 1892–1980*. Stockholm: Atlantis.

Maclean, Mairi, Charles Harvey, and Jon Press (2006). *Business Elites and Corporate Governance in France and the UK*. Basingstoke: Palgrave-Macmillan.

Matis, Herbert, and Dieter Stiefel (1995). *The Schenker Dynasty. The History of International Freight Forwarding from 1872–1931*. Vienna: Wirtschaftsferlag Carl Uberreuter.

Mazzarella, Merete (1981). *Att spela sitt liv*. Helsingfors: Söderström.

Miller, William (1962). "The Business Elite in Business Bureaucracies. Careers of Top Executives in the Early Twentieth Century." In William Miller (ed.), *Men in Business, Essays on the Historical Role of the Entrepreneur* (pp. 286–305). New York: Harper & Row.

Newcomer, Mabel (1955a). *The Big Business Executive. The Factors That Made Him 1900–1950*. New York: Columbia University Press: New York.

Newcomer, Mabel (1955b). "The Professionalization of Management." *Business History Review*, 22(1): 54–63.

Nordlund, Therese (2012). En osynlig företagshistoria: Direktörshustrun i svenskt näringsliv, Lund: Sekel.

Reed, Michael, and Peter Anthony (1992). "Professionalizing Management and Managing Professionalization: British Management in the 1980s." *Journal of Management Studies*, 29(5): 591–613.

Rose, Mary B., ed. (1995). *Family Business*. The International Library of Critical Writings in Business History 13. Cheltenham: Edward Elgar Publishing.

Rose, Mary B. (1998). "Networks and Leadership Succession in British Business in the 1950s." In Wilfried Feldenkirchen and Terry Gourvish (eds.), *The European Yearbook of Business History 1998*. Aldershot: Ashgate.

Stanworth, Philip, and Anthony Giddens (1974). "An Economic Elite: A Demgraphic Profile of Company Chairmen." In Philip Stanworth and Anthony Giddens (eds.), *Elites and Power in British Society* (pp. 81–101). Cambridge: Cambridge University Press.

Stewart, Alex, and Michael Hitt (2011). "Why Can't a Family Business Be More Like a Non-Family Business? Modes of Professionalization in Family Firms." *Family Business Review*, 25(3): 1–29.

Stjernschantz, Göran (1991). Ett förlag och dess författare: Söderström & Co Förlags Ab 1891–1991. Borgå: Söderströms & Co.

Taussig, F.W., and C.S. Joslyn (1932). *American Business Leaders. A Study in Social Origins and Social Stratification*. New York: Macmillan.

Tortella, Gabriel, Gloria Quiroga, and Ignacio Moal (2010). "Entepreneurship: A Comprative Approach." In José L. García-Ruiz and Pier Angelo Toninelli (eds.), *The Determinants of Entrepreneurship: Leadership, Culture, Institutions* (pp. 81–104). London: Pickering & Chattoo.

Virtanen, Sakari (1993). *Lapin leivän isä. Kemiyhtiön historia*. Kemi: Kemiyhtiö.

Wilson, John F., and Andrew Thomson (2006). *The Making of Modern Management. British Management in Historical Perspective*. Oxford: Oxford University Press.

Wilensky, Harold (1964). "The Professionalization of Everyone?" *American Journal of Sociology*, 70(2): 137–58.

Index

Printed by BoD™in Norderstedt, Germany

9 781107 480513